Empire's Edge

Empire's Edge
Travels in South-Eastern Europe, Turkey and Central Asia

SCOTT L. MALCOMSON

VERSO

London · New York

First published in the USA in 1994
by Faber and Faber Inc. Boston

First published in Great Britain in 1994
by Faber and Faber Limited
3 Queen Square London WC1N 3AU

First published in paperback in the USA in 1995
by Verso
180 Varick Street New York NY 10014-4606

A catalog record for this book
is available from the Library of Congress

ISBN 1-85984-098-1

*For Rebecca,
and in memory of
Wes Anderson (1952–1991)*

CONTENTS

Men [should] despise no men for the diversity of their laws. For we wot not whom God loves ne whom he hates.

> —John Mandeville, *The Buke of John Maundeuill, being the Travels of Sir John Mandeville, Knight (1322–1356)*

The First and the Second Worlds are being reunited into something which has no name yet, nor a number: perhaps it will just be the World. . . . There is only one world left with serious claims to development and hegemony.

> —Sir Ralf Dahrendorf, *Reflections on the Revolution in Europe (1990)*

Men, we have created you from a male and a female, and made you into nations and tribes, that you might get to know one another.

> the Koran, sura 49

On the Bosphorus

ON A MILD SUMMER EVENING, after dinner, you walk down the slope of Üsküdar toward the Bosphorus with Dina. The root of her name means "religion." "That makes it easy to remember," she says, which is true if you know Arabic. (She's a historian, from Lebanon.) You walk down darkened streets to the quay and board a motorboat for the ride to Beşiktaş.

Üsküdar is on Istanbul's "Asian side," as it's called; Beşiktaş is on the "European side." Neither Europe nor Asia exist anywhere outside the imagination, of course. Traditionally we call each a "continent," though they are no more separate, geographically, than Canada and the United States. A long time ago someone stood in, say, Beşiktaş, pointed toward Üsküdar and said, "That's Asia. It's differ-

1

ent from here." You can swim across the Bosphorus when the tides are right.

We leave for Europe in our little boat-taxi, called a *dolmuş*—it means "stuffed" or "filled." The boat-taxis that cross the Bosphorus putter slowly, tossed by the wakes of huge freighters plying between the Mediterranean and Black Seas. Both the Asian and European sides of Istanbul rise steeply from the shore. Istanbul has been the capital of three great empires, pagan, Christian, and Muslim: Roman, Byzantine, and Ottoman. Now it wants to be part of a united Europe, since it knows that being outside of this new empire would leave it in the Third World, or whatever the not-powerful part of the globe is to be called. Over dinner you talked with Dina about the book you were going to write (this book), about the places you would describe—Romania, Bulgaria, Turkey, Uzbekistan—and how people in them have lived on the borders of empires, always wrestling with the prospects of membership in the Roman or Greek, Persian or Muslim, Christian or Soviet or EuroAmerican worlds. Dina enjoys this kind of conversation. She, like you, has observed the end of the Cold War with anxiety as well as joy, for both of you dislike the arrogance of victors. You fear the rise of a new Rome. (Hadn't a French tycoon, in the *Herald-Tribune*, nominated then-president George Bush as "the new Augustus"?) This post–Cold War empire would have its heart ineffably in Europe, with the United States and Japan as outriggers—in short, in the West, another place not visible on any map. Lebanese naturally know much about empires and the struggle for power. Dina is capable of saying something like "Imperialism is always monotheistic" and meaning it, and laughing. Or did she say, "Monotheism is always imperialistic?"

At this point, though, neither of you is talking, because it is nighttime on the Bosphorus and intensely pleasant to rock up and down on the creaking *dolmuş* in silence. Dina smokes her cigarette, you close your eyes. This is your favorite place in all of Istanbul, a floating point between two imaginary continents, delicate, deliciously landless.

The foreigner allows you to be yourself by making a foreigner of you.
—Edmond Jabès, *A Foreigner Carrying in*
the Crook of his Arm a Tiny Book (1989)

Romania

1

THAT WAS AT THE END of your journey. This is at the beginning: in Moldavia, part of Romania, near the old Soviet border. You wander with young, semi-employed Dan Radu through the streets of Iaşi. The princes of Moldavia had their ancient capital at Iaşi; it sheltered a lively diplomatic community in the run-up to World War I, and was the site of a famous massacre of Jews during the second war; old Moldavia is now split between Romania and ex-Soviet Moldova. A year and a half after the murder of Romania's Communist dictator, Nicolae Ceauşescu, you and Dan walk down a steep street at 5:30 in the morning as men walk up it, coming from the train station, silent, looking bleary and rough in worn-out clothes. Dan gestures toward these men, then opens his arms wide to embrace the pale dawn growing before you, the vista of countless apartment blocks, and declares, "We must create a new man! We must build the workers' nation!"

2

IN BUCHAREST, ROMANIA'S CAPITAL, Bogdan Bogoescu meets you at his office with a firm handshake and an air of confidence. Carefully shaven, tall, a youthful forty or so, he sports a fashionable suit and haircut. Most Romanians in Bucharest are neither fashionable nor

3

confident; they tussle in breadlines, scrambling and tearing, though one hears the situation is much improved from the previous winter.

As the city's chief architect, Bogdan Bogoescu's primary responsibility is to complete the massive urban rebuilding project begun under Ceauşescu. The dictator, in his later years—in his period of uncontested power and splendor—ordered much of the old city destroyed to make room for a new city built of radiant white stone. His architects determined the length of the Champs-Élysées and planned a Boulevard of the Victory of Socialism to be even longer. Lining it would be white apartment buildings in an odd style (French-neoclassical, yet modernist) with fabulous shops on the ground floor. At the head of the boulevard would stand the House of the People, the largest building in the world.

Baron Haussmann built the Champs-Élysées and many other great Parisian boulevards for Emperor Napoleon III, who wished to destroy the tangled, rebellious old Paris and replace it with one straightforward, orderly, and easy to patrol. "We had a group of French architects visiting," Bogoescu says. "They were very severe when they saw our plans. But then I said to them, 'This is just like Haussmann, this is an opportunity even *greater* than Haussmann's.' And they stood back.

"What happened in Paris is now happening here." Bogoescu compares the House of the People, now called the House of the Republic, to the Pentagon—"It's a Taj Mahal, it's a Cheops!" All of Ceauşescu's project will be complete, he hopes, in two years. It will go, more or less, according to the dead man's plan. But while the House of the People will look the same as intended, its use will be different. Parts of it may be given over to private offices, since the government hopes to make the building "profitable"; another, considerable part will house Parliament. Bogoescu's great dream is to make the building "converse" with a "European village" next to it. Each of the European Community members would have its own building, "in dialogue with" the House of the People.

"We're the only ones in Europe with the potential to accomplish this. We need to improve our image, and break with the image of the past." Bogoescu says the main problem he has confronted is the mentality of Romanians, who are not facing the future with eagerness or

4

a sense of possibility, and whose aesthetic understanding remains primitive.

"It is very important to change people's mentalities. They must learn what is beautiful. They must be educated—educated in culture, in mentality. Every culture has times when it...*structures* itself. And that is what we are doing."

Let's walk down the Boulevard of the Victory of Socialism for a while—it's never crowded—and talk as we go, approaching in a leisurely way the House of the People. It is obviously difficult to learn what is beautiful and to have one's mentality changed. It is difficult for a culture to structure itself. The dictator had tried to do all these things. He saw (he hoped he saw) in every Romanian a blank slate on which he could draw. He struggled to create a "new man."

An important paradox was at work: the new man had also to be, profoundly, an old man, or rather a pure, essential, pre-existing Man. The new man had to live *already* in the heart, waiting for his historical moment—the moment Ceauşescu worked to create—to emerge and declare victory over the shell (bourgeois, nationalist, capitalist, religious) that had been preventing his full and free existence. Ideally, all socialists would stand up and announce that they had, at last, become what they already were. (And the dictator's city would be the glittering, prosperous, modern, European city Bucharest should always have been but wasn't.) In this way the "creation" of a "new man" would in fact be the liberation of the essential Man. The dictator wished to show men their true selves.

How did he know what the true self was? The question has been a devilish one, puzzling tyrants and normal people alike, for ages. The dictator decided it as most people do: he took the system he knew (Stalinism), assumed that the true self would be in harmony with this system, then applied it to the people around him on the principle that he was liberating them to their true natures. In other words, he attempted to rationalize a human society. A document from the 12th congress of the Romanian Communist Party makes this clear. It speaks of progress and civilization, of the new man and a "new humanism." It declares that ethnic differences, for example, must be resolved by "liquidating inequalities and discriminations of whatever kind." It mentions a "program of urban and rural systematization" and "increasing homogenization." Ceauşescu himself notes, "[I]t is

5

an anachronism that in this great epoch of the technical-scientific revolution, when the people affirm themselves as the knowing creator of all material and spiritual values, there yet exist people, even members of the party, who still believe in a supernatural force." Ceaușescu was expressing a common communist ethics, vestigially Christian, but with God replaced by Man—aided by the state and science—and with sin removed from the hearts of people and deposited at the border with capitalism, which was the expression of human sinfulness. After this congress, systematization and homogenization became firm policy as villages were slated to be razed, ethnic minorities repressed, and a very long road built toward the world's largest building.

Which we now approach, the new humanism fixed in our minds. The House of the People is enormous and not pretty. The dictator was always changing his mind about this feature or that; the result looks like a collection of things from other buildings. The dictator's house looms huge in its indecision. When you stand in front of the house and look back down the boulevard, you can see what was supposed to be here. The boulevard was supposed to be bustling with cars, water should be splashing from the fountains, plants growing vigorously, the electric lights blazing, happy people shopping and savoring their happiness. All this is possible, in principle. But what you see instead are a few Romanian cars groaning and wheezing.

Look at that crazy building! The dictator must have thought it was beautiful. Now it will be a symbol for yet another structuring of the Romanian people, one that will be "in dialogue with" a united Europe. "Let us return to Europe!" was one slogan of Romania's 1989 revolution. Romania's first post-revolution prime minister emphasized that Europe is a continent to which Romania "has never ceased to belong, owing to its being a neo-Latin, Christian, democratic and tolerant country inhabited by people open to human values in general." In other words, Romanians will again become what they have always been—new men, free to express their essential selves. How will they recognize their essential selves? They will be educated to learn what is beautiful. They'll change their mentalities. They'll become Europeans, taking what they're told about humanity and applying it to themselves, aided by the state and science, and the free market. There will be no sin, only crime.

6

3

NICOLAE CEAUŞESCU LOVED TO HUNT. There are videotapes of him and his friends hunting bear: that is, tapes of him and his friends getting ready to hunt bear, and interminable shots of dead bears lined up face-down on country roads. One sequence shows the men pushing the women into the snow in a jolly manner.

There's also a ritual that is repeated many times at different locations. Ceauşescu and his friends, all men, are in a hunting lodge. (He had hunting lodges throughout Romania.) A dead bear sprawls on the floor. A man goes down on all fours and straddles the bear. A second man takes a switch and playfully whips the first man on the buttocks. Everybody laughs. Usually Ceauşescu does the whipping, though once he too is whipped, gently.

4

WHEN THE REVOLUTION CAME Petre was twenty-three and working in a factory. He was very depressed at the time—"brain-damaged," he says. He'd finished polytechnic, was making lousy money, and had no friends. He heard on Radio Free Europe about the revolt in Timişoara—a city, near the Hungarian border, where citizens had been protesting for weeks on behalf of a priest whom the police had sought to evict from his home. Then on December 21, 1989, while Petre was listening to Ceauşescu give a speech on the radio, the transmission was interrupted and music began to play. Petre switched on the TV and turned to the Soviet news. A map of Romania appeared on the screen. Petre doesn't know Russian, but he recognized the words for "Bucharest" and "tanks."

The next morning he was at the factory and, at eight o'clock, heard on the radio that the head of the army, General Milea, had committed suicide. "I said to the others, 'This will be bloody.' And they said, 'How do you know?' I said, 'I've read books about Latin America, I know about history, and it repeats itself.'" The radio played music until 10:30, when the workers took a break and heard announced, "Romanians! We are free! We have won!" Then there was static for five minutes. "We figured Securitate had got him. But then it came on again. 'We are free!' It was like a nervous breakdown: people cried or laughed. I laughed."

Later Petre says, "I was so happy when Ceauşescu was killed. It happened and—*ahhhh*, I could relax. I guess it isn't very civilized to be happy to see someone's blood. When I saw him dead I laughed, though most people at the factory shrank from it in fear."

5

ALTHOUGH MOST ROMANIANS experienced their revolution on, at best, radio and television, not all did. Lucian, for example, a twenty-ish aspiring grifter. At this moment he is standing in the central plaza of Bucharest, ringed by the old Hotel Athenée Palace, the even older university library, the royal palace, a church, and the relatively new Communist Party Central Committee headquarters. Cars zoom around him; it is midday. "This is where we would come to praise Ceauşescu," he says, looking at the Central Committee building, a blank, imposing edifice in white stone, and clapping his hands. Lucian takes you rapidly over to a corner along the wall. "I was here when Ceauşescu left. I could see Ceauşescu, he was behind that window with the grate." You walk away from the wall and Lucian points upward. "Then he went out onto that roof, got in the helicopter, and the helicopter flew away."

That was December 22, 1989. The day before, Ceauşescu had been giving a speech from the balcony when the crowd turned against him. Ceauşescu looked confused. His wife, Elena, looking furious and offended, said to the crowd, "Be quiet!" Ceauşescu shouted, "*Alo!* Sit down and be quiet!" But the crowd didn't sit down. The dictator and his wife were taken inside, where they spent the night. Late the next morning, the helicopter took them from Bucharest. Its pilot abandoned them on a highway. One of their two bodyguards commandeered two cars. The civilian drivers managed, by various ruses, also to abandon the couple. One of the bodyguards then slipped away. The remaining guard commandeered yet another car, which was being washed by its owner. This man drove the Ceauşescus to an agricultural research station, whose manager, by yet more ruses, succeeded in delivering the couple to the militia, who in turn handed them over to the army. The Ceauşescus were given a very brief trial by several people whom they knew well, and whom they treated during the trial with contempt. Then on Christmas Day the dictator and his wife were taken to a courtyard and shot. It is said that some two hundred rounds were fired to kill them. Their bodies are generally believed to lie in a Bucharest cemetery. People come every day to lay flowers on the unmarked graves.

Lucian walks you around the plaza. There are bullet holes all over the library and the Athenée Palace, the grand hotel of prewar Romania. Some of the hotel's exquisite interiors remain intact: the waiters wear black tie, prostitutes gather in the disco.

"These are the holes where they fired during the revolution?" you ask.

"Yes."

"Why?"

"Because there were terrorists there. Boom-boom-boom. You see that door? Here, I was here." Lucian scurries to a sheltered spot. "I was here. Over there was a tank. You know the word 'tank'?"

"Yes."

"Good. The tank fired—boom!—against the door."

"Why?"

"Because they thought there were terrorists inside."

You walk along the library, surrounded now by scaffolding. "They're rebuilding it," Lucian says. The library's interior was gutted during the December events.

The Central Committee building, by contrast, was neither burned nor fired upon. Presumably no terrorists lurked inside. No one ever found any terrorists, despite exciting rumors about Libyans and other Arabs. Nor did anyone otherwise identify the people who were shooting at the army during Romania's revolution. The killers came from some cultural black hole and returned there, remembered only as "terrorists" because no other word existed to describe them.

Inside the unharmed Central Committee building there was, however, a group of plotters, including the future president (Ion Iliescu) and future prime minister (Petre Roman). Various plots had been hatched by disaffected Communists through the 1980s. One of

9

them, eventually, worked. Iliescu, Roman, and their colleagues were inside the Central Committee building when Ceauşescu was spirited away. They soon announced that the rising in Timişoara was part of a popular revolution led by themselves. One may never know how much of the Romanian revolution was spontaneous, how much planned. In any event, Iliescu went on to rule free Romania.

6

YOU STAY IN Madame U.'s son's room in Bucharest. One wall is covered with pages clipped from in-flight magazines, duty-free catalogs, and other catalogs—advertisements for foreign cigarettes and liquors, for perfumes and stereo equipment. From the window of this sixth-floor room you see only other high-rise apartment buildings, identical to the one you are in.

Madame U.'s room has almost no decoration. Some mementoes of her husband, a hunter who died, young, of cancer. (A stuffed pheasant, antlers.) But in her desk is a drawer filled with photographs from their life together. This was, of course, their life together under Communism. Small black-and-white pictures of weddings and funerals; herself, youthful, with her graphic-artist colleagues in the Scinteia ("Spark") building, the state publishing center (she recently retired); her and her husband and friends at a party; him posing in his hunting outfit; her with her husband while he was dying; her with her son, their only child, when he was about six; her standing alone in the snow at Buşteni.

She can't stop showing you these photos. There's such a pile that ones you've seen on top slip and sift to the bottom, then come up again, and she shows them a second time.

7

IN ROMANIA THE HISTORICAL RECORD has been far too controversial, and far too useful, to be left to disinterested historians. On the borders of so many empires, Romania has ever been torn between being itself, whatever that is, and being part of something else. The territory now called "Romania" had its first significant appearance in recorded history when the Romans annexed part of it, marking Rome's farthest advance to the northeast. Before departing in A.D. 271, the Romans left their language (contemporary Romanian is much like Latin), some roads and buildings, and the rudiments of Christianity. Even prior to Rome's evacuation, "Romania" was being invaded by peoples from the east and north. Following imperial withdrawal, it was overrun by Goths, Huns, Avars, Bulgars, Magyars, Mongols. Romania was less a coherent zone than a primeval highway to somewhere else. Eventually in 1460, another empire—the Ottoman—forced the central Romanian principalities of Moldavia and Wallachia to become vassals. (Transylvania, more than a quarter of modern Romanian territory, was under Hungarian rule from the 11th to the 16th centuries, then Austrian, then Austro-Hungarian into the 20th.) In the 19th century, as Ottoman power waned and nationalism became a very active principle of Continental politics, Romanian patriots emerged to demand independence. They got it in 1877. However, poised as it was at the intersection of Ottoman, Austro-Hungarian, Russian, and even German influences, Romania could not remain alone. It joined the Central Powers in World War I and, enthusiastically, the "New World Order" proposed by Joseph Goebbels, and led by the Nazis, in World War II. After the war, of course, it became part of the Soviet empire, donated by Churchill to Stalin at the Yalta conference. Now it is to be part of "Europe."

History has many uses; Romania's history has more uses than most. What is striking today is that the most recent period of imperial membership—the Communist—is widely seen as useless.

You note this while visiting three history museums: in Oradea, on the Hungarian border; in Bucharest (the national museum); and in Constanța, near the mouth of the Danube and close to the Bulgarian border. In all three, the situation is the same. The Romanian people are shown to have descended from a root stock of people living so far back in time that they can hardly be identified. Although Romanian territory has been invaded constantly from the beginning of recorded history well into the present century, the "proto-Romanian" and then Romanian people never varied, preserving their national essence. Romanians adopted all the good aspects of the many peoples who overran Romania, and none of the bad ones.

This uninterrupted, quasi-genetic process of accretion and self-improvement, according to the displays and explanations in these three museums, continued without interruption through the Second World War. After that, the process stopped. Romanian history is presented in a series of rooms. At the end of the series of rooms is an empty room. That empty room contains the history of the Communist period, which is to say it contains the history of most people now alive in Romania.

8

THE FEMALE HALF of this elderly couple spent three years as a girl in Transnistria, east of Romania. From 1941 to 1943, the Romanian government (with German assistance) transferred tens of thousands of Jews to Transnistria, which is part of Ukraine, and settled them in work camps. Her father and sister both died there. She is now a large, nervous, demanding woman living in a decrepit apartment block outside Bucharest. Every night we watch TV – "Moonlighting" and, with particular ardor, "Dallas." And the news. On a sticky, buzzing summer night, German chancellor Helmut Kohl appears on the screen leading a somber procession down a broad German avenue. This is, the news reader says, a "private" event, marking the transfer of the remains of Frederick the Great from one place to another. The reburial is meant to symbolize something about reunified Germany healing its wounds and overcoming the Communist past. Frederick the Great (1740–1786) had succeeded in enlarging and strengthening Prussia at Poland and Austria's expense; the only decoration in Adolf Hitler's bunker suite at his death was Graff's portrait of the king. The news reader repeats several times that Frederick the Great was "the father of Prussian militarism." He also repeats poll results that show a large percentage of Germans have no idea who Frederick was. Chancellor Kohl looks very solemn. "Thank you very much!" the woman says, watching TV. "Good work!" And to her husband she says, "What does this mean? What will happen to us?"

12

9

HERE'S A STORY you hear from an acquaintance: "Like many Romanians during the war, this guy I was telling you about was a fascist. After the war, he went up into the mountains [the Carpathians] and continued to organize with other fascists. They staged guerrilla actions up until 1959. Eventually the Communists sent in small groups and the fascists collapsed—though a lot of these guys are still up there, and they remember a lot and have a lot of stories to tell.

"So this guy went into regular life, and one day in the late sixties he visits West Germany with his son. They drive around. They see how beautiful everything is, how prosperous people are, how orderly and clean and happy life is.

"And they park the car at some point, the old man's looking at all this around him, he says to his son: '*This*. This is what we wanted to do.' "

10

LYA BENJAMIN, together with the historian Sergiu Stanciu and various amateur helpers, works at Bucharest's Center for the Study of the History of Romanian Jewry. The center is in a small, old building on a broken street, surrounded by high-rises in various states of construction—part of Ceauşescu's urban project. Three mangy dogs and their keeper guard it behind an iron fence.

Benjamin is a diminutive, forceful, charming woman with a desk in the center's chaotic, tiny library—tiny, but vital, as documents on Romanian anti-Semitism aren't easy to find. (The most important single work, Matatias Carp's *Cartea Neagră* [Black Book], was published privately just after the war and is quite rare. The best account in a major language, Radu Ioanid's *The Sword of the Archangel*, is itself difficult to acquire, even though it was published in 1990.) Following the 1989 revolution, Benjamin, the center, and the rabbinate cooperated to put together an exhibition concerning the history of Romanian anti-Semitism. They wanted to bring to the Romanian people a revealing aspect of their history, a gift for which many Romanians were deeply ungrateful.

13

You follow Lya Benjamin from the center across fields of rubble. "I think perhaps that living in a border country is the best thing for an intellectual, a person of culture," she has said earlier. "It is more tranquil. You can see things perhaps more clearly from the border than you can from the center." She has told you about being surrounded by hate in a small town when she was just a little girl. Now she walks ahead, balancing on upturned slabs of pavement, you fear she might fall.

The exhibition is in Bucharest's Great Synagogue, the same temple that was torn apart by Iron Guard fascists one night in 1941. Photos, documents, and explanatory texts cover its four walls. They concentrate on the period from 1940 (with the pogrom at Dorohoi, claiming some 136 lives, and the subsequent establishment that September of a fascist government under Marshal Ion Antonescu) to 1944 (when Marshal Antonescu was overthrown and Romania joined the Allies). You learn about the massacre at Iaşi in June and July 1941, which claimed some eight thousand lives. A map has been prepared outlining the routes of the "death trains" between Călăraşi in the south and Iaşi at the Soviet border. Photographs show corpses being unloaded along the way. Poster reproductions announce laws mandating Jewish registration, restriction of movement and of employment, rationing of food and other supplies.

Romania never sent Jews north to the German camps, despite repeated and firm requests. (The Hungarians, who occupied a large part of Transylvania that is now in Romania, did; well over one hundred thousand Transylvanian Jews died in the camps, mainly Auschwitz, after a sudden, massive deportation in 1944.) The Romanian government was above all nationalist and would not have the Germans taking over its Jews.

The Romanian holocaust was largely an act of displacement rather than straightforward murder. This was true in many European countries, but the Romanians took it to a peculiar extreme. There were, of course, many small-scale killings, particularly between 1940 and 1941. But the Romanian government's greatest goal for "its" Jews was expulsion, to purify Romania. The vice president of Romania's assembly believed that "we are living at the historical moment most propitious for a total ethnic emancipation, for a national revision, and for the purification of our Nation from all those elements foreign to

14

its heart. . . . If need be, in order to complete the enterprise of ethnic purification, the governments of the provinces will consider measures of forced immigration of the Jewish element and all of the other foreign elements, which must be made to cross the frontier. . . ." So Jews were placed in trains, without water or food, the doors were locked, and the trains moved slowly on their way to Romania's border.

In a sense, once the Jews were placed on trains they were no longer "in Romania" but in transit, like immigrants without visas. Dying in the labor camps of Axis-occupied Transnistria was a death *outside* Romania. Even if Jews were killed by Romanian troops in Transnistria—as one hundred thousand were in Odessa—this was, from the Romanian point of view, an entirely different thing than killing them in Romania itself. And so their deaths were not quite the responsibility of Romanians, for they had taken place in non-Romania. This distinction may be insane, but it was not a form of excuse cooked up by clever Romanians with an eye toward the future. The engineers of the Romanian holocaust, from the neighbors down the street to Marshal Antonescu, did not carry it out thinking that the united fascist powers would lose and that one day they would have to justify their taste for murder. The engineers of the Romanian holocaust acted, in their time, with sincerity. To pretend that their actions were sneaky and abashed, done behind the backs of a generally innocent humanity, is very much to miss the point.

At the exhibition, Benjamin hastens to show you various documents. The historian Jean Ancel discovered a remark in Goebbels's diary, dated August 1941, that Goebbels attributed to Hitler: "A man like Antonescu proceeds in these matters in a far more radical fashion than we have up to the present." Antonescu himself addressed his Council of Ministers later that year: "There are still in Bessarabia [just east of Romanian Moldavia, and then part of Romania] 10,000 Jews who in a few days will be taken across the Dniester [river] or, if circumstances permit, even beyond the Urals." And in point number three of his four-point 1941 decree for expropriating the urban property of Jews: "This decree is, in this time, evidence of the integration of the Romanian people in the nationalist spirit that has traversed Europe, establishing a forward-looking and healthy base for the ancient nations."

15

Benjamin shows you other documents, other photographs. She stresses that Jewish soldiers fought bravely for Romania in World War I. When you entered the synagogue, you had been given a yarmulke. Benjamin pinned it in place for you, but it keeps slipping anyway. When you are at the head of the synagogue she wanders off for a bit and you want to say a prayer, or something, but you were raised Christian and a Christian prayer somehow seems like it would be blasphemous – the fascists' rhetoric could be militantly Christian. You get no further than clasping your hands and hoping you can remember all that Benjamin tells you.

11

A PICTURE AT THE EXHIBITION: A man is standing tied to a stake labelled "The Stake of Infamy." This is near the city of Constanţa, in winter. Under Ceauşescu, this photograph was used to illustrate the repression of "democrats" in the fascist period. But the man was in fact a Jew, and he was tortured at the stake, and died there, because he was a Jew.

12

ANTI-SEMITISM HAS DEEP ROOTS in Romania. When the great powers agreed in the late 1870s that Romania could have independence from the Ottoman empire, they insisted that Romanian nationalists enforce a clause guaranteeing ethnic and religious rights in the constitution. This fired the anti-Semitism of the newly independent elite. Philosopher Vasile Conta (a pioneer of wave theory) told the national assembly that "the Jews made up a nation distinct from other nations, whose enemy they are." Jews, like Gypsies (who would also be killed), had no state uniquely their own and so their allegiance had to be guessed at. Anti-Semites associated Jews with communism and with capitalism, given that both emphasized class, not national, loyalty. Romania's elite were desperately afraid of class war, obsessed by borders, and understandably xenophobic given that Romanian terri-

16

tory had always been the plaything of greater powers, and still was after "independence," and would be for decades to come.

Mihai Eminescu (1850–1889), Romania's revered national poet, the modernizer of Romanian and bard of the infant state, believed that his country was caught between socialism and liberalism and should avoid the dangers of both in favor of feudalism, "the system of greatest freedom, of decentralization, of communal autonomy, of the independence of classes. Men were not equal, and for that very reason they were free." Feudal Romania was a place of healthful purity and, needless to say, free of Jews. "The Jew does not deserve rights anywhere in Europe, because he does not work." Jews in Romania were "foreign in its body," a "race whose immediate aim was to get hold of the Romanian's real estate, and whose long-term goal was to get hold of his country."

"Whatever one may say," Eminescu wrote, "between us and the Jews there is a racial difference that does not allow us to have any feelings toward them in circumstances where honor is at stake—but contempt, and nothing but contempt." The poet, like many Romantic Europeans of his era, did not hesitate to invoke science: "[T]he ethnographer Hoffmann maintained that the development of the cranium in the Romanian race was admirable, that those crania deserved to be in the forefront of civilization.... Virchow, a celebrated naturalist, assigns the Albanian cranium first place among all the pure-bred crania from the ancient empire of the East, and the Albanian is identical to that of the Romanian race, to that of our people today."

The successful reproduction of eminent crania necessitated, in Eminescu's view, an historical process of selection: "In general, the happy struggle between races—the blessed struggle that elevates souls, that awards the palm to superiority of character, the struggle that engenders serenity and communion—is war."

Bogdan Hasdeu, whose work was the crowning achievement of 19th-century Romanian folkloric studies, noted that "the Jew drowns in avarice and grows moldy in filth." The great historian Nicolae Iorga, whose prolific output created Romanian historiography virtually *ex nihilo*, was sympathetic to fascism in his early years, warning the assembly in 1910 that it was "tolerant to a ridiculous degree" of Jews and founding, that same year, the National Democratic Party. His co-founder, Alexander Cuza, an academic from Iaşi, believed

Jews to be "an altogether inferior ethnic combination, bastards, as their physical and moral features show." How he must have feared them. Eventually, in 1938, Cuza would head the first straightforward fascist government, together with Octavian Goga. Goga was "the most promising and popular of the younger Roumanian poets," British historian R. W. Seton-Watson wrote in 1910. "Mr. Goga is to every Roumanian what Mr. Yeats is to cultivated Irishmen." (Seton-Watson laid the groundwork for English-language Romanian history.) "Our shepherd's swastika," Goga wrote in 1936 with a poet's instinct for the flexibility of metaphor, "is the most ancient blazonry in all Europe."

13

THE TRAIN FROM Bucharest to Iaşi today covers much the same ground as the death trains of 1941 once it turns northward through the rich, gentle landscape of southern Moldavia, then suddenly east at Tîrgu Frumos ("pretty market"). Ancient Iaşi—sometimes called, in translation, Jassy—was built on seven hills, inspiring wishful comparisons with Rome. The largest numbers of Jews emigrating to Romania came to Bukovina (north and northwest of Moldavia, now divided between Romania and Ukraine) to Bessarabia (across the river Prut, which constitutes the eastern border of Romania with the old Soviet Union; Bessarabia is now the republic of Moldova), and to Moldavia (also called, in Romanian, Moldova), the main city of which is Iaşi. These immigrants were, generally speaking, in flight: from the Hungarians in 1367, from Spain in the 16th century, from Poland, Ukraine, and Russia in the troubled period of 1648 to 1658 and later (notably in the 19th century, whenever Polish or Hapsburg or, above all, Tsarist persecution became sufficiently unbearable). Those Jews who were educated town-dwellers tended to settle in Iaşi—which thus became, in the 19th century, the birthplace of modern Romanian anti-Semitism. This is where Mihai Eminescu held forth, often carousing in a popular wine cellar that still exists, a congenial place where, ninety years after the poet, you get drunk with your own writer friends and toast the end of Communism.

14

IN IAŞI YOU MEET the retired pharmacist Dr. Kauffmann and his daughter, Odette. Dr Kauffmann is old and tired, sitting at a desk in a Jewish center, kept company by several other elderly Jews lucky enough to have survived the 1941 massacre. "The present generation doesn't know much," Dr. Kauffmann says, and the others nod their heads. Three of his brothers were killed.

Dr. Kauffmann tells how he was saved. "A pharmacist—he was also some kind of a Romanian Army officer, and he had heard there would be a killing of Jews that weekend," Dr. Kauffmann says. "He invited other pharmacists, Jews, to a party on Saturday night at his house. I went with my wife. At the end of the party, he said, 'You will stay here with us tonight.' We stayed, Saturday night, Sunday, to Monday evening. And so we survived."

Dr. Kauffmann, his daughter, and their friends are not particularly eager to speak. After Ceauşescu's death a nationalistic, anti-Semitic press appeared, very quickly. Cultural organizations and political parties were formed to promote Romanian ethnic self-esteem and to protect the nation from Westward-looking cosmopolitans, Jews, Hungarians, Gypsies, and others. The post-Ceauşescu efforts by Romanian Jews to publicize long-suppressed information about the Holocaust in Romania met with even stronger efforts by nationalists to downplay the deportation and/or murder of several hundred thousand people and to improve the reputations of various fascist figures, especially wartime dictator Marshal Antonescu, whose memory the post–Communist chamber of deputies honored with a minute of silence.

Dr. Kauffmann remembers a man who had led the Iaşi lawyers' association and was "an intellectual anti-Semite." After the war, he fled, only to reappear years later as a priest. Others came back with new names. Others grew beards.

(Someone in the room laughs.)

"So," Dr. Kauffmann says, "there were some *intellectual* anti-Semites. But there was no difference between intellectual anti-Semitism and nonintellectual anti-Semitism. Their aim was the same."

"It may be that the intellectuals were worse," another survivor says.

19

"They had the *responsibility* for the *ideas*."

"Just like now," the other man says. "It's the intellectuals who have the ideas. But they certainly don't know what the people will do with these ideas."

15

YOU WALK ALONG the streets of Iaşi with F., an intellectual. You pass a bookstore and in the window is a new book by Marshal Antonescu, who was executed in 1946: *Românii: Originea, Trecutul, Sacrificiile şi Drepturile Lor* ("Romanians: Their Origin, Past, Sacrifices and Rights"). The book, a digest of the marshal's views on history and his claims (against Bulgaria, Hungary, and the Soviet Union) for a Greater Romania, was first published in 1919.

You walk along the streets of Iaşi with F., a book in your hand — *Martiriul Evreilor din România* ("The Martyrdom of the Jews in Romania") — that contains photographs. It is a fine day, a little cool. You want to find some of the places in those photographs.

"Eighty percent of students were in the Legion," F. has told you, referring to the fascist Legion of the Archangel Michael that would later become the Iron Guard. Iaşi is still a university town. "Corneliu Codreanu, 'the Captain,' who headed the Legion, was a Pole originally, named Zelinsky." At least that's what his enemies said. Codreanu was born in Iaşi in 1899 and studied law. He learned about history from Nicolae Iorga and sociology from Alexander Cuza, both of whom had taught in Iaşi. His earliest political activity was rallying fellow students for attacks on Jews and Communists — organized Romanian fascism was, in its beginnings, a youth movement. Codreanu made his reputation at age twenty-five by killing Iaşi's police chief and not going to jail for it. "He said, 'We want a country without corruption. We want everything to be normal.' They weren't fascist, they were nationalist. His mistake was the anti-Jewish stuff. But...Iaşi was half Jewish. They controlled everything. They were peaceful; but they were like a little mafia. Very friendly with each other, very helpful to each other."

You've asked F. to help you find the places in the photographs. You stop on the high street, well known because several blocks of lovely turn-of-the-century buildings still stand there. You're holding a photo that shows a dozen Jews standing with their hands against a wall. "Yes," F. says, looking around, "it was probably right here." You notice a poster from a contemporary nationalist group with the slogan "Romanians, Don't be Humiliated!"

"Many Iaşi Romanians hid Jews," F. says as you walk along. "Romanians are not aggressive, they're a very tolerant people. Romania was like an Eden for Jews. They didn't have to wear stars."

(Actually they did, but the policy wasn't consistent.)

F. takes you to a large plaza dominated by a statue of a man on a horse. "The Russians gave that to us as a gift. They said it was Stephen the Great." Stephen (1457–1504), as prince of Moldavia, fought constantly with his neighbors in the feudal manner and signed on as a vassal of the Ottoman empire; he is one of Romania's national heroes. "Pretty soon we realized it wasn't Stephen at all. They must have had an extra monument around and sent it over here as 'Stephen.'"

F. takes you to a famous ancient church, inside which is a famous ancient corpse. It is covered in cloth. People are praying before the corpse and touching it for luck; scattered around it are slips of paper, each with a wish. "Once a year," F. whispers to you, "they pull the cloth back and you can touch the saint's hand. This is a miracle, because the body has not decayed. Most young people don't believe in this anymore, except at exam time. Then the church is filled with students."

You're particularly interested in one photo from *Martiriul Evreilor*, dated June 30, 1941, that shows a group of Jews cleaning the cobblestoned courtyard of the Iaşi police prefecture. They were washing off the blood of Jews killed the day before. On the right side, you see a man carrying a pail; in the courtyard men are on their knees, scrubbing. F. takes you to a courtyard that looks like it, but he isn't sure. You go down an alley and arrive before a tiny, very old house with a miniature garden in front. Most people in Iaşi live in high-rises, and this minuscule house seems like a tidepool from the last century. An elderly woman appears at the door. Her chickens flutter. F. greets her and asks, Is this courtyard over here the one where the Jews were killed? The old police station?

She says, I think so, you mean during the war? Yes, I think...

She calls out to her neighbor, an equally ancient woman inhabiting a squalid hole in the wall. They both appear to be living alone. She calls out, Is that courtyard the old police station courtyard? Where the Jews were killed? During the war?

The second woman is fairly sure it is.

You go back and look at it again, look at the old photograph in your hand.

16

WHAT WAS THE HOLOCAUST in Romania? The Iași massacre was by far the largest on Romanian soil. One hundred twenty Jews were killed in Bucharest during the Legionary rebellion in 1941; eight hundred in Nouă Suliță (later another sixty), one thousand in Marculești, eleven in Vilovca, nine in Milie. In towns, villages, or hamlets, a few Jews might be killed by police, German soldiers, local fascists, or practically anyone. Their corpses would be stripped. The naked bodies might gradually surface as the snows melted in spring; there are photographs of this, too.

Law after law was passed, to restrict movement of Jews, identify them, limit their access to food and to jobs. Professional associations would forbid Jews from membership. The first to do so was the Bucharest Bar, putting 1,302 Jewish lawyers out of work in September 1940. Half of Romania's doctors were forbidden to practice. You can see how such an idea gathered momentum: the Bar was quickly followed by the Sports Federation, the Opera, and the Journalists Union, and soon every organization was passing a resolution—you can imagine their directors meeting to pass such rules, adapting to the spirit of the times—so that Jews were barred from the tourism association, Picturesque Romania (October 26), the Directorship of Boxing and Wrestling (November 8), and finally the Association of Deaf Mutes (November 10).

In 1940, the Romanians and the Soviets were agreeing upon a new border in the northeast corner of Romania, to the advantage of the Soviets. When the border was closing, one hundred Jews from the former Romanian territory were transferred to just inside the new Romanian border then detained at the frontier railway station in Burdujeni. The new frontier was mined. The Jews were divided into groups of twenty or thirty.

Then the Jews were told to make their way back to their old homes, secretly, at night. When they reached the border they were either shot by Romanian or Soviet border guards, or else blown up by the mines.

17

BETWEEN THE WARS, nearly everyone who wrote for a public wanted to make Romania a clean and pure place, an unconquerable fortress, its people animated by a unified will, expressing their true selves, filled with purpose. The nation had existed but a short time. Its history, prior to 1877, had been one of fragmentation, occupation, and vassalage. Independence itself had come about largely due to territorial chess-playing among greater powers. After 1877, Romania's neighbors continued to covet this region or that.

Culturally, there was precious little the nation could claim as unique to itself. If you include Transylvania in the Romanian nation—as Romanian patriots certainly did, though it pertained to the Austro-Hungarian empire—the ethnic Romanian majority lived with large minorities of Hungarians, Germans, Saxons, Szeklers, Jews, and Gypsies, as well as numerous smaller groups (Czechs, Ruthenians, Turks, Tatars). The nation had four sizable religions—Catholic, Uniate (a compromise mix of Orthodox and Catholic), Jewish, and the dominant Romanian Orthodox—with a scattering of smaller Christian groups and Muslims. Even the weakest argument of nationalists—that they are an honored part of some larger, significant group—was difficult for the Romanians, poised as they were between Europe and non-Europe, Slav and Latin, Catholic and Orthodox, Western and Eastern.

The resulting debates were at once fierce and confused. Believing in the very idea of Romania required an act of will, and so, within Romania's literate class, acts of will were the common coin, Romanianness the common pursuit. This would be as true in the 1990s as in the 1880s, or the 1930s. Among the Romanian Academy's stated goals in 1937 were "to promote the spiritual consolidation of national unity" and "to civilize the ethnic territory...through the creative power of the national genius."

Perhaps the most influential philosopher in the early part of this century was professor Nae Ionescu (1890–1939), generally considered the spiritual father of Romanian fascism. ("The victory of the Legion [of the Archangel Michael] advances as a necessity of Destiny.") Ionescu was preoccupied with his people's "organic spiritual structure" and emphasized the role of Orthodox Christianity. "To be Romanian, not 'a good Romanian' but Romanian pure and simple, also means to be Orthodox.... To be Romanian means to be in a natural state." That Romanian state of nature, Ionescu believed, was under threat, necessitating "a wholly revolutionary politics" that would entail "decoupling us from world politics; closing us up in our own borders as completely as possible...and laying the foundations for a Romanian State of peasant structure, the only form in which we can truly live according to the indications of our nature and the only one we can implant that will enable the powers of our race truly and completely to bear fruit."

Ionescu's contemporaries, such as the minor theologian Nichifor Crainic (born 1889; real name Ion Dobre) and the eminent philosopher/poet Lucian Blaga (born 1895), shared his interest in Romanians' spiritual structure. Crainic was preoccupied by Orthodoxy and what he considered Orientalness: "Everywhere it is said that light comes from the East. And for us, who find ourselves geographically in the Orient and who, through our Orthodox religion, hold to the truths of the eastern world, there can be no other orientation than toward the Orient, that is, toward ourselves." Crainic believed that Hitler would aid the growth of Orthodox Christianity, calling him "the restorer of the Byzantine splendor of the Orthodox Church" and "the new athlete of Christ against atheistic barbarism." When Crainic became minister for propaganda under Marshal Antonescu, he defined the state as a "homogeneity of blood" and emphasized that "the ethnocratic state accepts the doctrine of the Orthodox Church without discussing it."

Lucian Blaga, not nearly so lurid a writer or thinker as Crainic, shared the desire to pin down a national soul, analyzing the various possibilities with urgency: "Our Latin symmetry and harmony are often battered by a storm that rages in the Romanian spirit at near-metaphysical depths; and this storm is the revolt of our non-Latin

24

soul. . . . Why should we violate our true nature, corset ourselves in a formula of Latin clarity, when so many other possibilities for development lie within us in that barbarian unconscious?" Blaga wrote at influential length on the varied but unified nature of Romanian culture, rooting it (as did Crainic and many others) in village life and folklore.

Not all interwar intellectuals or politicians were enthusiastic about fascism as such. Blaga moderated his statements about national soul and the "barbarian unconscious" when he saw the purposes to which such rhetoric could be put. Historian Nicolae Iorga was killed by the Iron Guard, though for political rather than ideological reasons. But the general sentiment, not to say obsession—that a nation was a part of nature and had an indivisible soul, that the duty of a nation was to conform to its essential nature and express its single soul—was remarkably consistent, even among the few Communists. And the great majority of interwar intellectuals and politicians were either fascists or made alliances with fascists.

Fascism, like many things, was purest among youth. The philosopher Ionescu was particularly influential, and his young students—notably the philosophers Constantin Noica and Emil Cioran, and the novelist and historian of religion Mircea Eliade—carried his ideas to greater levels of intensity. Noica wrote, "He who does not believe that nations too have a soul, does not see, does not touch, this extraordinary beginning that constitutes the legionary movement." Noica idolized Ionescu, as he idolized the legion's Captain, Corneliu Codreanu. Early in the Antonescu dictatorship he instructed his readers: "You are not permitted to doubt. Believe in the resurrection of legendary Romania." Emil Cioran did not believe in legendary Romania, but rather in that contradictory, complementary aspect of fascism, the mystical violence of modernity. "I have no ideas, only obsessions," he wrote in 1934, at the age of twenty-two. "Anybody can have ideas. Ideas have never caused anybody's downfall." Cioran stated that "Man should stop being—or becoming—a rational animal. He should become a lunatic, risking everything for the sake of his dangerous fantasies, capable of exaltations, ready to die for all that the world has as well as for what it has not. Each man's ideal should be to stop being a man. This can only be attained through *absolute arbitrariness.*" Three years later, just before Antonescu came to power, he wrote, "Whoever doesn't know how to hate with passion doesn't have the political instinct.... To hate is the political virtue par excellence.... We don't want an ordered, dutiful, and well-behaved Romania, but a Romania that is agitated, contradictory, furious, and menacing." Cioran told his readers, "What I think we must learn from Germany ... is the conscious cult of force, unlimited obsession with power, organized megalomania."

"We are waiting," wrote Mircea Eliade, who would later have an illustrious career as a historian at the University of Chicago, "for a nationalist Romania, frenzied and chauvinistic, armed and vigorous, pitiless and vengeful." Explaining why he believed in the legionary movement, Eliade wrote of the "tide of love that the legionnaires pour out," arguing that "the legionary movement has a spiritual and Christian meaning. If all the contemporary revolutions have as their goal the conquest of power by a social class or by a man, the legionary revolution aims, on the contrary, at the supreme redemption of the nation, the reconciliation of the Romanian nation with God, as the Captain said. That is why the legionary movement has a different meaning with regard to everything that has been done up till now in history; and the victory of the Legion will lead not only to the restoration of the virtues of our nation, of a hardworking Romania, worthy and powerful, but also to the birth of a man who is in harmony with the new kind of European life."

For Romania to harmonize with European life, a new man needed to be created. "A new man? By God, the new man is our salvation," Eliade wrote in 1934, "he is the meaning of our existence.... One makes the new man, one does not wait for him. The new man signifies above all a complete break with the hypocrisy and cowardice of the society in which we live. A young man, tied down to nothing, without fear and without stain, with his eyes turned toward the future...."

18

ONE IS STRUCK, in reading the interwar literature, by the richness of its contradictions. The fascists wrote movingly of ethnic identity and the national soul, of defending the nation from predators; but they also wrote of being a part of something else, something beyond the nation. Captain Codreanu spoke of Romania's "historic mission in the world: the defense of the Cross, of culture, and of Christian civilization." The fascists could be at once nationalist and imperialist. Theoretician Nicolae Roşu wrote in 1937, "The nationalist ideal is a myth that presupposes unceasing improvement, psychological and biological, of the Romanian nation, transcending the limits of an epoch, prolonging itself into eternity, on the paths of imperialism." (The same expansionary urge was, of course, part of Hitler's nationalism, and of Stalin's. Both men in turn admired British imperialism, which had also been nationalistic but still managed to cover much of the globe.) The fascists could be at once anti-communist and anti-capitalist. Nicolae Bogdan wrote in the late 1930s that Marxists "adopt an infernal principle of life – class struggle"; he felt that "this form of life represents a catastrophic regression in the history of humanity. Bolshevism signifies the return to the state of barbarism, systematic and scientific brutalization of all humanity, reduced forever to slavery, condemned to serve forever without appeal a closed caste of terrorists, of sadistic criminals, of maniacal kikes." Yet fascists would also call for "the socialization of the means of production," and describe themselves as "antibourgeois and anticapitalists." They could speak of a new Europe and go to war with half of it. They could combine medievalist nostalgia with futurism, belief in a "new man" with a craving for ancient roots, cold science with a romance of the irrational, fraternal equality with a yearning for hierarchy, burning chaos with order, cleanliness with destruction, life with death. Their philosophers could embrace arbitrariness but see no role for chance. The fascists could describe "our country of wheat, of ewe lambs, and of fairies" and shoot people at the edge of the forest, could envision both the "tide of love" and streets washed with blood.

One is struck, in reading the interwar literature, by the notion of race. Most fascist groups, not just Romanian, emphasized the purity, destiny, and greatness of their respective races. "In reality," Horia Sima, successor to Captain Codreanu, said in a 1965 interview from his Spanish exile, "the nation is not the product of history, on the contrary it is the nation that creates history. Like human individuals, the nation has a soul, a consciousness, an existential center." In 1935 Nicolae Roşu wrote, "Nationalism is a fluid that takes its source from the very substance of natural things"; six years later, as the murder of Jews and Gypsies got under way, he noted, "Only works that draw upon tradition, with roots that run deep into the race and the past, can aspire to permanence. Tradition in culture always flows into the matter of race."

The Romanians faced a problem, however, namely that the Nazis, their allies, believed that the Aryan race (themselves) was superior to other races. Did this mean, then, that the Romanians were inferior?

The German Nazis had themselves confronted this problem. Their solution was a typical mix of theoretical precision and political prudence. The basic principle, of course, was that Germans were the culmination of an Aryan race, destined, since its initial expansion four millennia earlier, to rule the world. The Germans could then cite as predecessors the German tribe of the Goths, who overthrew Rome (the Nazis' logical predecessor). They could cite the German Franks, who kicked Rome out of Gaul and established what would become France. They could cite the Angles and Saxons, who traveled from Germany to conquer England. And so on. In this retrospective schema, the German race found itself at the center and apex of world history.

Conveniently for the Germans, this racist world view possessed enough flexibility to integrate other European powers—hence the obsession with a new *Europe*, a vague space in which German particularities of tribal history and genetic makeup could be both diffused and embedded. After all, hadn't the architects of medieval Europe, the inheritors of Rome—Clovis and Charlemagne, Alaric, the Goths and Franks and Saxons—been Germans? Building a Nazi Europe would be to return Europe to its primordial unified greatness, reclaiming an opportunity bungled in the 5th century. Germany found its allies in those countries ruled centuries before by German tribes: Spain, France, Italy. One of Hitler's less remembered dreams, stated repeatedly before and during his reign, was alliance with England, which he saw as only natural.

In the scenario of German/European world domination, there were other races destined for slavery, first and foremost the Slavs. Characterized as *Halbmenschen*, "half-men," they were neither Aryan nor European. Nazi racial expansionism always headed East, into the Slav territories of Czechoslovakia, Poland, Russia, and Ukraine. The

West was a space to be integrated into the new Europe; the East was a space to be conquered and repopulated with Aryans, that is, to be *racially* as opposed to *politically* conquered. The distinction, rarely dwelt upon in the West, held great significance for the Slavs.

There remained the Jews and the Gypsies, who were neither German or European in origin nor Slavic. They were not even *Halb-menschen* but *Untermenschen*, "under-men." Their fate was extermination.

"Europe," however, was not quite so seamless as the Aryan vision suggested, and this raised problems for various local fascists, including the Romanians. For example, the tension between Germanity and Latinity was especially sharp in Romania. Germans, in the 20th century as (supposedly) in the 5th, could picture themselves as inheritors of Rome, but they were manifestly not Latin. That non-Latinity was basic to the Nazis' Romantic idea of barbarian vigor, among other things. The Romanians, on the other hand, were Latin, or at least they spoke a Latin language and had once been colonized by Rome, and their own Latinity was often crucial to their nationalist self-esteem. Without Latinity, the Romanians would leave themselves open to charges of Slavness (an argument made by Russian Slavophiles, and later by Russian Communists, in the course of their ideological planning for the takeover of Romania), or even to lesser charges of Bulgarianness, Serbness, etc. Romanians needed their Latinity to protect themselves, ideologically, from invasion. But pure Latinity would have placed them at risk with regard to the Germans. And so Romanian fascists came up with various novelties in order to mold their notion of themselves to the new realities. They pondered, as seen in the remarks of Lucian Blaga, their "barbarian unconscious." They resuscitated the argument that Romanians were a mixture of Latins and Dacians, the latter being a tribe conquered in parts of "Romania" by the colonizing Romans. "The mass of the colonizers were not of Italic origin," wrote Alexandru Randa in 1941, adding "we must not forget that the Dacian element has a superior range as compared with the Latin element in the racial structure of the Romanian people." (Historian Maurice Sartre has shown recently that many of the Roman colonists were indeed not "Latin," but rather from the Middle East, notably Syria; this is not what the interwar thinkers had in mind, though.) They could even imagine themselves as Aryans, extolling "our Aryan and Mediterranean race" or, as Horia Sima called Romania, "this old Aryan land." Randa wrote that "Romanianness today represents the rearguard of the great Aryan mass that descended 4,000 years ago into Greece, Asia Minor, into Persia, and into India," and that "the land of Thrace [meaning parts of Romania and Bulgaria] is the most important racial reservoir of the Aryan world."

19

CAN WE GO BACK a ways now, leave behind the mangled interwar period with its terrible consensus, its bloated corpses, its stealth and triumphant murderers?

We can go back on a drizzly day to Sarmizegetusa. As you stand beside a small, empty outbuilding of green metal, which guards the entrance to Sarmizegetusa, a family of geese waddles along and two boys on bicycles pedal by on a narrow road in the rain. Verdant grass grows vigorously around the edges of cut stones lying scattered. A sign, explaining what you might see at Sarmizegetusa, has fallen down. Inside the guardhouse are many plastic bags filled with ceramic shards, and an old brassiere gradually decomposing into the wet ground.

Past the guardhouse you enter Sarmizegetusa proper, a field of low ruins, perhaps two hundred meters square. The road defines one side, the three others are marked by gardens or empty fields. Piles of hay stand here and there among the excavations; they're damp and sweet-smelling. The excavations themselves are gradually being taken over by vegetation. The most spectacular, heavily restored, is the gladiator school, which, a sign reveals, had both hot and cold running water; next door was a glass factory. Some distance from the gladiator school lie the impressive remains of a religious site. A sign calls it "the most imposing cult edifice in Roman Dacia" without saying what the cult was.

Across the road from the ruins is a two-storey museum. Sarmizegetusa was the capital of the Roman colony of Dacia, which at its height encompassed much of modern Romania. According to a museum exhibit, Sarmizegetusa was built between the years 107 and 110 A.D., "on the location of a legionary encampment from the first Dacian war (101–102) by Decimus Terentius Scaurianus, first governor of the province." Its initial name was Colonia Dacica, but in 118 Hadrian renamed it Colonia Ulpia Traiana Augusta Dacica Sarmizegetusa. He called the new capital Sarmizegetusa because an earlier Sarmizegetusa, a long day's walk away, had been the capital of the Dacian king Decebal. It was Decebal who had forced the Roman emperor Trajan to fight on and off for six long years (101–106) before conquering Dacia. At the end, Decebal's head was exhibited on the Gemoniae Steps in Rome then thrown into the Tiber river, and the Romans erected a great column to commemorate Trajan's victory. Dacia was the last colony to be integrated into the Roman empire before its decline, and marked the limit of Rome's expansion toward the northeast.

Life at Sarmizegetusa was probably what one would expect. Farms, worked by slaves—the Roman economy, like the Greeks' before it, rested on slavery—surrounded the town, which occupied itself with administration, trade, pleasure, and worship. The most arresting feature of the exhibits at Sarmizegetusa's museum is the wealth of gods. You see altars or inscriptions to Hypsistos, Nemesis, Kore, Caelestis, Apollo, Apollo Grannus, Jupiter Optimus Maximus, Juno, Queen Juno, Minerva, Neptune, Serapis, Hercules, Fortune, Vulcanus, Liber and Libera, and Medusa; you see a beautiful faded portrait of Nemesis, her head framed by scales, a statuette of Isis, a mosaic of Priam with Achilles and Hector, a relief of Mithras killing the bull; you read that there were temples to Asclepius and Hygiene, to Silvanus.

Who were all these gods? Hypsistos is a Greek name for Eliun or Eljon, an old Syrian god; the Jewish/Christian/Muslim God is also called *el eljon*, "the most high god," in Genesis. Nemesis was a Greek goddess, an apportioner of justice; in the Roman empire she also became associated with racing. Kore was one name for the Greek Persephone, daughter of Zeus and Demeter, wife of Hades. Caelestis was the Libyan name of Juno Caelestis, the tutelary goddess of Carthage (now in Tunisia). Apollo was a famed Greek god, perhaps originally from Asia Minor (i.e., modern Turkey), the son of Zeus and Leto, while Apollo Grannus was a version of the Celtic Grannus, a god of healing (as was Apollo). Jupiter Optimus Maximus was a version of the sky-god Jupiter, or in Greek, Zeus; Optimus Maximus was specifically the Jupiter who acted as the supreme god of Rome. Juno was an Etruscan, later Roman, goddess of marriage and the protector of

31

married women. Queen Juno, in the period of the Dacian wars, was worshipped by Romans as the protector of the entire empire. Minerva was an Italic goddess, the deity of craftsmen and teachers. Neptune was the Italic god of flowing waters, equated with the Greek Poseidon; he too, like Nemesis, made appearances at racecourses. Serapis was the Greek version of Osiris, imported into Egypt by its ruler Ptolemy I, a successor to Alexander the Great and, like Alexander, from Macedonia, in the Balkans; a god of fecundity, Serapis then would have traveled from a region just south of modern Bulgaria, across the sea to Egypt (specifically Alexandria, the city founded by Alexander in his conquest), then back north again to Romania. Roman Hercules, in Greek Herakles, was the son of Zeus and the mortal Alkmene; in the Roman empire, he came to embody all the virtues of imperialism. The Roman Fortune began as a goddess of women then moved on to be the goddess of good luck. Vulcanus, an Etruscan god, then Roman, was the deity of fire and dear to blacksmiths. Liber was originally an Italic god of animal and vegetable fertility, later equated with the Greek Dionysos and thus a partisan of wine-drinking; his sister Libera was equated with the Greek Persephone. The Latin word *liber* means "free." Medusa was one of the three Gorgons, Greek deities and daughters of the sea-god Phorkys; the only mortal among them, she was beheaded by the hero Perseus. Isis was an Egyptian goddess whose manifestations are legion; in the period of Sarmizegetusa's occupation, she was especially associated with seafaring. Priam was the king of Troy, Hector his son, and Achilles the best of the Greek warriors who went to war with Troy (now in Turkey) and destroyed the city. Mithras is the Greco-Roman name for the Iranian god Mithra, himself equated with the Indian Mitra. Both were associated with daytime and light, and were guarantors of contracts. (The Indians also had him as a god of friendship.) Mithras was extremely popular with Roman soldiers at the time Sarmizegetusa was founded, and they spread his cult throughout the empire. He is often portrayed, as in Sarmizegetusa, slaying a bull; this action brought fertility and may even have created the world itself, and light. Asclepius, like his father Apollo, was associated with medicine, while his daughter Hygiene was worshipped to bring good health; both carried snakes. Silvanus was the Roman god of fields and woods, perhaps related to the Etruscan Selvans.

Evidently there was no shortage of gods in Sarmizegetusa. They came, to use modern place-names, from Tunisia and Libya, from Egypt, from Syria and Turkey and Iran, from Greece and various parts of Italy. Sarmizegetusa was a United Nations of the spirit world. And since new gods, like new wine into old bottles, so often take on the attributes of their predecessors, who knows what lives these deities had before the Etruscans and the civilizations of the Nile valley and Mesopotamia?

And who knows what lives they had after Sarmizegetusa, after the emperor Aurelian withdrew Rome's troops in A.D. 271, never to return? A display at the museum mentions "a paleo-Christian symbol (monogrammatic cross)" which "demonstrates the continued Roman presence in this complex after the retreat of Aurelian." Plenty of archeological evidence indicates continued communication between the empire and former Dacia after 271. This cross, however, does not. It merely shows the characteristic desire of the museum's organizers to assert that Romania was a part, however obscure, of the Western mainstream – which, in the typical catechism of European history, is constituted by Greek and then Roman imperialism up to roughly the time Sarmizegetusa was abandoned, then afterward by expansionist Christianity. (Forty-two years after Aurelian's withdrawal, emperor Constantine recognized Christianity as a legitimate cult.)

The museum's ordering of history does not, for example, recognize the mosaic of Mithras killing the bull as an example of continuity with imperial Rome, though at the time any border–dweller eager to prove enthusiasm for Rome would have been wise to choose Mithras over Christ. Mithraism enjoyed a tremendous vogue among imperial soldiers, who would gather in underground *mithraea* to perform their solemn rites. Mithraism emphasized the struggle of good against evil and the possibility of immortality, and enforced a rigorous ethics. Early Christian churchmen found Mithraism, with its popularity and unnerving resemblance to Christianity, to be particularly evil. But with that brilliant combination of intolerance and quick-wittedness that has often characterized the Christian church, the fathers hoisted Mithras by his own petard. They noted that the birthday of Mithras was celebrated with wild excitement by many people. This day was also the birthday of the sun among some non-Mithraic believers in Egypt and Syria, who appended to it a belief in a Virgin – her son was the sun. The church fathers further noted that Christ had no birthday. So why not make Mithras's birthday Christ's birthday, mixing in some business about the Virgin Mary? The people might gradually be led to believe that they were all celebrating Christ's birthday rather than Mithras's, and Christianity would replace Mithraism. In this way, the tradition of Christmas was born—Mithras's birthday was the 25th of December. Some Egyptians wanted to observe Christ's birthday on January 6, but the Western church eventually put its weight behind December 25, making January 6 the date of Christ's baptism, the Epiphany. All this became fairly clear about four centuries after the death of Christ, "the Sun of Righteousness," by which time Mithraism had declined dramatically.

As had Dacia, where, a museum display explains, "the Roman life continued, without interruption, but in a more modest form"—or, in Sarmizegetusa, "life continued among the ruins." Christianity, at least, eventually triumphed.

At the museum that rainy day you speak with the director, a bulky, almost florid, yet nervous man with little to do. Tourism, he says, dropped precipitously after the revolution, from sixty thousand in 1989 to ten thousand the following year. He asks repeatedly if you would like to exchange some dollars for local currency. He offers a bad rate. Outside on the road in the rain you speak with a Gypsy farmer who says the museum director is lying. "He was big in the Communist Party. There were never many tourists here. He just misses the old days."

20

CAN ONE ENDLESSLY till the ancestral graves to bring forth some new story? The residents of Constanţa, a lively Romanian port in the Danube delta founded as "Tomis" by Greek colonists in the 7th century B.C., are proud of their relationship with the Roman poet Ovid. He was the only eminent Roman who did not come to what is now Romania as a conqueror. Ovid came to Tomis/Constanţa as an exile in A.D. 9, when the city was a far outpost of Greek traders, feebly tied to Rome. He had angered the emperor Augustus with his unusually didactic *Art of Love* and with another, vague "fault" that has never been determined. Ovid alludes to something he saw in Rome that he should not have seen: "because my unwitting eyes beheld a crime, I am punished, and 'tis my sin that I possessed eyes." This accidental act of witness, he wrote from exile, was somehow an "injury" or "wound" for Augustus. It was at least the proximate cause for Ovid's ending up in "Romania."

"Alas! How near to me is the margin of the world!" Ovid wrote to Augustus of "clinging with difficulty to the edge of thy empire," isolated among "barbarian" people who understood neither Latin nor Greek, among "the Sauromatae, a cruel race, the Bessi, and the Getae, names how unworthy of my talent!" The main population seems to have been the "shaggy [hirsutis] Getae," who "laugh stupidly at Latin words": "No race in the wide world is grimmer than the Getae."

In the 19th century, Romanian nationalists would construe the Getae as among their ancestors. Struggling to acquire that double patrimony typical of European nationalism, they argued that Romanianness had existed in an unbroken line from Getae through Dacians and on up to themselves—but also that the Roman, and earlier Greek colonizers firmly tied "Romanians" to transnational Western "civilization." (They rooted this civilization, of course, in the classical world, with Caelestis, Hypsistos, and Mithras—Africa, the Middle East, and Asia—carefully removed). Legitimacy, in the paradoxical poetics of Euronationalism, had to be both national and universal (i.e., European).

Ovid, reflecting on his fate among the shaggy Getae, knew something about the psychology of membership in an ethno-geographical unity that sought to assert an imperial center in a spherical world. His only hope for rehabilitation by Rome lay in a thorough self-abasement. Salvation would come when he had implanted in his soul the imperial judgment and learned amicably to stroke the hand around his throat. "O sire, with what restraint thou hast used thy power!" he wrote to Augustus in the Tristia. Later, in the Epistulae ex Ponto, he would meditate upon a medallion decorated with the faces of emperors. "For my head shall sooner leave my neck, sooner will I gouge out my eyes from my cheeks, than be deprived, O deities of the state, of you." Ovid's embrace of mysterious guilt, his love of the empire that crushed him, was exacerbated by the approach of death. As the Epistulae wind down, he finally adopts the desperate role of colonial poet. "I have even written a poem in the Getic tongue, setting barbarian words to our measures: I even found favor—congratulate me!—and began to achieve among the uncivilized Getae the name of poet. You ask my theme? You would praise it: I sang of Caesar."

Not even this could gain Ovid a reprieve. He did outlive Augustus, but died alone in Constanţa in the year 18, during Tiberius's reign. A 19th-century statue of Ovid broods over the town square. He doesn't look very happy there in his toga, head down, facing a parking lot, a low fence, and the open sea. "I, who lie here, with tender loves once played" reads the Latin inscription, a line from the *Tristia* and a rather cruel joke, since it appeared in a poem to his wife and was intended to be the epitaph on his tomb *in Rome*. "Beneath this stone lies Ovid," the inscription concludes in Romanian, though no one really knows where the poet's bones are.

What once applied to Rome may also apply to Europe. In the realm of ideology, "Europe" has recently acquired amazing normative weight, a complement to its economic and military power. One is given to believe that there is a single valid way of life, which is commonly called modern or in many cases European. The terms tend to wander. They terminate in the belief, common among Romanian intellectuals, that there is a "normal" life. As a Romanian, you have to concentrate hard and figure out how to *become* normal. You acquire institutional qualifications: elections, freedom of capital movement, private property, the forms of normalness as offered by the normal nations back West. Yet you know, even if you prefer to think otherwise, that the West has its peculiarities, and if you are ever to become normal you will have to be peculiarly normal. And so further ideological layers are trowelled on, things like "neo-Latinity" or Christianity.

But there is still one more step, a subtle, decisive movement of the heart. You must erase your past, that is to say, your life. A Westerner has a normal life. Your own life, by contrast, has been abnormal. Since you can't live it over (though you may lie), you'll have to kill it. Fueled by your desire, not to say desperate material need, to "return to Europe," to leave your exile for a normal hearth, you will have to obliterate your past. You will have to take up residence in the last, empty rooms of your museums. Ovid, to end his exile, had to suffuse himself with a questionable guilt; as a Romanian, you must convince yourself of your innocence. It may amount to the same thing. Faith in the existence of a normal life gains its strength from the pleasant obliteration of history, which appears, from the normal present, to have been a series of mistakes. Communism, which was born and grew and died in Europe, is now seen to have been a mistake. Fascism, which had a shorter life among the same people, was also abnormal. Some Romanian nationalists now argue that neither was "natural" to Romania, but rather a foreign imposition. So many abnormalities, so many mistakes. "I have lost all," Ovid wrote when he finally accepted the permanence of his exile. "Life alone remains to give me the consciousness and the substance of sorrow." But in our new world all will be washed away and Ovid will return to Rome.

21

IN THE LOBBY of the Bucharest Intercontinental, an American couple watches over a baby in a stroller. Next to them an American woman holds another baby. They speak in big American voices. They have flown here to purchase infants for themselves. The solitary woman says, "We've had a lot of babies in and out of here, haven't we!"

The man says, "We don't even know who the father is!"

His companion says, "They said he was tall and handsome, but I'm sure they say that to everyone." She asks the woman, "Is this your first?"

"First and only! He's going to be spoiled rotten." She looks down at the infant. "He's my new little boy." Then she nods toward the couple's baby and says, "He likes the stroller."

The man says, "I hope he likes carseats."

The woman laughs, "I'm sure he hasn't been in one!"

The man says, "Everything will be new."

22

EIGHT TATARS SIT in chairs on a wide terrace next to the mosque one waning afternoon, conversing in Romanian. They explain that, although they all know Tatar Turkish and, in fact, are eager to have it taught in schools, it is easier and faster to speak in Romanian.

They're members of the Democratic Union of Romanian Tatars, Constanța branch. Tatars are relative newcomers to Constanța, having first arrived in numbers as a result of Russian expansion into the Crimea in the 18th century. The Tatars on the terrace this afternoon were part of a later migration, fleeing Stalin's pogroms after the fascist withdrawal from the Crimea and Transnistria. This terrace is like an aerie, on a sharp finger of land pointing into the sea.

The Tatars are happy about rejoining the European mainstream. One of them draws a map of Eurasia. He makes a circle in the general area of Belgium and marks it with a B. He then cordons off the far corner of Siberia and marks it, too, with a B.

"If the Belgians were here [Siberia], then that would be part of Europe," he says. "At bottom, Europe is an economic concept. Europe is the most economically successful area right now. The European concept has won, so of course it expands east. Once the Asian concept was stronger, and it went west." Now he draws an A, for Asia, somewhere east of the Ural mountains, an E on top of Western Europe, and arrows pointing back and forth across, roughly, Poland. "If Asia again becomes stronger it will expand. It's a question of which economic concept is stronger."

Does this mean that you, as Tatars, are European?

"It's clear that the European concept won."

But are you European?

"We are in Romania, and Romania is returning to Europe, so we are European."

Where does this leave the Crimean peninsula, whence several of these Tatars came and which two of them have already revisited after long decades of exile? They both compare it to Israel. The Jews, one says, "waited two thousand years to get their nation back." And the man who put Belgians in Siberia perks up. "Yes, look at Israel. It's in the East, but wouldn't you say it's a European country?"

23

WHEN GYPSIES FIRST APPEARED in Western Europe, in 1417, puzzled locals frequently called them Tatars. "A certain strange, wandering horde of people, not seen hitherto, came out of eastern lands to

Alemannia," one Cornerus wrote from Lübeck concerning the events of that year. Europeans of the period had a sketchy knowledge of ethno-geography. "Tatars" was applied broadly to eastern peoples and infidels, as was "Saracens"; Gypsies were called both, and also "Egyptians" (hence Gypsies), "the family of Ham," "Samaritans," "heathens," and variations on the Byzantine Greek *Atsinganoi* or *Atzinganoi*, which itself may refer to an heretical sect (Athinganoi) probably destroyed in the 9th century.

Taking advantage of late-medieval piety with regard to pilgrims, the Gypsies entered Western Europe posing as a tribe of Christians doing penance. "The reason for their wandering and travelling in foreign lands was said to be their abandoning of the faith and their apostasy after conversion to paganism," Cornerus wrote. "They were committed to continue these wanderings in foreign lands for seven years as a penance laid upon them by their bishops." These bishops were said to have resided in "Little Egypt," a nonexistent land. The Gypsies' ruse worked well, and they would continue using it for much more than seven years. One of their first stops in 1417 was Rostock, a north German coastal city – the same Rostock where, in the early 1990s, Germans would attack Romanian Gypsies seeking asylum.

Gypsies had lived in the Balkans since at least the 14th century, having come originally from the Indian subcontinent (from where exactly, or when, is the subject of scholarly dispute). Gypsies were particularly prominent in the Romanian principalities of Wallachia and Moldavia, for the simple reason that the princes and church leaders enslaved them. Gypsies in the two principalities would not be fully free until 1856. Meanwhile, other Gypsies would spread throughout huge stretches of Eurasia and, in due course, to the Americas.

Like the Jews, Gypsies have long been something of a special case as far as nationalism and ethnicity go. This ensured their fate during the Nazi era. In 1937, Dr. Robert Ritter, a psychologist, took over Berlin's Research Center for Racial Hygiene and Population Biology, which led German research on Gypsies. By 1940, a confident Dr. Ritter could report: "Further results of our investigations have allowed us to characterize the Gypsies as being a people of entirely primitive ethnological origins, whose mental backwardness makes them incapable of real social adaptation." By 1943, "despite all the difficulties engendered by the war," Ritter announced that the "number of cases clarified from the racial-biological point of view is 21,498."

"The scientific establishment," Angus Fraser writes in his *The Gypsies*, "welcomed the opportunities offered by the new regime. Professor E. Fischer, Director of the Kaiser Wilhelm Institute of Anthropology, wrote from the heart in the *Deutsche Allgemeine Zeitung* in 1943: 'It is a rare and special good fortune for a theoretical science to flourish at a time when the prevailing ideology welcomes it and its findings can immediately serve the policy of the state.' " Various methods were considered for murdering Gypsies, including putting them in boats then bombing them. A plan from Heinrich Himmler for preserving some Gypsies of pure blood as a scientific resource was mooted and rejected. In the end, most were killed in special camps. While estimates vary widely, probably at least a quarter of the one million or so Gypsies in the Axis countries were murdered by war's end.

In Romania, at least twenty-six thousand Gypsies were deported to the east and few returned; Romanians also killed smaller numbers in local attacks. In Romania, too, the possibility of a Gypsy preserve was mentioned, this time by one Ion Cialcea, who wrote in 1944 that "we are for a total segregation of the nomadic Gypsies. A portion of them must be set aside in a nature preserve so that the country may keep a rare species. . . . The ballast, the majority of rustic Gypsies, living in villages but especially in the cities, will have to be colonized in a peripheral region of the country, sent out beyond the Dniester, sterilized if necessary, so they can no longer proliferate, and thus stifle the qualities existing in the heart of our population. Let us not forget the bastard resembles more closely the inferior nation."

The Gypsies still struggle in Romania. "The Romanians never wanted to have anything to do with us," Gypsy sociologist Vasile Burtea says one afternoon in Bucharest. "The fact that they think Gypsies are from some other planet shows an incapacity to understand anything about our culture."

Since the 1989 revolution, Gypsy homes have been burned by Romanians. Gypsies have been chased from villages, beaten, and killed. Gypsies in Romania are more visible now because they've involved themselves in trade, an activity viewed with suspicion by many Romanians, especially if Gypsies make money by it. This trade is commonly called *bişniţa*, which means "business" but carries implications of shadiness and double-dealing. Any Gypsy who works in business is said (by Romanians) to be in *bişniţa*. "In terms of business," says a Gypsy merchant proudly, "we were pioneers. We still are." He stresses, however, that not all Gypsies are the same. Some are more civilized than others, some more nomadic than others, and some darker-skinned than others.

"The Romi [a name variously applied, including, roughly, to Gypsies from Romania] are an ethnic minority, not a national minority," Burtea notes. "Unlike other groups, Romi don't have a state. The concept of a state has never existed. There isn't any place to have a state, unlike with the Jews, though our histories are very similar. We have perhaps been held back, marginalized, because of our lack of a state concept." But Burtea sees this as the wave of the future: "Europe will be federal, there won't be any states. The condition of the Romi anticipates this. We will be the very first uniquely *European* minority."

At least they will no longer be known as Tatars. Although, as it happens, the true Tatars you met in Constanţa referred disparagingly to the Turks in their city, with whom they're often confused by Romanians, by saying, "Every group has its Gypsies."

24

COMMUNIST ROMANIA HAD essentially two leaders, Gheorghiu Gheorghiu-Dej and his successor, Nicolae Ceauşescu. Gheorghiu-Dej was a Stalinist and internationalist. Ceauşescu was a Stalinist and a nationalist. Because of his nationalist opposition to the Soviets, Ceauşescu received honors from the great leaders of the free world such as Richard Nixon, David Owen, and Queen Elizabeth.

Ceauşescu's nationalism—most spectacularly, his refusal to support the Warsaw Pact invasion of Czechoslovakia in 1968—was a risky endeavor, for the Soviet Union did not like its allies to disobey. Why was Ceausescu such a maverick? Because, anthropologist Katherine Verdery persuasively argues in her groundbreaking work *National Ideology Under Socialism: Identity and Cultural Politics in Ceauşescu's Romania*, he had little choice. Romania in the 1960s, like other Soviet bloc countries, faced tremendous difficulties. The rapid industrializa-

41

tion of the postwar years had begun to stall, not least because overall Soviet-bloc planning, which had initially sought to industrialize Romania, now wished to fix Romania as a source for agricultural products and light consumer items – a subordinate role many Romanians were unwilling to play. Furthermore, the legitimacy of the Communist government (as an anti-fascist movement, however overrated; as a force for modernization), the excitement of its ambitious reordering of society, the novelty of a New Romania: all these things had begun to fade. Political opposition – which had been destroyed, not least through murder, by the Communist Party following its takeover in 1947 and its expulsion of King Michael – had reappeared, however feebly. One gradually realized that Communism was not going to spread triumphantly over the world any time soon. On the contrary, the world was divided into two camps, and the camp one found oneself in was not necessarily the stronger or more prosperous. Or more free. A generation of Romanians too young to remember the interwar period – too young, in particular, to remember the bankruptcy of the old "democratic" parties, with their buying and selling of votes and cooperation with fascism, too young indeed to recall the fascist nightmare itself – was growing up and claiming its place. The promise of Communism stood ready for fulfillment, leaving Communists in the worst possible position for politicians, as they had made many promises.

Finally, the Communist party itself had consolidated into regional power bases, raising the question of national unity. As Verdery points out with great originality, localism had long been a distinguishing problem of the Romanian state. If we were to begin in Constanța, capital of the Danube delta region known as the Dobrudja, and travel counterclockwise, we would pass through Moldavia, Bukovina, Transylvania, Satu Mare, the Banat, Oltenia, and finally Wallachia – or Țară Românească, "Romanian Land" – the principal city of which is Bucharest. Since Romanian independence in 1877, with Bukovina and Transylvania added after World War I, people in Bucharest have sought to govern these regions as "Romania." They haven't always found it easy.

Certainly Nicolae Ceaușescu didn't. "Counties," Verdery notes, "came to resemble independent fiefdoms, held together by the unending peregrinations of Ceaușescu much as Charlemagne unified his kingdom in medieval times." And so, beginning after the death of his predecessor, Gheorghiu-Dej, in 1965, more so in the 1970s, and with maniacal energy in the 1980s, Ceauşescu played the nationalist card. "How would it be possible for a Party which proposes to lead the people along the road of building a fairer system, the socialist system, not to know the past struggles?" he asked in 1966. "How could a people feel without knowing its past, its history, without honoring and appreciating that history? Wouldn't it be like a child who does not know his parents and feels alien in the world?" Ceauşescu argued that patriotism and Marxism were complementary. He encouraged in Romanians a sense of being endangered, by the Soviets (the *Slavic*, Oriental, barbarian Russian Soviets) to the east, and by the Hungarians (the cruel, Oriental Hungarians, descendants of bloodthirsty nomads of the Central Asian steppe, i.e., the Magyars, even more barbarian than the Slavs!) to the west. The old themes of pre-Communist Romanian historiography, literature, and politics—Romania as the bulwark of civilization, "a Latin island in a Slavic sea" (but also Dacian), a culivated outpost besieged by barbarians, heir to Rome—were resuscitated and refined by the dictator, the "Conducător." For Ceauşescu was referred to by the same epithet used for the fascist Captain Codreanu.

Verdery shows how, under Ceauşescu, Communist and anti-Communist intellectuals enacted a debate whose origins lay in pre-Communist, nationality-obsessed Romania. Ceauşescu simply "presided over the moment when the Marxist discourse was decisively disrupted by that of the Nation. From then on, the Party struggled to maintain the initiative in the use of this rhetoric. If national ideology struck outside observers as the most salient feature of Romanian politics, this was not because the Party emphasized nothing else but because the Nation was so well entrenched discursively in Romanian life." Thus Romania's intellectuals under Ceauşescu began to fight over the bodies of the dead.

This debate, the most suggestive intellectual quarrel of the Ceauşescu years—accompanied by more "Are We Dacians?" discussions and the rehabilitation of Marshal Antonescu—can be summed up as one between "protochronists" and "antiprotochronists." The protochronist intellectuals argued that many things of universal significance, as many things as possible, originated in Romania. That most Romanians, not to mention citizens of other countries, didn't know this only proved the importance of the protochronists' struggle. They railed against "spiritual vassalage" and "the defeatist doctrine that divides the world into major and minor cultures." Romanian writers "cannot keep limping along behind European civilization"; their culture "is not a subaltern culture and the road to our values does not pass through the West." Such statements put antiprotochronists in a difficult position, as they could hardly argue that Romania really was inferior: "The protochronist complaint is... often enough legitimate, to the extent that values from other national cultures— equivalent with the values of Romanian culture—have entered into the European circuit while ours have not. But this defect is not going to be remedied by overblown gestures such as the 600-page manuscript (rightly rejected by the publisher) proving that [poet Mihai] Eminescu discovered relativity theory before Einstein."

The protochronists and antiprotochronists, as Verdery says, "shared a common ground: the Nation and its proper values." This would be true in historical research as well, with the debate about Horea's revolt. Horea was a Transylvanian peasant who led an uprising against feudal overlords in late 1784. The protochronists argued that Horea's revolt was actually a revolution, one that in fact anticipated the French Revolution by five years. Although the French did not know it, they had merely followed in the footsteps of Horea. Romanians could thus leap from the backwaters of Europe to its vanguard. Once again, any "antiprotochronist" counter-argument had to rest on defending the objectivity of scholarship, not a very stirring cry. The shared ground—that there could be a true understanding of the national essence, and that discovering that truth was essential for the nation—did not change.

Not to be left out, philosophers had their own variation on the protochronist-antiprotochronist debate, wrestling each other over the work and legacy of Constantin Noica. Noica was born in 1909 to a wealthy family. He studied philosophy in the late twenties and thirties, in Romania, France, and Germany, receiving his doctorate in 1940. He briefly supported the fascist Legion of the Archangel Michael. The bulk of his writing was exegetical. The Communists imprisoned and otherwise persecuted him until 1964; in 1974 he settled himself in one chilly room in the Carpathian mountains and resided there until his death in 1987.

Noica's originality lies in his work on local identity. "[I] object to the practice of both traditional and modern logic, which subsumes the individual under the general; both Aristotle and modern set theory integrate the part into the whole and the member into the set. To such a logic of subordination...[I] oppose a logic...in which the part is *not* placed in the whole, but the whole together with the laws on which it rests is placed within the part." Noica said that his "obsession is to rehabilitate the individual, but not as an isolated individual, rather as the individual invested with the power of the general." Broadly speaking, this was not only his obsession but that of many, perhaps most, Romanian intellectuals since the species first appeared in the late 18th century. How can a nation be part of the larger world without being consumed by it, or at least belittled? Noica's answer was that the whole world existed in the nation, in Romania.

What a message for a people adhering neither to the Soviet East nor to the capitalist West, and ignored by both! Noica's protégé, the distinguished writer and editor Gabriel Liiceanu, summed up: "Noica burst into Romanian culture beginning in 1968, thus at the time when two distinct and parallel phenomena had taken place in Romania: on the one hand, a liberalization of thought, an acceptance of the fact that it is possible to think and to create culturally beyond dogmas; on the other, a preference on the part of official [Ceauşescu] politics for upholding national differences rather than supranational integrating theses. Noica's entire thought...was a response to a twofold objective need: to regain originality of thought, after years of mental monotony brought on by a dialectical and historical materialism reduced to the level of schoolbooks; and the need for self-definition, for regaining a national consciousness."

Both sides took Noica as their own. The protochronists saw Noica as a patriot reviving the glory of indigenous Romanian philosophy. This philosophy began, one protochronist wrote, as "an *implicit philosophy*, unsystematic, a state of the spirit, a spiritual attitude, a protophilosophy, on the basis of which there will develop an *explicit philosophy* as an exercise of the spirit, as doctrinaire thought.... [Noica] refers to this wisdom as the beginning of knowledge, as the prehistory of philosophy." Romanian philosophy has been "a perennial value of Romanian spirituality."

The antiprotochronists, those in what they called "the Noica School," sought rather to place Noica and themselves in a larger ethnic group whose traditions were more systematic and explicit: Western Europe. Noica, they pointed out, had emphasized throughout his career the professional necessity of grounding one's philosophizing in the Western tradition from the Greeks onward. "Noica," Liiceanu wrote, "sent us to the great texts and instruments of European culture, . . . as wellsprings for a spirit that is not closed up in provincial frustrations and vanities." This "ritual of liberation," he continued, "was and still is the form in which certain great values of today's Romanian spirituality will survive." The Noicans used "professional standards" as a sword against the Noica-stealing nationalists' patriotism. But both sides shared crucial presuppositions: that the ethnic and spiritual realms overlap (at least), and that Romania's national spirit was embattled and even in danger of disappearing into the maw of universalism (whether Communist or Western European).

Such were among the most vigorous intellectual debates of the Ceauşescu era. Following the dictator's execution, protochronists and antiprotochronists alike rose to prominence. The ex-Communist National Salvation Front brought various antiprotochronists into ministerial positions. (Many later resigned when the new regime became repressive.) Some protochronists also entered government, though their most vivid work has been in journalism. Protochronists Corneliu Vadim Tudor and Eugen Barbu founded newspapers which soon specialized in anti-Gypsy, anti-Hungarian, and anti-Semitic tirades of astonishing virulence; folkloric and religious (Romanian Orthodox) essays; fawning, sentimental articles featuring Marshal Antonescu and other fascist figures; furious denunciations of the Russians, Americans, Masons, and the European Community; and appreciative commentary on the reign of Ceauşescu himself. None of this outpouring has been the least bit Marxist. The national essence has survived its would-be vessel, the Party. State Communism's clunky prose has departed in favor of something much more exciting. Strangely, that Marxist language had served reasonably well to express many of the nationalist, even racist ideas of the Ceauşescu period. Now the pre-

1989 language is retired, like a weapon that has become outdated and useless in battle, a wooden sword. The new swords are of steel.

25

HIS LIFE IS OVER and he knows it and it doesn't make him happy. He'd specialized in agricultural technology. He is, for the moment, still head of a small operation that takes machinery to farmers except there isn't any machinery left and the farmers couldn't afford it if there were. Besides, he explains, the farmers all have their own plots now. They aren't interested in re-forming the old cooperatives (though Romanian farmers elsewhere are), so most of the farms are too small to justify the use of machinery anyway.

So he goes to work in the late morning, starts drinking, then keeps on drinking until he comes home and collapses. You are at his home one evening, with his two teenage sons and his lame, somewhat feeble-minded wife, when he returns in a rage. What had you been watching on TV in that darkened room? The news? A soap opera? He stands in the middle of the tiny living room, no longer healthy or very strong but animated by anger. He comes at you: "Malta! Yalta!" he shouts. "Malta" refers to the summit meeting between George Bush and Mikhail Gorbachev; "Yalta" refers to the meeting in 1945 of Winston Churchill, Joseph Stalin, and Franklin Roosevelt in that resort on the Crimean peninsula. At both, he believes, the fate of Romania was decided. His shouts turn to screams. "Churchill! Roosevelt! Stalin! Bush! Malta! Yalta! Yalta! Malta!" He begins slightly to cry, he staggers, he collapses onto the couch. Malta! No one moves. A whisper: *Papa.*

26

IT IS SOMETIMES SAID that the essence of a people, their true spirit, can only be found in a rural setting. For pre-Communist Romanian intellectuals, who generally spent little time in villages, the unshakeable authenticity of peasants constituted an article of faith. In the early Communist period, industrialization was the order of the day and so the proletarian became the authentic (internationalist) Romanian. Since Romania had been an overwhelmingly agricultural country, these proletarians were mostly ex-farmers. Under Ceauşescu the situation became quite problematic. On one hand, the Party wished to force industrial production upward, and Ceauşescu's plan for "homogenization" and "systematization" entailed razing villages and moving the inhabitants into apartment blocks. On the other hand, Ceauşescu prized the national (village) spirit. But true village life had to go. At least Romanians could visit the museum of rural life, built in the 1930s next to a pretty lake in Bucharest. A melancholy place, the museum features various dwellings arranged by region. Each had been torn from its village setting and moved to the museum so modern Romanians could appreciate their rural heritage without having to travel all over – though with systematization even travel would not, eventually, have led to any pretty villages.

Yet Ceauşescu died before bringing about the destruction of village life. Caşvana, for example, still lies in Bukovina, near the present Ukraine border, just as it did when founded by Stephen the Great. The people of Caşvana, maybe seven thousand in all, are, as they themselves emphasize, extremely *harnici* ("hard-working," from Bulgarian *haren*) and *gospodar*. This second word is both common and difficult to translate. A Romanian source traces it to Bulgarian or Serbian, though it may well come from Little Russian *hospodari*, Russian *gospodari*; the basic meaning is "lord" or "master of a household." The princes of Moldavia and Wallachia in the Ottoman period were known as Hospodars. The modern Romanian noun *gospodărie* refers to the totality of a rural household: the buildings themselves, the goods they contain, and the people who live in them. *Gospodar* would describe someone who has all these things. The Communists tried to put this word to socialist use, giving it connotations of "collective" and "communal," but found little success, for *gospodar* can really only refer to a family and its private property. In Caşvana, *gospodar* would, ideally, only be applied to a living-working compound entered via a carved wooden door – a large door, too high to see over, with a smaller human-sized door or doors at its base. The compound's exterior would be decorated with bright paintings of flowers and plants. Within the compound and facing its center would be, at least, various rooms for living, a separate kitchen, and a barn for animals and fodder. The exterior and interior walls should also have decorative paintings of flowers. Nearby would be an extensive garden with vegetables, fruit trees, herbs, and flowers; the fields, primarily of fodder crops with some vegetables for export, would be perhaps a mile away. Within the compound walls should live at least a mother and a father and their several children. All would be *harnici*, happy, healthy, well-fed, and full of love for each other. Thus the most important, abstract sense of *gospodar*, the sense in which it is used by the millions of Romanians living in cities who came from the countryside, its mournful sense: *gospodar* means "what one should be," that is, "what one has lost."

The dimensions of south Bukovina's landscape are perfect. The hills are high enough, the ravines steep enough, that the slightest motion will reveal to you a fresh vista of forest or a field of grain. The hills are low enough that they will never stymie you; they will always be part of your view but never obstruct it. They are gentle enough to be tillable but not gentle enough to be overwhelmed by the plow; they allow agriculture without inviting it. The Bukovinan landscape places you in a symphony of undulations where you are always somewhat lost but never frightened; and you're free.

While in Caşvana you stay with a farming couple and their son Gabi. The couple rise every morning at dawn, shoulder their long scythes, and leave for the fields. They return at dusk or a bit later. After dinner they have an hour or so to relax before bed. A Western visitor might find them quaint or picturesque, because they are short, bent, and weathered from a lifetime of outdoor labor; they use medieval tools and wear clothing that Westerners associate with the last century. But it is most difficult to live with people and find them quaint or picturesque.

The father explains the recent changes in land tenure. "In 1962, the farms here were collectivized. They were mechanized, and fields were devoted to a single crop." While farmers were not happy about losing possession of their land, they had little choice. Moreover, they were told that this was the way of the future and that they would all become richer. "There was a period when collectivization was very good, in the 1970s, say from 1972 to 1978. The process was complete and the collective was profitable. Then it just got worse and worse." Mechanization meant less need for farm labor. The people of Caşvana were able to survive in part because their sons would go to other countries, primarily Yugoslavia but also Western countries, and do construction work. The sons brought back currency and foreign goods. (Many Bukovinan villagers are more cosmopolitan than city dwellers.) But the backbone of the village, its land, was breaking. After 1989, the government redistributed land to the farmers.

"The fields are less profitable now than they were before," Gabi's father says in his clear, even voice. "Everyone has their own small farm. They're too small for you to use a tractor, so all the work is done by hand now. More work for less production." The government doled out land on the basis of a 1962 register and farmers' memories.

Were there disagreements about which land was whose?

"Yes. After thirty years — of course. People would say, 'This was mine,' and someone else would say it was theirs. But we managed to work it out."

Surely there were people before collectivization who had no land?

"Yes, yes, and it was better for them with collectivization."

What happened to them when the land was turned back into private property?

"Each of us was required to give five percent of our land to those people who didn't have any."

What do you think will happen in the future?

"Well, in the future, some farmers will work hard and buy the land of others. The richer farmers will then be able to use technology and make their farms profitable. And then they will become even richer. And so on."

Gabi takes you to meet the local priest. His pretty *biserică* is midway up a steep hill and receiving a coat of paint. The priest — a tall and stout man with the obligatory Orthodox beard — appears confident, points out his favorite interior decorations, sits you down at a table and asks questions about America. What is the land area of the average farm? How many animals would it have? What kind? His Romanian is languorous, yet probing, forming itself with studied ease into full sentences or even paragraphs; he is, in other words, a rural man of the cloth.

"The Romanian people are ill, ill from the cancer of Communism. They need to return to God." He's not a terribly interesting

50

man, but, as a visitor, one is expected to meet the priest. "Before, every citizen was free to worship or not to worship, though this was more a theory than a practice. The Communist Party directed a great deal of propaganda against the church, and against God." The priest does not mention that the Party had favored his own Romanian Orthodox church over the Catholics (mostly ethnic Hungarians and Germans), the Uniate church (combining aspects of the Orthodox and Catholic rites and encouraged by the Hapsburgs in hopes of separating Transylvanians from Romanian orthodoxy), the Jewish religion (the regime had had a good business exporting Jews for hard currency), Lutherans, other loosely Protestant sects, the proscribed Transcendental Meditation and Jehovah's Witnesses churches, and Islam. "After 1989, religious freedom was guaranteed by the state." And, though he doesn't mention it, state television began to air hour after hour of Orthodox programming, images of churches much like this one accompanied by a droning narration concerning spiritual values and the immutability of God's truth. Under Communism, priests were paid by the state, though they supplemented their incomes, sometimes substantially, by charging for baptisms, marriages, and the like. Romanian priests in general have a mixed reputation: *gospodar*, certainly, but not always *harnici*. "The church was full before," he says, smiling, "but now it is more full." And he goes off to greet two young, timid women in white head scarves and full skirts who bear with them a tightly bound, utterly immobile infant. The priest escorts them to a small anteroom lit by candles, opens and reads from a Bible, and makes the sign of the cross many times, baptizing the infant a Christian in the eyes of the Lord.

Caşvana also has a museum, founded in 1986, next to a famous tree said to be six hundred years old. You visit the museum with Gabi, his pal Cîrcu, and the founder and head of the museum, local teacher Gheorghe Pîtu. The museum consists of two rooms, one with display cases containing old coins and other memorabilia, the other an "average peasant home." The average home has a miniature bed, a cooking area with iron implements, a bassinet, colorful aging textiles. It is meant to be a memory but the memory is very recent for residents of Caşvana; some of the poorer villagers, those who did not own land before the reforms of the 1960s, probably still live in such rooms.

We discuss Caşvana-scale geopolitics. Pîtu taught history to

51

most of the children of Caşvana. "Hungarians are bad people," he says. There are about two million Hungarians living in Romania, mainly in Transylvania. "If you go where it's all Hungarians, you'll find the signs in the shops are all in Hungarian. Some of them don't even *know* Romanian."

Do many Romanians speak Hungarian?

"Very few.... This business of nationalism — anti-Magyar, anti-Semitic, whatever — is more something of the city. We're all Romanians here. There weren't really people from other countries here in Caşvana."

Were there any Jews here?

"Very few, two or three. But they left; they returned to Israel."

People seem relatively well-off here, compared to the cities.

"This was part of the Austrian empire, and it's partly that that makes the people wealthy — the discipline, the organization. People here are very *harnici*."

But you're Romanians, not Austrians.

"No, of course, there aren't any Austrians here. They had a higher civilization than we did, so naturally we took from them what seemed best."

You, Gabi, and Cîrcu leave the professor, walk around the six hundred-year-old tree, and stroll through the village. In unison you greet every single person who comes along the road, whether they are on foot or in horse-drawn carts. The only people you don't greet are those infrequent souls who drive by in cars, for they move too fast to greet anyone on a village road.

Gabi is detached in a good-natured way, aware of his responsibilities in guiding a foreign visitor. He worries about the future, but not too much. He is acutely in need of a wife. He divides his time between Caşvana and a machinist's job in the nearby city of Suceava. He feels pride about nearly everything in Caşvana and wishes to present a happy picture. He does not want to speak, for example, about the old days or about Securitate, the Communist intelligence apparatus. The Communists are gone, like a foreign army, the land has already been returned to the farmers, the current government, while corrupt, is still an improvement: that's that. Cîrcu, however, is thinner than Gabi, more thoughtful, and more distressed. He is willing to speak about Securitate. "They were from outside — professors, engineers, they'd work a little, listen. After the revolution they all left. I had a friend who worked for Securitate in Sibiu." In the southern Carpathians, on the rim of Transylvania, Sibiu is famed as a particularly lovely city with an intellectual tradition. "My friend was from Caşvana. He was an electrical specialist and was compelled to join Securitate. And he told me a bit about how it worked. They'd come into town and get a job, but they wouldn't have to do much. They'd work a few hours and spend the rest of the time"—Cîrcu cups his hand behind his ear—"listening."

"The Communist Party activists weren't old. They were young people. The Party worked to recruit more intellectual people—teachers, engineers. And of course it *was* the route to advancement." Cîrcu notes that in those days there had been rules for social behavior, whereas now, it seems to him, people live—his phrase is a common one—"outside of borders" or "without borders" (*fără de graniţă*). "There were two kinds of Communist activists: those who joined to help the people, and those who actually believed in the ideology."

What happened to the Securitate and the Communists after the revolution?

"The big ones just fled, like my friend fled Sibiu and returned here."

There weren't any fights?

"Well, yes, there were many cases. The police chief was beaten up. There was a fair amount of beating in the first weeks. People either left or, eventually, things calmed down. Though with Securitate, you can never really be sure who was, so you're never sure who is now." Most Romanians speak as if Securitate still exists. The postrevolution government laid off many Securitate employees and a new organization—the National Information Service—took over Securitate's tasks.

Another young man, Nicu, joins your group. Dusk slowly overtakes the village, and farmers trudge past carrying scythes over their shoulders. They will return home, the men will sharpen the scythes with a whetstone and perform various other tasks, the women will prepare dinner. Someone will turn on the television the moment he or she gets home, and it will probably stay on until bedtime.

Alternatively, especially if one is male, one might go out drinking. We go to a dirt lot separated from the dirt road by a low wall.

Farmers arrange themselves with liter bottles of Romanian beer. One group gathers around a two-wheeled cart that has broken down. They discuss what to do about it. Another group stakes out the low stone wall and sits there mutely. A few drink alone. The remainder stand in the lot in small bunches and talk.

As we do. Nicu, short and agitated, fond of the bottle, is in his element. "Obviously," he says, "Western Europe is interested in us because we're cheap. We can do what the others used to do." By "others" he means the Turks, Spaniards, Italians, Algerians, Moroccans, and other "others" imported by Western Europeans, notably since World War II, to do the low-paid, dirty, or otherwise demeaning work that proper Western Europeans felt was beneath them. "Before the revolution, we were members of *Eastern* Europe, like we were closer to Asia." Since the revolution, according to Nicu, Romanians' predicament no longer has to do with space—East instead of West—but with time. At present Romania is awkwardly positioned in time. "We're in the 18th century," he says. "Country life is very hard—up at six, and you work until dark."

"Villagers," Cîrcu says as Nicu pauses, "aren't interested in much apart from their own possibilities. Life here is very hard. You work all day and then you're tired."

"There's so much to tell you!" Nicu interjects. He hesitates, then: "We have a king!" Gabi and Cîrcu seem a bit embarrassed, but they really like Nicu. They all grew up together. And Nicu is good fun. "There—they say there are two kinds of music: Verdi and popular. The king is *popular* music! Maybe Verdi is better music, but I prefer pop.

"You need something *supernatural* at the center. That is the king. Democracy, and other forms of politics, are all made by men. You need something supernatural—nothing can *touch* the king. No man can touch the king."

Nicu invites us to his home, so we amble down the muddy lanes to his family's compound, an exceedingly *gospodar* collection of buildings nestled behind a high wooden gate. It even has its own well. Most villagers get their water from communal wells. Much of the home was built by Nicu's father, a strapping man with an excitable temperament softened by age, who ushers us into the sitting room and begins to pour his homemade *ţuică*, the fierce plum brandy fa-

54

vored by Romanians. Wife and daughters are introduced then sent away to prepare food.

Nicu's father saved a number of books from the local church and hid them from the Communists for decades. At Nicu's behest, he displays a volume from 1942, a celebratory photo book showing Marshal Antonescu in various poses with Hitler and Mussolini and King Michael. King Michael is still alive and, together with his capable daughter, Margarita, enjoys a fair amount of support in post-Communist Romania, particularly among democracy-minded opponents of the largely ex-Communist government. A king, so the argument goes, would link democracy with national identity and suture the pre-Communist past to the post-Communist future. Nicu loves the king. His book ties together Hitler, King Michael, and Antonescu with the successful "recovery" of Bessarabia (later lost to the Soviets). Bessarabia was the big political issue circa 1942, a key rallying cry and source of legitimacy for the fascist government of that time. The photos in Nicu's book are interleaved with fiery quotes from Mihai Eminescu about how Romania would never sell Bessarabia and Bessarabians. Eminescu was referring mainly to the Ottoman empire, which had received tribute from various parts of "Romania" for centuries. His emphasis on selling typifies the effort of many 19th-century nationalists, and later fascists, to emphasize that a nation's land could not be subject to the marketplace. Nationalist anxieties about being bought and sold run through 19th- and 20th-century rhetoric and point to a crucial reason why fascism took the form of national *socialism*. Both capitalism and communism were thought to be internationalist, or anti-national, both internally (because classes were pitted against each other) and externally (because internationalism was inherently expansionist and ethnically levelling). National socialism was supposed to be the compromise, a harmonious, soul-soothing alternative. People and land were not for sale.

Nicu also has a Bible, in Romanian, complete with Apocalypse attached, appropriately, at the end. He turns to chapter 17, which links Mikhail Gorbachev to a millennial plan for world domination. There is a reference to ten crowns—"That means the ten Soviet republics." To seven heads—"That's the seven leaders, including Gorbachev." "*Fiară* [wild beast] means Communism. And see here— *şapte munţi* [seven mountains]. In Russian, that's *semgorad*, which stands for Sergeyevich Mikhail Gorbachev. There! It's all right there in the Bible, in Apocalypse."

27

YOU VISIT THE NATIONAL LIBRARY in Bucharest looking for speeches by Nicolae Ceaușescu. Not long before, the librarians would have had no trouble finding such speeches. There were thousands and thousands of them. In 1989, an entire wing of the library was being designed to house Ceaușescu's speeches. But now, the speeches cannot be found. A large part of the library's staff mobilizes itself to help you. At one point, a middle-aged librarian is looking through some remote card catalogues when one of her colleagues stops by and asks what is going on. "I'm trying to find some speeches by Him." Catching herself, she looks up at her friend. The two of them laugh nervously, loudly. Him! Ceaușescu had been commonly referred to in conversation simply as Him, while Elena Ceaușescu was Her. Ineffable, all-seeing, all-knowing, the dictator and his wife had taken over even pronouns for Themselves.

In the end, you receive only a few small documents. What happened to the mountains of Ceaușescu speeches?

"They were burned," the young librarian says meekly.

Who did it?

"They were burned."

Yes, but *who* did the burning?

"It was done immediately after the revolution, on orders from above."

You mean the National Salvation Front ordered them to be burned?

"Something very much like that."

28

IN TRAVELLING AROUND ROMANIA one may encounter people who believe in democracy. Such people tend to be young and intellectual. They speak affectingly of having survived Communist dictatorship and of their hopes for a democratic and prosperous future now that the baffling, inexplicable, forty-plus-year period of evil is over. If one does not listen carefully, one may conclude that within the Romanian population there lives a group who are actually Westerners—displaced persons, so to speak, whom ill fortune deposited in Romania, but who will now (with luck) lead their country into the Western world of which (they presumably believe) it should always have been a part.

But which road should they take to heaven? Consider, for example, this thirty-five-year-old doctor in Constanța whose clothes are clean, who exudes the confidence of an educated person, who even speaks some English: "We need a monarchy," he explains, "because we need continuity. Presidents and prime ministers are here for a few years and then they're gone. Of course a democracy is best, but we are not ready for it.

"Now, a government knows it will be in office only for a while, so naturally it wants to make as much money as it can while in power. With such a system, soon the only reason to be in power is to make money yourself. This is natural. What we have now is simply corruption.

"A king would be good because he would establish continuity. He would be in line with the way we think as Europeans. He would bring us prestige internationally. Foreigners would realize that Romania is stable.

"Unfortunately, what we need in order to achieve a good monarchy is a dictator, a clever dictator, like Francisco Franco. Spain after the war was very poor, with a lot of stupid people—a low level of political education. Franco understood that Spain was right on the edge of being Communist. He knew what to do with the Communists, and he gave the country the slow political education it needed so that a democracy could work. He got rid of corruption—that is very important. You need a *clever* dictator."

29

AFTER THE REVOLUTION, Ana Blandiana, a dissident poet, helped found Civic Alliance, Romania's largest civic organization. Later she became its president. Her Civic Alliance is not a party, though one group within the alliance did decide to form an electoral party, also called Civic Alliance. Blandiana's Civic Alliance seeks to build what she calls a "permanent, critical opposition" composed of democratically minded people. Alliance members, like many Romanians, believe that the post-revolutionary government is not democratically minded, though it was elected by a majority. Civic Alliance also supports the return to power of King Michael.

"The biggest problem in Romania now is simply to learn the basics of democracy," she says. "After fifty years of dictatorship, we've lost even the ABCs. The person in power is there to serve the people who elected him. But for him to understand that, each one of them has to understand it as well."

Civic Alliance is trying to teach people how to be democrats. "Isn't it ironic," you ask, "that the Communists spent forty-five years trying to teach Romanians that they should be Communists, since that was the right way for people to be, and now you have to teach Romanians how to be democrats, because that is the right way to be?"

"Yes," she says. "It is ironic."

30

"THE CHALLENGE NOW," explains Florin, a professor who studies the work of French positivist Auguste Comte, founder of modern sociology, "is to convince people that they ought to be European, democratic, organized—in a word, that they ought to be normal. Regular Romanians are not civilized. They *cannot* be civilized after fifty years of Communism, of suppression! Before, Romania was like China or Africa. At this point, I think that Romania is some kind of no-man's land, not European at all, but not Asiatic at all."

Interestingly, Auguste Comte himself believed that convincing oneself that one is Western was the "final preparation for true humanity." "The human presidency," he wrote, "is irrevocably conferred upon the West." The civilization of the world, its gradual entrance into universal humanity, would, Comte believed, begin in France, the "core of humanity"; move on to consolidate the rest of the "white" world; then extend itself over the "yellow" race and finally over the "black" race. "The fundamental laws of human evolution, which establish the philosophical basis of the ultimate regime, are necessarily appropriate to all climates and races, except for mere differences in speed." The European government of this "ultimate regime" would "march openly toward the universal ascendancy of the religion of Humanity, which henceforth will tend to win acceptance for its regime as well as for its dogma and cult."

It is perhaps unfair to point out the similarity between Comte's conception and Ceaușescu's "new humanism." But both had similar roots in European tradition. They even share one classic inconsistency, what might be called "universalist patriotism." Comte saw France as leading the world to Oneness, while Ceaușescu and the protochronists saw Romania as the leading edge of humanity.

Florin, too, combines faith in "normality" with a nationalist bent, expressed in his case as concern about the power of Jews and pride in the Romanian Orthodox church. The Catholic church and the Catholic-Orthodox Uniate church are, in his view, anti-national. "The Orthodox church is very conservative and closed to outside influence. It is the only one that can absorb all the mythologies of early Christianity. Orthodoxy is very national because it lends itself to national thinking. Catholicism is international, proselytic. Catholicism is a *universal religion*. Only Orthodoxy believes the national spirit is important."

31

WHEN SIX COMMUNIST PARTY stalwarts decided, in March 1989, to send a letter to Ceaușescu protesting his policies, they put their complaint in this way: "Romania is and remains a European country, and as such it must move forward within the framework of the Helsinki process rather than turning against that process. You have begun to change the geography of the rural areas, but you cannot move Romania into Africa."

32

"YOU KNOW CHINESE HISTORY. You know that the Chinese are a cruel people," Alexandru Murgu explains over drinks at his home. "It's like that with the Hungarians. They are not a European people. They're Asians. Very cruel, brutal, heartless."

We sit around a lacquered table: Murgu, his wife, an engineer, a young medical student named Lucian, and a teenager visiting from Bessarabia who says nothing. Murgu notes that Transylvania was an autonomous region from 1940 to 1965, that after the ascension of Ceaușescu a policy of "romanization" gradually took hold. But, he says, even under romanization the Hungarians in Transylvania had been better off than the Romanians, with more money and more to eat. Immediately after the revolution, a Democratic Union of Magyars in Romania formed. Murgu perceived a threat. He became member number three of Vatră Românească, or "Romanian Hearth," which held its first meeting on February 8.

"We were afraid," he says urgently. "We were afraid we would be forced to learn Magyar."

"We would have to have a translator to go to the post office!" his wife shouts.

"Imagine going into town in your own country," Murgu continues, "and finding that people *refused* to speak your language, the language of the nation, and *insisted* that you speak theirs. It's as if the Puerto Ricans took over New York and everybody had to speak Spanish."

Everyone nods. The engineer wants to change the subject. His main concern is that he has no money. The only people that have money are ex-Communists, all of whom are now taking care of each other such that the old ruling class has transformed itself into the new ruling class, exchanging power for money, i.e., power. "So *now* we will be ruled by a class of capitalist communists!"

"For us," the engineer continues, "the 'left' is Russia and China, the 'right' is the U.S., with Europe as a fief. I know that in the U.S. 'left' and 'right' are defined differently. This is how they're defined here. It's probably hard for you to understand."

Murgu interrupts: "We are not extremists."

The engineer adds: "We are not extremists."

Murgu's wife shakes her head vigorously: No, they are definitely not extremists.

You leave with Lucian, to go to the home of his wife's parents. His father-in-law, an army sergeant, pours homemade *pálinka*—like *țuică*, made from plums, but here given a Magyar rather than Romanian name—and explains that "the Communist Party was always led by foreigners. Hungarians, Poles, Serbs, Jews, Gypsies. Ceaușescu's family was part Tatar Gypsy."

"Look," young Lucian says, "the Hungarians want to rule. They want to oppress Romanians completely. There was no policy of romanization. On the contrary." He uses medical education as an example. "They go to Hungarian schools, they have university professors who teach in Hungarian. So obviously there will be hospitals where you have to speak Hungarian. I don't like it. I don't want to learn Hungarian. When I graduate I think I'll go to Pretoria in South Africa."

Lucian, his in-laws, Murgu and his wife and his friend all live in Tîrgu-Mureș, a pretty and ancient town tucked into the folds of several hills. Tîrgu-Mureș is one of Transylvania's major cities, its population roughly split between Hungarians and Romanians. On March 20, 1990, within three months of the revolution, a series of seemingly minor events—protests and counter-protests involving the use of Hungarian in classrooms and the under-representation of Hungarians at the medical school, the placing of a Hungarian sign next to a Romanian sign on the wall of a pharmacy—somehow led to a full-scale riot and ancillary clashes in which several people died and many dozens were wounded. These events briefly received attention outside Romania as further evidence that Romanians are uniquely demented among the former Soviet bloc peoples. Then they were forgotten, though not in Tîrgu-Mureș.

One morning you have a meeting scheduled at the Grand Hotel with Murgu and Dr. Virgil Hobai, a member of the Vatră Românească executive board, Tîrgu-Mureș branch. Before they arrive, you have an opportunity to chat with the waiter.

Say, isn't this the hotel that was torn up by a mob during the March events?

"Yes, it is!" he says, smiling, with a hint of pride. "They ripped everything."

61

Why?

"I don't know why."

There are still slashes through the wallpaper and broken windows. The Grand was reputed to be a Vatră stronghold.

Murgu, a tallish though not prepossessing man, arrives with Dr. Hobai, who is short, well into middle age, and tends to look away from you when he talks. Murgu begins: "The Romanian people are sick from dictatorship. They are very different from the Slavs. Slavs have a mass mentality, they are easy to manipulate. Romanians don't have a mass mentality. Romanians are a people difficult to lead. The Russians did try, with arms."

Dr. Hobai: "In fact Romania was occupied. They forced us to cooperativize, and that just wasn't part of the Romanian way. The early [Romanian Communist Party] leaders were Jews, Magyars, Poles. They weren't Romanians. The Soviets were politically internationalist. This was Comintern policy. The International maintained that Romania was an ethnic conglomerate, therefore not really a country."

Murgu: "You have to understand, Romania is a Latin island in a Slavic sea. The Soviets, the Russians, motivated by pan-Slavism, wanted to dismember this island. Anti-Soviet and anti-Communist, I would say that is the Romanian spirit."

Both Murgu and Hobai think of themselves as intellectuals, and proceed to give a brief history of intellectual life in modern Romania. The initial influence, they say, was French. People knew Romania as the Belgium of the East. After World War II—neither man mentions the interwar period—most intellectuals fled. Those who stayed were watched. Later they were denounced and sent to work on the misbegotten Danube canal, where many died. When Ceauşescu gained power in 1965, a liberal, more Western-oriented regime ensued. Unfortunately, Ceauşescu visited China and North Korea in 1971 and took from those countries a certain model of despotism. Elena Ceauşescu, whose mental gifts were limited to shrewdness and implacability, began to acquire intellectual power. Party hacks could thenceforth get advanced degrees without studying (as Elena did). At this time, Ceauşescu announced the famous "July theses," which urged a proud nationalist isolationism. This policy, strongly anti-Soviet, gained him popularity. Then the economy started to decline.

The coal miners of the Jiu valley revolted in 1977 – the first strong opposition since 1947. They kidnapped the visiting minister of mines and demanded Ceauşescu come. He did. He doubled salaries; afterward, most of the miners' leaders died in various accidents. (Murgu mentions a Romanian proverb: "If your head is lowered it won't be cut.") In the 1980s, Romania's economy collapsed. Ceauşescu insisted that all the foreign debt be paid, which meant his subjects had to go without food, heat, etc. for long periods of time. "The situation," Murgu says, "became horrible. Men fought each other over food. People were the Helots of the *nomenklatura*. Ambulances didn't come for pensioners. Our rations were worse than in Auschwitz." This was a terrible period for intellectuals.

That period remains the most dramatic memory for Murgu and Hobai, as for many others. Murgu and Hobai fear it might happen again. They fear Hungarians might make it happen. "The Hungarians," says Dr. Hobai, "have the idea that they were more oppressed than Romanians. This is a very interesting point of view, since the situation was just the opposite."

Murgu: "The Romanian spirit is a tolerant one. We have welcomed everyone, Hungarians, Jews. The Hungarians have a very different mentality, of the steppes, a Mongoloid mentality. They are not a European people."

Dr. Hobai: "In Ceausescu's time, in Tîrgu-Mureş, all commercial posts were occupied by Magyars. Their community is very united. They eliminate Romanians at every opportunity. They have an intolerant spirit. But Romanians have failed to understand this situation. Moreover, the Party favored Hungarians, and the current government does too. Sixty percent of the current government is Jewish. Fact. There's no need to speak of 'anti-Semitism.' It's as if the U.S. president were Chinese and the vice-president Puerto Rican. But in the end, the Jews are not really a problem. There are only twenty thousand of them. Hungary itself is not even a problem. But the Magyars here [in Transylvania], *that* is a problem.

"When the Magyars organized after the [1989] revolution, it was immediately clear that their policy, unofficially, was the independence of Transylvania from Romania and Magyarization, excluding the Romanians. Their mentality is atavistic, barbaric. Just after the revolution there were killings of women!

63

"Vatră Românească was born as a cultural organization. It is a defensive organization. We are against the Magyars' pretensions to privilege."

We leave and go to Murgu's car, which eventually starts. The day is moist and green. You ask whether there are former Securitate in Vatră Românească. Dr. Hobai says there had been but they were purged in April and May of 1991, more than a year after the group began. He says Vatră has split between the Tîrgu-Mureş branch, which is nationalist and allied with the Romanian National Unity Party, and the branch in Cluj, a university town and the intellectual heart of Transylvania.

How do you know the Securitate people are all gone?

"We know!" Murgu said. "We worked with them all the time! It was a great distinction to be a member of Securitate."

We leave Dr. Hobai near his office and drive on. "You can't really know," Murgu then says. "That's why I left Vatră. Because you couldn't ever really know."

It is difficult really to know much of anything in Tîrgu-Mureş — especially concerning the 1990 riots. After the pharmacy-sign fracas on March 16 that year, an anti-Hungarian meeting of Romanian medical students and the burning of the mayoralty's Hungarian nameplate on the 17th, and a meeting of Hungarian high-school students on the morning of the 19th, the situation quickly deteriorated. Romanian villagers with crude weapons arrived on the afternoon of the 19th to join Romanian protesters in the center of town. A few hundred Hungarians gathered nearby at the Democratic Union of Hungarians in Romania headquarters, eager to move on to the town square. Instead the Romanians came to them. Over seventy frightened Hungarian leaders hid in the attic. Retired Colonel Ioan Judea, head of the local council, urged the leaders to come outside and get away in a truck under the colonel's protection. A few did so. They were severely beaten — two reportedly lost their eyesight — before the truck took them away. The remainder stayed in the attic until well after nightfall, by which time they could escape.

The following morning, the Hungarian union called a general strike. By early afternoon, some ten or fifteen thousand Hungarians had massed before the Town Hall. A smaller crowd of Romanians, perhaps three thousand, gathered nearby in the town square. Hungarians shouted "Down with Vatră." Romanians shouted "Europe is with us." Romanian villagers began to arrive with clubs and axes. In mid-afternoon, a small police force placed itself between the two sides.

From that point, things became confused.

At Lucian's house you watch a videotape. Lucian tries to point out the important parts. The videotape was made by an Irish journalist, a young man. You see him standing in front of the camera. "A Hungarian minority asserting its nationality"—he motions to the cameraman. He has made a mistake. They try again. "A Hungarian minority asserting its nationalism. . . ." Is that better? You see a truck coming from the Hungarian side, out of control; it crashes into the steps of a church. (One of its passengers, a Romanian, dies later, having injured his neck in the collision.) You see a young Romanian man—what was he thinking?—dodge through the police line only to be beaten on the other side. Jump-cut. You see Hungarians surging toward the Romanians. The police have disappeared. An old Romanian man is lying in the street on his back. From the Hungarian side an elderly man in a dark suit ceases running to stomp the supine man, over and over, on the genitals. The body doesn't move. More kicks, to the side, the head. A placard is placed over the still man's face, the crowd moves forward. (The man survived.)

Lucian explains that this video proves the Hungarians are barbaric and that they started the fight.

The next day you visit the Hungarian union headquarters. "You should see our videotape," a Hungarian man says in Romanian. "It shows that the Romanians started everything." This video incorporates other footage with parts of the Irishman's tape. You see the elderly Hungarian senator and writer András Sütő bloodied by the crowd on the 19th. Some of the Irishman's footage appears. Suddenly you see the old man lying in the street. Your Hungarian acquaintance fast-forwards the tape.

What was that?

"You'll see everything later on," he says.

You ask again and again about the scene. It reappears several times. It is always zoomed over by the Hungarian with his hand on the fast-forward button. "You'll see everything."

You see a confused scene of sudden agitation. "See, they started everything!" You see a dark tableau, from street level: crowds all around, in the background a road with trucks coming down it, trucks with villagers carrying clubs. "Those are Romanian villagers," the Hungarian says. In the middle ground, someone is handing heavy wooden sticks down from a window. Who is that? "Those are Hungarians arming themselves to fight against the attackers."

The video, its fragmentary quality exacerbated by the sudden fast-forwards, ends with a grand, leisurely scene from Budapest. Many thousands of Hungarians gathered there to commemorate the outrages committed against their Transylvanian brethren. In Budapest you can buy maps showing a Greater Hungary that includes Transylvania; the 1920 treaty of Trianon, "bloody Trianon," is remembered annually as the piece of paper that gave away Transylvania to the Romanians. In the video people gather with candles. Behind the podium hangs a huge Hungarian flag. A woman sings a lovely, very sad, Catholic song.

33

SINCE THE MARCH EVENTS in Tîrgu-Mureş, various things have happened in and around town. Two Hungarian men were fishing when sixteen young men led by someone nicknamed the Shepherd attacked them and took their fishing-poles. A Hungarian activist lawyer was beaten in a stairway by unknown men. A Hungarian boy broke someone's window with his slingshot by accident; the police abused him at their station and took his watch. Three drunk Hungarian boys urinated near the statue of Romanian national hero Avram Iancu and lived to regret it. They were initially sentenced to two and a half years in prison. The police, military, and legal institutions of Tîrgu-Mureş are all dominated by Romanians.

34

YOU'RE RIDING IN A CAR with an educated young Hungarian woman in the Tîrgu-Mureş night. Her greatest fear is that groups like Vatră Românească and the Romanian National Unity Party will gain power. The key for Hungarians, she believes, is not to compromise with Romanians. She says, "You must not forget that there are also economic reasons for these difficulties. It began when this area became part of the Austro-Hungarian empire. Hungarians are very hard-working, different from Romanians. We don't want to be given something."

Why is it that Hungarians are more hard-working than Romanians?

"Oh, it's just our mentality. A Hungarian always thinks how he can go up."

Later the editor of the Hungarian newspaper *Freedom* explains that everyone knows it is "utopian" to think Transylvania might be part of Hungary. "Magyars and Germans feel more European than Romanians and Gypsies. Hungarians and Germans here need to raise Romanians to their level."

35

IOAN TAKES YOU into his bedroom, with its precious packets of foreign cigarettes taped to the walls as decoration. Ioan is enormous. He lifts weights for hours every day. His dream is ever to become larger and stronger. He is already fantastically strong, absurdly, uselessly strong. Watching him do normal daily tasks is like watching Zeus balance a pea on a fork. He likes American pop music, which he listens to on a reel-to-reel tape player. "Not in America such machines!" he says, smiling with disdain and gesturing violently, muscles rippling, at his prized possession. "In America you would spit on such a machine! You would throw it away!"

After listening to some music he takes you outside to get a beer. You walk together through the empty streets of his forgotten provincial town, a day's hike from Hungary, dim apartment blocks all around. The bar is a little undecorated terrace on a corner. You each have a bottle of warm, flat Romanian beer. He gestures at a nearby building, four storeys high. "Not in America such buildings!" he shouts. "This is *nothing*, a small building, not even one home. In America you have buildings fifty storeys tall! No, *one hundred* storeys tall! This building would never even *exist* in America!"

36

PROFESSOR MARGA IS A PHILOSOPHER in Transylvania. He opposed the Ceauşescu regime in its later years and now sees a chance to start afresh: "In the first place, we need John Locke. In our situation now, it is very important to know the philosophy of a natural law of social life. In Romania, Marxism took Hegel's critique of natural law. My generation was under the influence of a Hegelian standpoint. But with Hegel we cannot build a democracy. In the last twenty years, Heidegger has been influential. But with Heidegger, too, we cannot build a democracy. Heidegger was a critic of democracy. In this situation, I find John Locke is a solution, with his philosophy of natural law."

37

IN JUNE OF 1990, hundreds of coal miners descended upon Bucharest to break up anti-government demonstrations following the first post-Communism election. They had been invited by the president, Ion Iliescu, and were greeted by him upon their arrival.

You go to a mine and ask a miner who had been to Bucharest what happened: "After my shift I went home and ate with my family. I looked at the TV. At a certain moment the program was interrupted, around six o'clock. After the interruption, it was announced that the TV station [in Bucharest] was being attacked and the government was in danger. The president made an appeal. He appeared on TV and called on people to come help the government. I called the mine, and I asked who was at the mine so they could give us men.

"Outside, miners had gathered in the street. People said, 'Come on, let's go to Bucharest,' and that sort of thing. So I dressed in my miner's clothes—so we could identify each other, because our clothes are different from other workers' clothes.

"We were shocked by the fact that things there [in Bucharest] had gotten so bad—that people were acting like that. It didn't appear to me democratic. Because I don't understand democracy as something where you go out, block the streets, keep people from reaching their homes and jobs, and oppose a government accepted by the nation. I was overcome. I work hard, and I want to enjoy my family and my home. And at home [on television] I see the same faces, shouting 'Down! Down!'

"I got a car from the mine and went with others to the station. There was a train from Deva with seven or so wagons. In the night we arrived in Craiova. Men had come [to the Craiova train station] prepared with hot bread, jam, water, food. There was another train already there with other miners. I don't know why, or what negotiations had taken place to get the train.

"At four A.M. we arrived in Bucharest, at the North Station. We didn't know where to go. It wasn't organized. We went in columns to University Plaza—we had some people who knew Bucharest. First we went to the seat of government. On either side and in front of the building were tough-looking boys with lanterns, chains, and wooden poles. About fifty or sixty boys. I didn't want them to have anything to do with us. Either [President] Iliescu or [Prime Minister] Roman then addressed us, saying 'Thanks for coming.'

"We headed for the plaza, without those boys. I saw things on fire. Let me show you—"

The miner makes a drawing of the boulevard leading from government headquarters to University Plaza.

"This was the road to hell. The road to hell. I saw on either side punks with rough faces, who had sticks and chains. I thought they were going to attack so I ran up to join the other miners. But nothing happened. Even today I don't know who they were, or what they were there to do.

"Before the plaza, we saw burnt buses, and burnt cars. There were no cops anywhere. I entered the plaza. Everybody spread out. Some of them started to move the buses with a tow truck. At a certain moment, a car appeared with a megaphone. It said that miners had surrounded the plaza and told us not to let others into the plaza. I don't know who was announcing this.

"I, with a group of boys from the mine, left for the Ministry of the Interior to find out what to do. On this route, there were little pieces of broken glass all over, and blood. I had hoped not to see this. I'm a professional man, not a warrior, and in that moment I was afraid. I kept some guys around me. I was afraid that we would be attacked with incendiary bombs.

"At the Ministry of the Interior there was an arsenal. In back, a military car was burnt. I saw Molotov cocktails around the military car, unexploded. I saw many traffic tickets. And windows broken. This was the work of someone. We entered the building and saw, outside, a civilian man who had been beaten. He came in and collapsed on a desk. There was no one in the ministry, no cops.

"Okay. Meanwhile, there was a house. Some people from Bucharest told us, 'Hey boys, come in here, there are Peasant Party people here, it's a conspiracy house.' We miners entered. There were pink and yellow papers around, and written on them something like 'We're going to overthrow the Iliescu government, come out onto the street.' The boys wanted to burn the place but I said no, it would start a fire. I'd been to Bucharest before.

"I left for the plaza, where there's a fountain, where...It had been taken by Marian Munteanu [a prominent student leader]. Miners surrounded it. Then I went to an ambulance and I said to the driver to go pick up Marian Munteanu. And the driver said, 'Marian Munteanu? The one who started all this?' And he started the ambulance and took off. I said to the others, 'That's what people from Bucharest are like.'

"Meanwhile, from the university building, I saw a miner come with a load of sport guns. He put them by the fountain. I knew him. By this time it was nine or ten [in the morning]. Traffic had begun to circulate. The miners surrounded the plaza and wouldn't let anyone in. The burnt vehicles were gone, a truck came to clean the plaza. At one point, people tried to force their way in, and the miners wouldn't let them. I had an opportunity to see miners look in a sack. I saw a pistol. It belonged to a youngster. And he was beaten, of course. I didn't beat him, but the people who found the pistol certainly did. The police took him away. Traffic began to circulate. I left the plaza and went to the House of Sport. I got there around four P.M., and slept. In the morning I went back to the plaza. I could smell the urine of the thugs who had stayed there in front of the Intercontinental hotel. Many citizens of Bucharest came and said, 'Come get the Liberals and Peasant Party members.' The tents [where protesters had been encamped for months] were destroyed. Then in the afternoon I went home.

"Really I'm very sorry I went to Bucharest. I'm not a political person — and that was politics. Everything there was prepared beforehand. It was a drama prepared in advance. Now I know, and I shouldn't have gone."

Later, the miners reconciled themselves with Marian Munteanu, who embraced their leader, Miron Cosma. A loose alliance was formed with the opposition, notably with Civic Alliance. Over a year after the first trip to Bucharest, the miners made another. This time they shouted "Down with Iliescu" and demanded that the government resign. The prime minister resigned; Iliescu did not. He went on to be reelected as president. From one point of view, the second trip to Bucharest was the opposite of the first. From the miners' point of view it was the same. They wanted to defend democracy.

38

THE ROMANIAN INTELLECTUAL holds forth in his cramped sitting room. "In the future," he says, "there will be a unity of races." All will take part in one "world civilization," such that there will be only "one race, which means there will be no races." Romania, he says, is turning to Europe because of its own European heritage, and because "European culture has authority. Africa, of course, doesn't have any philosophy."

39

AT A MOLDERING HILLSIDE MOTEL in a forest outside the coal-mining town of Petroşani, you sit in the reception room and listen to the clerk, who is lonely. "The Romanian people are panicked," she says, a slender woman, probably not yet thirty, dressed up a bit even though she is trapped in a dank room in a moldering motel populated only by a family of Gypsies (the men are itinerant goldsmiths). "We have no idea what kind of country we're in, what kind of government this is, what's going to happen. All we have is fear."

Her husband is in Austria and has been for three months. She flutters a teach-yourself-German book and sighs nervously. "Everyone in Romania wants to leave." One day she visited Hungary with her husband, and she thought Hungary was more beautiful than Romania. Her husband said that Austria was even more beautiful than Hungary. "Then I thought, after Austria is Germany, then France, then England, then — America. America must be very, very beautiful."

Forgetting, I would even go so far as to say historical error, is a crucial factor in the creation of a nation. . . .[T]he essence of a nation is that all individuals have many things in common, and also that they have forgotten many things.
　　　　　　　　　　　　　　　—Ernest Renan, "What Is a Nation?"
　　　　　　　　　　　　　　　(1882)

Bulgaria

1

HASSAN STOPS THE CAR at a road marker. You get out with him and Alibrahim and stand by the white stone. "This," Hassan says, gesturing toward open fields, one section plowed, another choking with plants, "was Romania. This"—another gesture—"Bulgaria." A truck passes by, and two old women in a donkey cart. The sky is overcast and you can feel the deepening of autumn. This part of far northeastern Bulgaria, a southern belt of the trans-Danubian Dobrudja region, was Romanian territory between the wars, reverting to Bulgaria after 1940. Neither Hassan nor Alibrahim has much to say. You loiter in smiling awkwardness, hopping to one side of the old border, then the other, laughing a little. Romania. Bulgaria. Romania. Bulgaria. Then you get back in the car and go to find a cafe and drink strong coffee in the remaining warmth of the day.

2

NORTHEASTERN BULGARIA IS a tidepool of Ottoman imperial history. Bulgaria was for the most part an appendage, or at least a subordinate, of the empire from about 1396 to 1908, when Prince Ferdinand

73

proclaimed full independence and named himself czar. In Bulgaria, as in so many other places, "nationalism" got under way in the early 19th century. Leaving aside the Muslims in Bulgaria, the non-Muslim population itself was mixed. Before the Ottomans, the Greek Byzantines had greatly influenced, and at times governed, Bulgaria, and a substantial minority of Greeks still lived in 19th century Bulgaria, mostly in the towns, following a different version of the Orthodox rite than did Bulgarians. So after four hundred years as a province of the empire, Bulgarians seeking to establish Bulgarianness had their work cut out for them.

The Ottomans had believed strongly that ethnicity, what they would have considered tribalism, was not a crucial aspect of personal identity. This belief dated back to Muhammad himself, who conceived Islam as above tribalism. From the Ottoman point of view ethnic tribalism was, at best, a very regrettable human tendency, one that made governing their vast empire unnecessarily difficult. This did not lead the Ottomans to stamp out ethnic identity, although—like other empires, like the Romans—they did go to war with tribes that rebelled. No, on the contrary, the Ottomans regarded ethnicity with condescension, perhaps even pity; for anybody who based his or her identity on something so trivial as ethnicity was clearly not broad-minded or civilized enough to be an Ottoman. Europeans liked to call the Ottomans "Turks," as if the Ottomans were some gang of brothers and cousins, a mere tribe, like the French or Germans. Not at all! Ottomans used the word "Turk" as a synonym for hick, hayseed, provincial. To describe oneself as a Turk would be to demean oneself, to make oneself disappointingly small, to abandon one's imperial, cosmopolitan role as defender of the true faith of Muhammad and a beacon for others—to trade in one's true humanity for the pathetic confinement of nationalism.

So a tidepool of Ottoman history such as northeastern Bulgaria would inevitably have a diverse group of inhabitants. There you meet, among others, an elderly man who knows Arabic and still remembers some Romanian from the interwar years. He is a leader of the Kızılbaş ("redheads"), a broad term which in this case indicates a wildly heretical subgroup of Shiite Islam, with its origins in 13th-century eastern Anatolia, Kurdistan, and Syria. Near his village you chat with two Pomak farmers; Pomaks are ethnic Bulgarians who converted to Islam in the 16th and 17th centuries. Later the same day you meet a middle-aged doctor, Margarita Georgieva, at a dinner party. She says her father is a Bulgarian who now lives in Turkey and has forgotten how to speak Bulgarian. Her mother is a Gagaouze. There's no solid consensus on Gagaouze history—"only speculations," as the doctor says—but the strongest opinion is that they are ethnic Turks from Anatolia sent to Bulgaria as frontier troops by the Byzantine emperor Michael VIII in 1261 under their chieftain Kay-Ka'us (hence "Gagaouze"). Around 1300 they converted to Orthodox Christianity. "I don't have any identity problems," Dr. Georgieva interjects cheerfully after a glass or two of whiskey.

Apart from the more commonplace Turkish Muslims, in northeastern Bulgaria one can even meet standard-issue Bulgarian Orthodox Christians, though they are in the minority—or, as they might say, with anger and resentment, a minority in their own country. But whose country is it? And what does it mean to have your own country? What does it mean for those of your neighbors who are not like you?

3

IN KLIMENT, A VILLAGE in northeastern Bulgaria, lives Hikmet Halid Mehmet, a big-hearted, burly man and probably the first entrepreneur in Kliment since the Soviet Union invaded and installed Communism in 1944. He had spent the last nine months of 1989 in Istanbul at a woodworking shop. Mehmet came back to Kliment after the fall of Todor Zhivkov, who had ruled Bulgaria for the preceding thirty-four years, and he set up a little shop of his own, making pallets from tree trunks. He looks like someone who spends his time maneuvering trees by hand.

Mehmet had not gone to Istanbul by choice. Like most of the men and some of the women in Kliment, and about 320,000 other Bulgarian Turks, he had fled Bulgaria after the Zhivkov regime decided that Bulgarian Turks weren't really Turks, but in fact Bulgarians who had been misled for the previous five hundred or so years about their true identity.

"In 1985 the police came with guns, and we were gathered in the center of town," Mehmet says at his home over the usual breakfast of fried unleavened bread and sweet brown dip. "They'd say, 'What name do you want?' I'd say, 'I don't want a new name.' They'd say, 'What's your name?' I'd say 'Hikmet.' They'd say, 'Hikmet...OK, now you're Hristo [Christ, in Bulgarian].' And they'd hold your hand and force you to write your new name." In Turkish, *hikmet* means "wisdom." When one converts to Islam, one takes a Muslim name. To abandon one's Muslim name is like deconverting, or abandoning the faith. Especially when the new name is Hristo.

Modern Bulgaria was forged in the 19th century in opposition to the Ottoman empire, the nationalist principle against the internationalist. "Early in life I understood that being a man meant bearing arms like my grandfather and father, and killing as many Turks as possible," Bulgarian revolutionary politician Kosta Todorov wrote in his memoir *Balkan Firebrand*. (Born in 1889, Todorov followed in the family line, participating in some guerrilla skirmishes in Macedonia and a comically botched attempt, run by Armenians, at assassinating the sultan in Istanbul—as well as both world wars.) Many Bulgarian Muslims, perhaps a third of them, fled to Ottoman territory during and immediately after the Russian invasion of Bulgaria in 1877, but a significant number stayed on to face various forms of repression that culminated in Zhivkov's exotic name–change policy, begun in earnest in December 1984. Mehmet was known as Christ for almost five years.

But with his anti-Turk policy the dictator Zhivkov at last overreached himself, as became clear in 1989, a bad year all over for Communist tyrants. Despite the years of steady repression, the Turks, Pomaks, Kızılbaş, Gypsies, and some Gagaouze rose in protest.

You drive out of Kliment one morning with a number of local men who want to illustrate for you some aspects of recent history. In May 1989, a meeting had taken place in Kliment, after which perhaps a thousand people struck out on the road to nearby Kaolinovo. Whole families chanted slogans about their right to keep their own names as they marched along a narrow country road.

The cars stop, you all stretch your legs on a road surrounded by tall and delicate trees swaying. A shepherd pushes along a half-dozen sheep with his stick. "You know," a man says, "this is called the 'Deli Orman.' " *Deli orman* is Turkish for "wild (or primeval) forest." According to some scholars, the wild forest extends well into Romania (known there as Teleorman). When one speaks of the northeastern Bulgarian Turks, one is mainly speaking of the *deliorman* Turks, whose Turkish has a number of peculiarities not found elsewhere, except among the Gagaouze of ex-Soviet Moldova. Some say the *deliorman* Turks are descendants of the Bulgars, a Turkic tribe that invaded Bulgaria from the north in A.D. 679, organizing the indigenous Slavs (who had arrived 150 years before) and giving Bulgaria its name; others say they descend from the Cumans, yet another Turkic tribe, who came from Central Asia and crossed the Danube in the 11th century. The first hypothesis would give these Turks just over 1,300 years of residence in the wild forest.

It was through this forest, along this road, that the Turks—most of them farmers, some workers—marched that day in 1989. "Behind these trees," D. says, "were the soldiers, maybe three hundred to six hundred of them. They hid there." At the edge of the wood a roadblock had been formed with tanks, and the soldiers ambushed the protesters. They dragged people off and handcuffed them to the slender waving trees. (A man illustrates, walking off and embracing a tree.) They beat people. (E. shows how he was beaten; he staggers and suddenly winces.) They killed a middle-aged man, shooting him in the lower back. (D. stands in the deserted road, bends slightly, and points to his own back, to a place just right of his spine. "Right here.")

The day after the ambush, you're told, a wedding took place in nearby Todor Ikonomovo, a largely Turkish village. Soldiers were stationed here and there, notably on a rooftop facing the mayoralty. The soldiers, apparently, were interested in a young man who was among the wedding party gathered before the mayoralty to celebrate. A scuffle occurred, and the soldiers fired their machine-guns from the rooftop into the crowd. Three people were killed—Mehmet Sali Sarac, thirty-six; Hassan Sali Arnaut, forty; Mehmet Sali Lom, fifty-two—and seventeen wounded. It was following these events that Hikmet Halid Mehmet and hundreds of thousands of others left for Turkey.

You lay wildflowers at a monument to the three dead men. Everyone gathers before the stone, first kneeling in the Christian manner, though none is Christian, then standing and holding their hands over their stomachs, as Muslims do. No one knows enough to say a prayer. D. takes you to his car, which is now parked in front of the mayoralty. He opens the back door and points to the floor. "I brought one of the people who'd been shot to my car to take him to the hospital. He bled onto the floor, there. You can't see the stain anymore."

4

THE WORD *deli* has other possible associations. In modern Turkish, its first definition is "insane, lunatic." The raiders who prepared the way for Ottoman troops on the march were sometimes called *deliler*. They weren't necessarily insane in the bad sense. Rather they possessed a reckless courage and the firm sense of conviction that often accompanies (or encourages) a certain madness. So we might consider Deli Orman the "forest of lunatics."

The Ottoman empire was founded by Osman (or Uthman, hence Ottoman), born around 1258 in the tiny town of Söğüt, about two hundred kilometers southeast of Constantinople (Istanbul). In later times, the story spread that Osman's family was descended from Süleyman Shah, leader of a Turkoman tribe that governed a small region in northeastern Iran. Süleyman, so the story goes, fled the advancing Mongols of Genghis Khan with his sons only to drown in the Euphrates. One son, Ertuğrul, supposedly moved on into Anatolia with four hundred followers and entered the service of the Seljuks of Rum, yet another Turkic group originating in Central Asia, who then ruled a substantial part of central Anatolia. These Seljuks gave Söğüt to Ertuğrul, who passed it on to Osman.

It appears more likely, however, that Osman's roots were among the many nomadic Turkoman tribes which entered Anatolia following the Seljuk Turks' watershed victory over the Byzantines at Manzikert in 1071. The Ottomans claimed a relationship with the Seljuks probably because it gave them legitimacy, something they might otherwise have lacked—since being a Turkoman tribe was, at the time, no great distinction. There were countless Turkoman tribes wandering around. They would hire themselves out in battle to both Christians and Muslims, look for good pastures, plunder, and mix into their religion a bewildering variety of Muslim, shamanistic, pagan, and Christian tenets. They were, in other words, *deli*.

These *deli* Turkomans often fought each other but, in principle, were still more interested in fighting the Christian infidels, for the expansion of the *dar ul-Islam* (abode of Islam) into the rest of the world (*dar ul-Harb*, the abode of war) was thought to be a good thing. We see that the *deliler* had much in common with Christians—except that they were, perhaps, less divided by their many variations on the One Faith than the Christians were by theirs.

Osman was born at the right time to fight the Christian Byzantines. The Greek Orthodox Byzantines were not at all friendly with the Western-church, Latin Christians, who sought to expand at the Byzantines' expense. In 1204, fifty-four years before the birth of Osman, the Christian knights of the Fourth Crusade had sacked Constantinople and pillaged its ancient buildings. "They have spared neither the living nor the dead," Nicetas Choniates wrote at the time. "They have insulted God; they have outraged his servants; they have exhausted every variety of sin." The Latins would control Constantinople until 1261. Michael VIII Paleologus succeeded in restoring something of the empire, but sundry western Christian powers were always trying to grab this bit of land or that, sundry Muslim powers were chewing up Byzantine territory from the south and east; Bulgarians and Serbs grabbed land in the Balkans; and the Byzantines themselves were forever quarreling. The gap between rich and poor widened severely and imperial income plummeted. The 1320s was a period of horrible civil war, followed by worse strife in the 1340s, when the regents of John V Paleologus tangled with John Cantacuzenus over who would get the throne.

As if overwhelming political chaos weren't enough, the Byzantine church itself was divided. In the 1330s Gregory of Sinai wandered about Byzantium preaching a mystical practice known as hesychasm. A hesychast pursues *hesychia*, a silence of the heart, particularly by repeating constantly to himself the "Jesus Prayer" ("Lord Jesus Christ, Son of God, have mercy on me") while holding his breath. The hesychast could achieve unmentionable ecstasy and see directly the divine light of God, the very same light which Jesus' disciples had seen on Mount Tabor. Gregory was a *deli* Christian. Hesychasm found favor at Mt. Athos, site of the Byzantines' preeminent monastery, and was taken up by the great theologian Gregory Palamas. Bitter controversy ensued. Gregory Palamas wrote of God: "He is both being and non-being; he is everywhere and nowhere; he has many names and he cannot be named; he is ever-moving and he is immovable; and, in a word, he is everything and nothing." Gregory Palamas's ideas on union with God would have been familiar to many Muslim mystics and theologians of his time, for whom the Jesus Prayer (probably without Jesus) would have been a form of *dhikr*, mystical incantation. But these were not the times, at such high political levels, for cross-cultural clasping of hands. Pro- and anti-hesychasts added their theological fuel to the social fire.

Against this turbulent background, Osman and his sons began to carve their little empire. From 1300 on, Osman moved at a measured pace from town to town, fort to fort, almost always against Byzantine nobles; he would defeat them in battle, or arrange marriage alliances, or buy their territory. Over a period of twenty-six years, he slowly encircled, then strangled, the strategic city of Bursa. On April 6, 1326, it fell to an army led by his son Orhan. Osman died, Orhan took over. He had coins minted and the Friday prayers recited in his name.

What distinguished Orhan from other Turkoman leaders, apart from talent, was his plan to extend his empire across the water and into the Balkan peninsula, that is, into "Europe." If he had not decided to do this, the Ottomans would be no more significant to the West than, say, the Safavids, Abbasids, or Mamluks. As it was, "the Turk" became in Europe a synonym for the infidel Muslim, the hateful Oriental.

The lines of ethnic loyalty were not so clear in the 1320s, 1330s, and 1340s, however. Orhan expanded his territory in Anatolia to a point where he could be taken as an ally by Byzantine factions. John Cantacuzenus, fighting John V Paleologus, asked Orhan for help and had him enter "Europe." After some successful raiding and John Cantacuzenus's ascension to the imperial throne as John VI Cantacuzenus, Orhan received the Christian emperor's daughter Theodora as wife. In 1349, Orhan, at Cantacuzenus's request, sent twenty thousand troops to Salonica against the Serb leader Stefan Dušan. Ottoman forces raided far into the Balkans, sometimes aided by an alliance with Genoa, which was seeking to counterbalance Venice...The Ottomans established their first permanent European base at Gallipoli. This angered John VI Cantacuzenus, but he wasn't in a position to do much about it.

From then on the Ottomans, under Orhan and, later, under his son Murat, advanced northward. Murat conquered western Thrace, Bulgaria, Serbia, and Macedonia, raiding into Bosnia and Albania. He also extended his domain in battles against the Turkoman powers at his rear, and against what remained of Byzantine resistance in Anatolia outside well-fortified Constantinople.

Murat's success raised a difficult question: How could he, as an essentially nomadic, traditional Muslim frontier warrior, control such a vast territory? One answer was to make Christian princes into Ottoman princes, allowing them, in accordance with the Koran, to preserve their own religion and their Christian communities. Christianity survived in Bulgaria and elsewhere not least because the Ottomans let it survive.

A second answer, in Europe, lay in the very *deli* quality of the Ottomans' warriors, the quality that made them such good fighters and such recalcitrant subjects. In war and in religion, there's much to be said for lunacy. The *deliler* were wild in their enthusiasm for Islam, so wild and hungry that they absorbed many things that hadn't the slightest connection to traditional, state-sanctioned Islam, with its hierarchies and canonical texts. Like roaming Gregory the hesychast, they had a lover's passion for God—true, deep, mad. Unlike Gregory, they combined their ardor with open-mindedness. Some believed, for example, in such non-Muslim notions as the migration of souls and the absolution of sins by means of confession. Some practiced adult baptism and a form of Communion involving not only bread and wine but also cheese. All believed in saints and saintly miracles, not as things of yesteryear but as realities of the present and future, as manifestations of God coming to visit their very own hearths, their own forests.

The *deliler* made excellent colonizers. Their nomad training, tribal solidarity, and religious fervor enabled them to withstand hardship and isolation; the flexible lunacy of their faith enabled them to convert the common folk they encountered. Islamic law requires, in general, that Christians and Jews be left free to follow their beliefs. Thus it leaves little scope for conversion. But nothing prevents the more *deli* among Muslims from sharing their soulful wares with others—their poems, dances, and songs, their arcane theories about numbers and colors, their secret rites, their tales of heroic saints and of miracles, their holy sacrifices, their dreams, their rhapsodic visions

81

of God. This fervid, bubbling Islam was what the *deliler* brought northward during the early years of Ottoman expansion, northward across the Balkan range and, eventually, into that remote section of northeastern Bulgaria still known today as the Deli Orman, or lunatic forest.

5

COMMUNIST BULGARIA WAS A country built for an imaginary people. The Party built its country for ethnic Bulgarian, vestigially Orthodox Christian, Communist believers. These people were not necessarily the majority. It built the country for people who lived the ideal modern life, complete with leisure time, cars, ample food and drink, sturdy ready-made clothes, a taste for refined culture, and a general sense of satiety and well-being. These people barely existed at all. So when one moves about the architectural spaces of modern, now post-Communist, Bulgaria one feels dislocated, puzzled, and strangely insufficient, as if one were riding a bicycle down an airport runway.

There are so many roads without cars. In Sofia, a huge esplanade leads to a mammoth national arts center; but no one is there. Broad ramps lead off the highway, then stop. You see the middle of a bridge, but neither its beginning nor its end are built, so that it appears to you not as a bridge but as the symbol of a bridge. On a brilliant afternoon you pass a large park, with a spacious lot for cars and a playground for children; no one has come, there is not a single car or child. You walk down an elaborate stairway to a tunnel; but there is no tunnel.

6

AFTER GAINING AUTONOMY, thanks to Russian arms, in 1878, Bulgarians tried various means to purify their new nation of Ottoman and Muslim institutions, of Muslims proper, and of Greeks. The Greeks posed a lesser problem; they were dispatched by pogroms, deportations, population exchanges with Greece, and discriminatory laws. In 1884 there were over fifty thousand Greeks in Bulgaria. By

1934, the number had dropped beneath ten thousand. The ethnic Turkish population in 1884 was over seven hundred thousand, nearly a quarter of the Bulgarian total. The Ottomans offered land to immigrants from the former province, and emigration kept a steady pace. But hundreds of thousands of ethnic Turks remained, offering a challenge to the Bulgarians' perilous sense of Bulgarianness.

Bulgarian intellectuals worked hard to purge their Slavic language of Turkish elements (just as Romanian intellectuals had labored, somewhat earlier, at cleansing their Latin language of Slavic, and Turkish, elements). Thousands of Turkish place-names were replaced by Bulgarian ones. Mosques were on occasion destroyed, and Ottoman gravestones used as building material.

But given the steady turmoil and unflagging nationalism throughout Europe in the period between 1878 and 1945, life could have been far worse for the ethnic Turks of Bulgaria than it was. No Bulgarian regime was strong enough to afford alienating either the Muslim minority or the Ottoman (later Turkish) government next door. Even the postwar Communist state, tempered by international-ism and lacking popular support, acted cautiously with regard to its Muslim subjects. Yet, by the 1960s, the government under Todor Zhivkov had seen the utility of chauvinistic nationalism. At the same time that Nicolae Ceauşescu elaborated his own nationalist program, and for some similar reasons, Zhivkov began a policy, tentative at first, of ethnic-religious purification. (Zhivkov and Ceauşescu often went hunting together.) Initial efforts were directed in particular against the Pomaks, who were especially problematic for Bulgarianness because they were ethnically Bulgarian while of the Muslim faith. "There will be a struggle," Nikolai Vranchev had written with unwarranted confidence in 1948, "between ignorance and deception, on the one hand, and knowledge and truth on the other. The bearers of the former are the old Bulgarian Muslims [Pomaks], and the bearers of the latter are members of the younger generation. Some day the older generation will pass away and take their ignorance with them. The young will remain and consolidate the new system with enlightenment and culture. And then there will not be even a memory of the Bulgarian Muslim problem that troubles us today."

Beginning in the 1960s, the Zhivkov government forced Pomaks to change their names to Bulgarian ones. Their mosques and Muslim schools were closed, Muslim rituals forbidden, and those Pomaks who resisted were imprisoned. As the official *Sofia News* explained in 1985, "[T]he 1960s witnessed the first big wave of resurging national self-consciousness among Muslim Bulgarians, which found expression in the renunciation by tens of thousands of people of the once assumed personal names of Arabic and Turkish origin." The official argument was that the Pomaks had been forcibly converted to Islam, a belief for which there is no scholarly base despite reams of pseudo-scholarship published in Bulgaria at the time.

The principle applied to the Pomaks was then transferred to the Turks and Gypsies, or at least those Gypsies, a majority, who were Muslim. In 1971, the 10th Party congress emphasized that citizens "of different national origins will come ever closer together." The Party spoke of *priobshtavane* ("homogeneity") and *edinna bulgarska natsiya* ("a unified Bulgarian nation"). The government and its scholars argued that all of the non-ethnic Bulgarians in Bulgaria were in fact ethnic Bulgarians deluded long ago by the Ottomans and (temporarily) made unaware of their true nature. "All our countrymen who reverted to their Bulgarian names are Bulgarians," Minister of Internal Affairs Dimitur Stojanov declared in 1985. "They are the bone of the bone and the flesh of the flesh of the Bulgarian nation; although the Bulgarian national consciousness of some of them might still be blurred, they are of the same flesh and blood; they are children of the Bulgarian nation; they were forcibly torn away and now they are coming back home. There are no Turks in Bulgaria."

7

RAIN IS FALLING AGAIN in the mad forest and you ride along with your friends to visit a tomb. The rain has fallen steadily all day on the undercultivated fields, the abandoned factory, the depopulated town, the burial mounds of ancient warriors, the thickly wooded ravines along this crumbling road in Deli Orman. You stop at an unmarked spot and slip and slide together down a path, between dripping bushes with bits of thread or cloth tied to them, thousands of damp offerings, down to the bottom of a small steep canyon where lies the body of Demir Baba, "Baba Iron," a saint.

You enter the tomb compound through a gate. On the right is a small white two-storey building, well-timbered, in reasonably good condition, with fireplaces for heating and cooking and a *meydan* for meetings and prayer. Young Hikmet explains that everyone goes to this *tekke* (Muslim mystical lodge), Christians and Sunni Muslims, Pomaks, above all the Kızılbaş, the heretical redheads whose saint Demir Baba is. Tall, handsome Hikmet, a slightly cracked person, an unsuccessful artist turned tepid politician, his sense of humor strongly tinged with mockery, a boon companion: "I've been here three times before. Everyone comes to this *tekke*. You sacrifice a sheep here and you will never be sick, or no longer be sick." He smiles. The tomb compound is surrounded by walls, about ten feet high, made with large blocks of stone. "These stones," Hikmet says, "are too heavy to be lifted by humans. This shows the power of Demir Baba."

At one point in the wall there are two holes, the surface around them rubbed shiny. "Look," A. says. "You stand here." He stands on a stone, in the open air between the *meydan* and the tomb. The rain is falling, making one sound when it hits the leaves of the forest, another as it hits the stones, yet another when it strikes the earth. "You stand here, hold your arms in front of you, pointing your index fingers. You close your eyes and walk toward the holes." If you fail to place your fingers in the holes, it might mean that you are *şeytan*, Satan—the root meaning is "the adversary"—or it might just mean that you are flawed. A. walks nervously along the path then puts his fingers in the holes. Hikmet tries after a bout of grinning; he walks confidently and succeeds in penetrating the holes. You try. You hurt your fingers. You all laugh! Hikmet suggests some supervision to make sure people aren't peeking. A. nods cockily, tries again—he doesn't come very close. Everyone tries again, with someone standing by the holes and watching. Everyone fails.

The tomb of Demir Baba lies in a domed stone building, perhaps twenty-five feet high at its zenith, with thick walls that begin, at the rear, to merge with the steep sides of the gorge. Inside, just above the door, someone has burned a curse in Bulgarian—"Your Mother." A candle gutters. Who lit it? Demir Baba must have been tall. His tomb stretches some eight feet, covered in green cloth, his headstone the distinctive Ottoman stele topped by the *taç* ("crown"), presumably a replication of Demir Baba's hat—it too is wrapped in cloth. Next to the tomb is a stepped platform for candles, the *tahtı Muhammad*, literally "throne of Muhammad." Hikmet lights some candles. The tomb is dirty, nearly undecorated, musty.

Outside again the rain comes down heavily, you stumble up the steep path, pulling on branches for support, you drive back, past the burial mounds, back to the sleepy town. It is now quite drenched, the roads have become watercourses, such that you and the few other people who can afford cars meet at the center of town, having half-driven, half-floated. The water is so high that it laps the exhaust pipes, you can't even open your doors, and you are trapped there waiting for the waters to recede.

8

"I CAME TO THIS WORLD. I am the iron pole of the *evliyalar*." The spiritual teacher, the *hoca*, intones this in rhyme. "After me, there will be no more *şeyhler* of my nature." This is the poem of Demir Baba. *Evliyalar*, originally "friends" (of Muhammad), is Turkish for saints; *şeyh* indicates the head of a religious order. The Kızılbaş *hoca* sits on a plain wooden chair before the wood stove in his sparse, dusty home. He wears a wool cap and cardigan vest, his soiled white shirt buttoned at the neck. When he speaks he looks away, sometimes closing his eyes. His wife stands irritably at the open back door with a switch, striking out at flies. Two younger Kızılbaş men sit and listen, as do you, together with two men from a nearby village.

"All wise men come from Khorasan." Indeed, much of Muslim intellectual and mystical history was led by sages from Khorasan, now a remote part of northern Iran. "There have been one hundred twenty-four thousand prophets since Adam. Of these, thirty-two are most important. These thirty-two can be reduced to four: Moses, David, Jesus, and Muhammad. Muhammad has four names. Different books call him different names." One of the young Kızılbaş men, anxious, and powerful in the shoulders, interjects: "In 1989 they came and took our book! It was a history of Demir Baba, hand-written! It told where all the *tekkeler* are. They took it and refuse to give it back!" The *hoca* sits unmoved; his wife says "Ah ah!" and waves her switch.

A child appears in the doorway, then walks off. The *hoca* tells his version of the story of Abraham and Isaac, and moves on:

"All wise men come from Khorasan. Ali Baba came from Khorasan to here. He was born in 1292 [thirty-four years after Osman]. There is an Ali Baba *tekke*. You see, all the leaders came here from Khorasan. On their way they met Jews and other travelling people. They were able to make room and to pass by the Jews and others. When Ali Baba came to this area, together with other *evliyalar*, he divided the territory. He established little *tekkeler*. Each territory got a *tekke* led by one of his followers.

"Demir Baba was not only a spiritual leader but a warlike man, with martial skills. He could stand on a horse and throw a lance. When he threw one and it fell someplace, that place would become a shrine, and people would pray there. He and his followers would set up towns.

"Demir Baba once lived atop the Šipka mountain, the mountain that separates north and south. It is the highest mountain in the Balkans. People said to him, 'Wherever you say, we will build a town.' Demir Baba threw a lance to the top of the Šipka mountain. 'Who,' he said, 'would come here to honor me?' The people said, 'Wherever, believe us. People will come.' He threw his javelin to the same place. 'Then that is where I will go.' If I get up at six in the morning, it is not until twelve that I can reach that spot.

"Once he said, 'Go here!' They said, 'Why here? There is nothing, it's deserted.' But they go, and they sleep the night, and in the morning they see that everything is green.

"And Elmalı Baba. He does gardening. Demir Baba approaches him and says, 'Why don't you bring us watermelons and cantaloupes?' Elmalı Baba says, 'But I just planted them yesterday!'

" 'Go and see.' And Elmalı Baba brings back watermelons and cantaloupes.

" 'Why don't you bring us some apples?'

" 'But they are very young; they are not ready to eat!'

" 'Go and look.' And Elmalı Baba brings back apples.

" 'From now on you will be known as Elmalı Baba [*elma*— "apple"], and when you reach forty years, you will be as wise as us.'

"All wise men come from Khorasan."

The *hoca* does not speak so much as intone, using old Ottoman words. His Turkish would be only faintly comprehensible in Istanbul.

"Four people emerged as real prophets—Moses, David, Jesus, and Muhammad. And there are four principles that we follow: *şeriat, tarikat, marifet, hakikat. Şeriat* is the law, *tarikat* is the way, *marifet* is spiritual knowledge, *hakikat* is truth. You have to use your talent and wisdom. Many go to one, fewer go to two, older people may go to three. Only very few can reach four."

You go with your two companions into the blazing heat of day. The Kızılbaş are supposed to be both Alevi and Bektashi, two extremely *deli* Muslim groups. "Alevi" describes Shiites (as opposed to Sunnis, the majority of Muslims) who have a particular attraction to Ali, Muhammad's cousin and son-in-law; they maintain both that Ali was Muhammad's successor and, theologically, that Ali, Muhammad, and God are three-in-one, a miraculous unity (a very disputed point). The Bektashi, too, are Shiite, more or less, but organized as a *tarikat*, or religious order, with their own practices, many related to a Paulician Christianity picked up from schismatic Armenians in the 13th century. The founder of the Bektashi *tarikat* was Haci Bektaş (1248–1337), who came from Khorasan.

The fact that one can be an Alevi-Bektashi Kızılbaş doesn't lead to scholarly clarity. But what, in the realm of saints and miracles, does?

"Ah," Alibrahim says wistfully outside the *hoca*'s home, "he is an old man. No one really knows these things anymore."

But who is Demir Baba?

"I'll tell you the story. When Demir Baba came here, he set himself up by a mountain. Villagers came to see him. They asked him what he had to say. He said, 'I've come here to live.' The villagers said, 'You can't stay here.' So one day Demir Baba took all his things and went to Mumcular. There he stayed. The villagers told him to go. Demir Baba said, 'Your villages will be broken up, and your cows will all be black-and-white.' The cows had been all white before. Demir Baba left for another village. In Mumcular, the cows all turned black-and-white. People came from all over to witness this. Demir Baba went back to Mumcular and stayed, and there he died."

Are there any more stories?

"There's always another story!"

9

SO WE WILL HEAR one more story from the crazy forest, the story of Bedreddin of Simav (1358–1420). Stories about Bedreddin tend to conflict. One likely version is that he was born in Simav and educated in Edirne (now in European Turkey), and that he tutored the sultan of Cairo. Reasonably conventional in his early years, Bedreddin was introduced to Muslim mystical practices (that is, Sufism) by a Turk from Azerbaijan. This apparently brought out Bedreddin's latent *deli* qualities. After heading his own *tekke* for a time, Bedreddin returned to Anatolia. There he preached a doctrine of social justice, demanding that wealth be divided equally among all people—Muslims and Christians and Jews alike—and insisting that Muslims and Christians and Jews were equal in the eyes of God. He rejected the doctrines of the Day of Judgment and the Hereafter. He seems to have leaned toward pantheism. "I will come out now and declare myself," Bedreddin wrote, "that with my believers I shall come into possession of the world. And with the power of knowledge and the revelation of the mystery of Oneness, we shall abolish the pretenders' laws and religions."

These views brought Bedreddin popular support and the hatred of traditional Muslim authorities. The times were ripe for both, because the Ottoman state had all but collapsed, threatening both livelihoods and religious orthodoxy. Tamerlane had defeated the sultan Bayezid in 1402 and imprisoned him. Bayezid died in 1403; Tamerlane departed eastward with hopes of conquering China only to die en route. This left Bayezid's sons, Süleyman, Mehmet, Isa, and Musa, to fight over the Ottoman throne. Süleyman was ensconced in the Balkans, making deals with the Serbs, the Italian seagoing powers, and the Byzantines. At first, it looked like Süleyman, the eldest, together with Isa, would triumph over Mehmet, feebly allied with Musa. But Isa disappeared on an Anatolian expedition. Mehmet sent Musa to Wallachia, just over the Danube from Bulgaria, to come down on Süleyman from the rear. Musa married the Christian prince of Wallachia's daughter, and raised a theologically chaotic army of Turks, Wallachians, Serbs, Bulgarians, and who knows what else. Given the different practices, some part of the army must always have been at prayer.

Nonetheless, the army proved strong and Musa a good general. They marched south, defeated and killed Süleyman, and Musa declared himself sultan in the spring of 1411, having coins minted in his name. With his distinctly mixed following, Musa turned to the distinctly odd Bedreddin for spiritual leadership, naming him *şeyhulislam*, the empire's supreme religious authority. Bedreddin's *deli* proto-communist, multicultural pantheism became state dogma. It didn't last long. The Turkish notables and orthodox leaders conspired against Bedreddin. By 1413, Musa was dead, captured and killed by his brother and ex-ally Mehmet's forces south of Sofia.

Bedreddin, however, lived, rallying his followers throughout the empire. From 1416 on, various uprisings in his name were crushed, by Mehmet or by his son, Murad. (One, in 1417, was led by a Jew, Torlak Kemal.) By 1418 or so, Bedreddin had arrived in Wallachia, possibly receiving financial support from the princely family there. Bedreddin went south to build a base. He went—where else?—to Deli Orman, to rally the grandsons (if there were any) of the Demir Babas and the Elmalı Babas. In the great tradition of Muslim mystics, who so often see the state and orthodoxy as obstacles between them and God, Bedreddin rallied the heretics of Deli Orman behind his own lunatic vision of an empire with complete freedom of religion and without classes.

Mehmet's grand vizier led an army north to Deli Orman in the spring of 1419. The army soon found Bedreddin in the wild forest, captured him, took him south, and executed him.

Five hundred years later, the Turkish poet Nâzım Hikmet would write "The Epic of Sheikh Bedreddin." A lifelong leftist and internationalist, Hikmet took inspiration from Bedreddin. He wrote the poem, published in 1936, while in jail. When the government found that young military cadets were reading the "Epic," it placed Hikmet in jail again, for a twenty-eight-year sentence.

> *"Well, Bedreddin!"*
> *I said.*
>> *"We see nothing but stars*
>> *above the sleeping sails.*
> *No whispers stir the air.*
> *And no sounds*

rise from the sea.
Only mute, dark water,
only its sleep."
The little old man with the white beard bigger than himself
laughed.
He said:
"Never mind about the stillness of the air,
the deep sleeps to awaken."

Stars and a sailboat alone
on a sea one night.
One night a boat sailed the Black Sea
headed for the Mad Forest,
the Sea of Trees...

We landed in this forest, this Mad Forest,
we pitched our tent in the Sea of Trees.
We flew a falcon from every branch to every village
with the message, "You know why we have come,
you know the trouble in our heart."

Every falcon came back with a hundred lionhearts.
They all came—the peasant burning the master's crop,
the apprentice the shop,
the serf leaving his chains.
All those like us in Rumelia came,
an army flowing to the Sea of Trees.

What pandemonium!
A blur
of horses, men, spears, iron, leaves,
leather, beech branches, oak roots.
Since the Mad Forest went mad,
it hadn't seen such revelry
or heard such a din.

Of Bedreddin's capture by the grand vizier's agents, Hikmet writes:

I know these hoofbeats.
One night
they
ride away from our tents at full speed.
They knife the sentry in the back,
and in one of their saddles,

arms tied behind his back,
is our most precious.

I know these hoofbeats,
and the Mad Forest knows them too...

10

BULGARIA IS CURRENTLY experiencing a religious revival. Muslims, whose church had been so harshly repressed in the final years of Todor Zhivkov, have begun to attend mosque again, though not in any great numbers. The Bulgarian Orthodox church, an autocephalous (self-organizing, quasi-independent) church within the fold of Eastern Orthodoxy, was not particularly repressed under Zhivkov, but is nonetheless thrilled at the collapse of atheistic Communism and attempting to gain some advantage from it.

A third church—one might better say "tendency"—has also sought to fill the spiritual void. Protestant evangelists from the United States can be found in every major city. They speak most often in Midwestern or Southern accents. Their clothes are clean. They look comfortable and well-fed; they do not resemble Bulgarians.

You are walking down a street in Sofia with a Bulgarian friend. Across the street stretches a large banner, in Bulgarian, with letters in red: "Jesus Heals and Saves."

"They've been filling the stadiums, these American evangelists," the Bulgarian says. "It's the biggest show in town. They have light shows and rock musicians. No one here can come close to that. No one has the money. I think people go to the shows because they think that, if they convert, they'll be taken to America and given money."

Do you remember that poster above the bed of the young Bulgarian student you knew—the one with the Turkish roommate? You slept in the extra bed right next to it. The poster showed a cartoon boy and a cartoon girl, in a forest with cartoon birds poised picturesquely. A cartoon sun shone on the horizon. Two large hands intervened at the base of the picture, unseen by the couple or the birds; and at the top was written, "Why Worry? You're in His Hands."

11

TWO BRITISH MEN sit at breakfast with two Bulgarian men at the restaurant of the second-best hotel in Šumen, an important city of 120,000 on the route between Varna, Bulgaria's main port, on the Black Sea, and the capital, Sofia. The four men have met here on time. They have clean pressed shirts, suits, and briefcases. They shoot their cuffs; they click their pens; they smoke foreign cigarettes. Perhaps they are planning to build the new Bulgaria? The British men are cynical and world-weary but amused to find themselves in Bulgaria. They tell their two local friends about the night before. There had been naked girls dancing and falling all over them. They drank champagne, so much champagne! Oh, oh! Better have some more coffee. The Bulgarians have already made an early tour of the villages. "The peasants," one says, "are too busy for politics. Besides, they can't tell one party from the other anyway."

You spend the day of October 13, 1991, with the two main opposition parties, the Union of Democratic Forces (UDF), which leads the anti-Communist ethnic Bulgarians, and the Movement for Rights and Freedoms (MRF), which effectively represents the non-Bulgarian and Muslim electorate. Both oppose the former Communist Party, now called the Socialist Party, which is in power. The MRF people crowd together in a small office, chain-smoke, drink coffee and tea, and talk constantly on the phone. There have been irregularities. The list of eligible voters was posted at 3:45 this morning. Many Turks and Gypsies (and some Bulgarians) are not on it. The main problem is that, following the collapse of Communism, many Turks and Gypsies have been changing their names back to the old ones, a process that creates many chances for error. They now find themselves between names. They gather at room fifty-one in the mayoralty—the former Party headquarters—and harass two anxious clerks. Some will get their names straight, and vote; others won't. The MRF people are trying to do something about it, but they, like everyone else, are accustomed to being paranoid, and when you're paranoid it's hard to concentrate on identifying specific enemies.

The UDF headquarters is more calm, mainly because the partisans there know they're not going to win. Except among the non-ethnic Bulgarians, Šumen is a communist-nationalist stronghold.

Also the campaigns in general have been very low-key, because nobody really has any idea how to campaign except to talk with those people who will probably vote for them anyway and ask them to be sure they do. The turnout will be over eighty percent, no thanks to the parties. The head of the UDF, a middle-aged, quiet man, explains: "None of the campaigns was very organized. I can't really say why."

Why should anyone vote?

"Because of democratic progress, to change society."

What are your economic policies?

"We don't have economic policies that I know of. It's a centralized structure, so I don't really know. In my opinion, in Šumen the Communists will probably win. Nationally, they won't."

On this sunny day you join up with Yany Milchacoff, a schoolteacher and candidate of the Radical UDF, a splinter group, and some of his friends. Yany is absolutely confident his party won't do well, and so he has plenty of time to ramble around and have a laugh. We drive up and up a steep road which leads to a strange monument that overlooks Šumen. The monument, called "1300 Years of the Creation of the Bulgarian State," was built of concrete in 1981. We read that Bulgaria was founded near here in 681 — to be precise, twenty kilometers away at Pliska. The first of the monument's enormous statues is of Asparuk, a Bulgar and therefore ethnically a "Turk," Bulgaria's first king. He looks exactly like a twenty-five-foot-tall cement robot. Above him are words in ancient Bulgar. "Only ten words of it survive," Yany says. Then come Boris and Simeon, frightening, accusing figures looming from the cement wall. "These," Yany says, "are our first intellectuals." Then we see Cyril and Methodius, who were charged by the Byzantine church to spread Christianity among the pagan Slavs. Antoaneta, one of Yany's friends, turns to you: "Even we don't understand a lot of this." So instead of trying to understand it you all go to a nearby lounge for coffee and brandy.

You ask: Yany, why wasn't there anything at the monument about the Ottoman period?

"Because we were under their slavery for five hundred years. The Turks — the Turks today think they're part of Turkey. Our — Bulgarians — our self-conceit is that we are part of Europe. President Mitterrand of France said Bulgaria would be part of the European Community in ten years."

What kind of life do you expect to have?

"Like Western Europe and the United States." Yany smiles, drinks, laughs. "I guess so. I mean, what else would it be?"

12

ON ELECTION DAY in Šumen, a Turk who was imprisoned under the old regime discusses the relationship between the Turks in Germany and the Turks in Bulgaria: "There's one big difference," he says. "We've been here over five hundred years. We're not here as foreigners."

13

LATE ON THE AFTERNOON of election day you head north from Šumen with a Gypsy couple. The man drives. "I don't see why there need to be distinctions of race!" he shouts. "We should be like the U.S.! Everyone can do what they want!" He has the Statue of Liberty tattooed on his arm.

The Gypsy drops you off at MRF headquarters in Kliment, a largely Turkish village. You meet up with Hikmet, the handsome unsuccessful artist, who is about to become mayor, and Alâydin, a school principal, who is about to become regional mayor. They take you to see the ancient village graveyard, which the government bulldozed in 1985. You walk by a tiny mosque. It is time for prayer. Where is everyone? "The young people prefer drinking now." They take you to a supporter's house for dinner. Your host bought a fish earlier that day in Varna, several hours away by car. You all sit around to watch TV, an excited group, all Muslims save for yourself and another guest. You drink whiskey, vodka, raki, and wine.

The ex-Communist Socialists lose. They come close, but they lose. The people of Bulgaria have overthrown the Communists by voting against them. On TV, the old bosses speak woodenly of their defeat. It's fun to drink and eat fish while the bosses eat humble pie. The UDF leaders speak dizzily of their triumph and the end of Communism. At the victory rally in Sofia young people sing songs, wave flags.

The MRF, too, does well—over eight percent of the popular vote, corresponding roughly to the percentage of Bulgaria's population that isn't ethnically Bulgarian. The MRF thereby controls parliament, as neither the Socialist Party nor the UDF have a majority. In just two years, from severe repression to the balance of power!

The next few days are filled with optimism. At Alâydin's house, his wife shows you wedding photos. She is proud of her husband and happy that the bad days are over. "I was known for five years as Christina." Her name is Fatima, the name also of Muhammad's daughter who married Ali. "I expect that democracy will mean many more things on the shelves. Everything will be available." Their shelves have bars of foreign soap propped up for display, as Westerners have fine china or crystal; also featured are bottles of shampoo and deodorant. On the wall they've mounted a poster of Michael Jackson, spelled Jacson. "He goes to the mosque, Michael Jackson," Alâydin says. "He studies the Koran."

You and Alâydin go to a bar with a young blond man, Mustafa, who looks more Swedish than Turkish. Much vodka is drunk. You toast democracy. Alâydin hopes that Bulgaria can become like the United States, where the rights of minorities are protected and non-whites can rise to high positions. The bar—a recently planted seedling of entrepreneurship—has a TV and a video player. Suddenly Madonna appears. All eyes rise to the screen. Alâydin raises his glass triumphantly. "Ah, democracy!" he exclaims, and we all drink to it again.

Nine months later you return to Kliment. You sit again in Alâydin and Fatima's living room, beneath the Michael Jacson poster. The bars of soap are still there in the display case, now augmented by plastic flowers. Young Mustafa comes by to discuss his prospects in post-Communist Bulgaria. He pulls a pile of papers from a plastic bag with Marlboro written on it. "I'm studying to be a *mencer*." The word appears to be a neologism, a phonetic rendering of "manager." Modern Turkish has its own words for manager: *müdür*, *yönetici*. But young Bulgarian Turks don't really know modern Turkish. There is an old Arabic word in Turkish, *menca*, defined as "elevated spot to which one can escape for safety from a flood; a fleeing (for safety); safety," which gives *mencat*, "means of escape." But a connection between that and

Mustafa's *mencer* seems doubtful. "I'm not really sure," he says, "what a *mencer* does, or what management is. I'm just starting this at school. I think a manager is someone who knows economics, politics, electronics—someone who organizes everything." He pulls out some papers. "Now this has to do with computers. It's very difficult for me. I have trouble understanding them. Oh, well—I'm just starting."

Hikmet arrives. He has been mayor of Kliment for nine months now. He doesn't like it. "It's very hard being mayor. People come and say, 'I don't have any work or money.' And I say, 'I can't help you.'

"All anyone talks about now is going away." (Young Mustafa nods.) "Going to America or Canada. Not so much to Europe. Now all the culture—films, videos—comes from the United States. It's the fashion.

"Muslims"—Hikmet points to his head—"have no culture. Now Christians, they have a culture. They have European culture. But"—his eyes twinkle—"you're a Muslim. Where does that leave us? Well"—he leans forward—"we're *Avrupamusulmanlar*." And he grins. Euromuslims : Hikmet has coined a new term.

In the afternoon you go chat with Osman, a farmer, and his sons, sitting around next to their small plot of tomatoes. All they want to talk about is money. Nine months before, everyone spoke of impending freedom; now they speak of existing poverty. Money is a mystery. Inflation, Osman points out, is running at sixty to seventy percent. His family survives because they grow their own food. But, apart from that, everything has changed around them. Their cooperative—once communist, now capitalist—no longer has a source of capital for improvements, so their decrepit machinery appears as an hourglass warning of inevitable collapse. "We have no money for another tractor," Osman says. "Besides, the available tractors are very old, Russian. They break down a lot and are inefficient. We want a John Deere tractor." Osman and his sons are quickly learning that the world is organized in a hierarchy of money; that nations and peoples have pricetags attached to them; that Bulgaria is somewhere near the bottom of this hierarchy and its price is cheap. *"Your* standard of living is way up here," an elderly man says, raising his hand above his head, "while ours keeps falling down and down." Because Osman and his sons do not wish to believe that the new world of money in which they find themselves is utterly emptied of justice, they argue that people with money must be better than people without it. "When people are rich," Osman explains, "they must be intelligent. That is why they are rich."

At dusk you watch Alâydin, in his capacity as regional mayor, pay each one of the farm workers at a nearby cooperative for their day's labor: the men who drove the tractor, the women who sat on rows of tiny metal steps at its rear, placing each of the seedlings into a rotary pincer mechanism which planted them in the furrows the tractor had made. (After initial planting, the women walk up and down the furrows, tamping each seedling and filling blank spaces the tractor missed.)

At dinner you eat quietly with Alâydin, Fatima, and Hikmet. Fatima has changed from nine months ago. Once effusive and witty, she's more reserved, speaking only of Alâydin. "He reads the Koran now, and even prays. He's even given up smoking! Every night he reads law books, trying to figure them out." Alâydin, his wiry body topped by an outsized head, chews and nods. "Every night I'm reading law books, thick books." Alâydin has changed. The energy that radiated outward during the campaign has reversed its course, as if Alâydin is trying to answer some basic question by turning inward, having found no answer outside.

Hikmet, however, has not changed much. He shows around a copy of *Paraleli*, a new magazine. *Paraleli*, he explains, means parallels, and the magazine is about parallel worlds. Its contents: UFOs, ghosts, the Bermuda triangle, naked or lightly clad female international celebrities, clothed male international celebrities, expensive cars and houses, European royalty, photo essays on wealthy foreign cities, and miscellaneous information concerning the occult. Hikmet produces a book, his favorite, about Baba Vanga. A blind Christian surrounded by lovely women, Baba Vanga lives south of Sofia and possesses extrasensory perception, enabling her to predict the future. "She's very good, very powerful, very intelligent," Hikmet says. "She can perceive things from afar and cure the sick." Alâydin adds, "She is like Demir Baba. When she dies a tomb and a *tekke* will be built and people will come to honor her." Like UFOs, international celebrities, luxurious cars and houses, wealthy cities, royalty, and ghosts, Baba Vanga exists in a world parallel to that of Alâydin, Hikmet, and Fatima, and one more powerful than theirs.

14

THE POPULATION OF rural Turks in Bulgaria has been divided more or less between Deli Orman and Dobrudja in the north and the Rhodope mountains in the south. The Rhodopes form most of Bulgaria's southern border with Greece and Turkey.

The village of Yeni Mağalı lies at the end of a road, near the crest of the Rhodopes. On a clear day one can stand in Yeni Mağalı and look down the valley to see the plain of the Maritsa. But most days, even in mid-summer, Yeni Mağalı is shrouded in fog. It's always green, and a little damp, and cool.

Except for the disco, the only one for miles, which is always smoky and hot. The disco—known as "The Disco"—occupies the ground floor of a building just behind and downhill from the mosque. As Ergin walks you down to the entrance he notes the oddness and shrugs, "Well, we are in Europe." You enter the disco and greet Necmi. A big, clean-shaven man, Necmi was the best friend of Mehmet, who built this disco in 1984. (Mehmet later emigrated to New Jersey.) Ergin, Mehmet, and Necmi are related, as are most residents of Yeni Mağalı with the exception of a few Gypsies, three or four ethnic Bulgarians, and some genetic mavericks. "Yeni Mağalı was started by the Şeyh family from Konya," Ergin says. Konya is now part of Turkey. "They were Oğuz Turks. Later the Şerif family came, possibly as Ottoman administrators. Almost everybody here is either a Şeyh or a Şerif." Ergin is a semi-employed sculptor. Short and powerful, he wears a black leather jacket, his strong features set off by flowing black hair. Like most everyone you have occasion to meet in Yeni Mağalı, he likes to drink and dance. Two to three hundred people will pass through the disco each night, weekday or weekend, from nearby villages or hamlets as well as from Yeni Mağalı itself. Young and old, men and women, married and unmarried, they will come and drink beer, wine, vodka, raki; they will dance to American and European rock, Turkish *arabesk*, plaintive Kurdish songs, Greek *bouzouki*. They will drink anything and dance to anything, with whomever they like and even with people they don't like, for Yeni Mağalı is a small village and people have to get along.

There used to be more young people here, but now many have left to seek work outside Bulgaria. "A lot of the young people work in Germany, Switzerland, and Sweden," Necmi says over a bottle of sweet wine. The sun has just set; dancing hasn't yet begun. "Some go to work in Turkey, but not too many, because Turkey is a Muslim country and they aren't comfortable there—Turkey isn't as European as here. Also, young people coming from a village find it hard in the cities." Ergin, too, believes Turkey is not home to Bulgarian Turks. "I feel that we are Europeans. We'll be joining Europe. It's true that we came from Asia, but that was a long time ago. We've been here for quite a while; we're Europeans. Look around you at this disco: we have a very modern life. This place used to be Oriental in design, before it became a disco. When Mehmet decided to build the disco, at the time of the name-change policy, he made it like this." Ergin indicates the walls with a sweep of his hand. They are nearly barren, certainly modern.

Mehmet built the disco in 1984 because local Party authorities had insulted him, saying that as a Turk he was incapable of achieving anything. They had laughed at his intention—he headed the young-Communist league—to build a disco. So he and Necmi built it, in this room beneath which lies the oldest cemetery in Yeni Mağalı, a cemetery for (so Ergin says) the Yörük Turks, a formerly, famously nomadic group that guarded the Rhodope passes.

Time to dance: Ergin brings you onto the floor. Raise your hands—this is how we do it—making gestures delicate now, then assured, or languid, so that one dance is nearly two, your hands with their own pattern, speaking to your feet, which speak back. Ergin will shout above the music: "Listen! We don't have any racial problems here! We'll dance to anything!" He'll laugh, you'll laugh, you'll close your eyes, inhale the music and listen to your heart. When the music is sad you may remember that in the late eighties soldiers would have been sitting a few feet away, with rifles, making sure that no Turkish music was played and that when people danced they didn't raise their hands in the Turkish manner but rather held them at their sides as if bound. Mehmet, what a reply you gave to their insults! For a time, back then, people danced like tin soldiers. Now they raise their hands and shout, laugh, make silly faces, as do you on a cool night in Mehmet's hot and smoky disco.

15

APART FROM THE DISCO, and one incident in which Mehmet was beaten up, the Turks of Yeni Mağalı did nothing to oppose the ethnic Bulgarians. A young man: "We didn't do anything because we were scared. We heard what happened elsewhere in Bulgaria, in the north, with people being killed. So everyone was quite scared. Also, we knew it wouldn't last because we listened to the radio from Turkey and understood this was a global issue. It couldn't last. So we waited in fear for it to end."

16

AYDIN ABAS IS also a young man from Yeni Mağalı, now a student of architectural engineering in Sofia. He has a mustache, a wrinkled, expressive forehead, a lively face with the preoccupied look of youthful seriousness. He says: "As a Turk, life for me in Sofia is a little rough. There aren't many Turks there, and very few in the university. From my village, only four people are in university.

"It's wonderful to go back to the village because there I'm surrounded by Turks. You can go there and be what you are. Everybody is at least your cousin.

"Life in Turkey is much different from here. Here—you've seen what it's like, very free, with men and women in the disco together, no problems. In Turkey that isn't the case. It's an Oriental society, very Muslim. That's not what we're used to. We're more European. Yes, among the rich in Turkey there is this freer life, where men and women can go to clubs and have a drink and there's no problem at all. But these places are expensive. For regular people such possibilities don't exist. For a Turk from Bulgaria life in Turkey is quite hard.

"Besides, in Turkey you have to work constantly, and if you don't, you're finished. The government won't give you a thing. Here, if you lose your job or can't find one, the government will pay you enough so you can have a home and buy food. [This would not last.] In Turkey, if you don't fight to live, you could die."

17

THE BYZANTINE HISTORIAN sits in his large office, smokes his pipe, invites you to have a seat on the couch. He has been working with a committee of seven on a report concerning the degree to which the Bulgarian Academy of Sciences was involved in lending academic support to "the so-called Revival and the policy of forced assimilation." They have nearly completed their report. They've found, to their pleasure, that the Academy's members were only dimly related to the program. While a coordinating committee did exist to supervise research into "problems of the Bulgarian nation from the 14th century to the present, that research — and this is the main point — was on normal and natural things in Bulgarian history, with nothing to do with Turks." For example? The Byzantine historian mentions the principal themes: the ethnogenesis of the Bulgarian people; the Bulgarian nation on the eve of the Ottoman invasion; church and religion in the Balkans at the end of the 14th century; demographic changes in Bulgaria from 1400 to 1600; the spread of Islam in the Balkans, 1400 to 1800. "I want to point out essentially that these subjects were not of a political nature." Place names; Bulgarian folklore; ethnographic problems of the Bulgarian people; Bulgarian history as presented in Ottoman sources; and the process of Islamization in Bulgaria. "The only unpleasant thing," he concludes, "is that these traditional areas of inquiry were nominally linked to the policy of forced assimilation."

18

AT MIDNIGHT IN Yeni Mağalı, you sit in Ergin's home with him and his mother. One candle lights the room. (The electricity is out again.) Ergin's mother shows you a photo of herself, young, in front of a band. She had been at university in the first Communist generation. At concerts, she sang while her late husband conducted. She was strikingly beautiful then, and still is. Ergin got his looks from her.

"Everything was very cheap then. Flour, oil, cheese. You could go to university — free."

"But Mom, you didn't get to *choose* those things. You always had to go to the government and ask. It was all *obligatory*."

"It was a very good life. You had what you needed. You didn't need money for everything, like now."

"Now you have choices, though."

"Things did change in 1984. But until then they were good."

"Good for ten years, that's all. Maybe."

"Fifties, sixties, seventies—thirty years."

"Ten!"

"Thirty!"

"Ten!"

"You did have choices. I could have worked in Plovdiv or Pazardjik."

"Mom! Communism was bad."

"It's a terrible thing to have democracy and no money."

"The system was bad, it didn't work, and in any case it's finished now."

"What we had wasn't Communism, but socialism. After eighty-two, it was Communism."

"Mom, the system was bad, it didn't work, and it's finished now."

19

WITH ERGIN, AHMET, AND CEVAT you hike upward into the summer pastures above Yeni Mağalı, moist dales or grassy upland humps edged by pine, fir, beech. When it rains you dip into the forest or run for shelter in one of the wooden huts used by shepherds. Soon the huts and pastures will be occupied, the rains will clear, the sun will shine. It is the 24th of May. You walk across a wide bowl with a view of Yeni Mağalı and the valley below. May 24 is Cyril and Methodius Day, a national holiday, an opportunity to celebrate the two Greeks who brought Orthodox Christianity north to the Slavs. Cyril and Methodius wished to preach in the vernacular, so they translated the Bible into Slavonic, creating along the way an alphabet—Cyrillic. Proud Bulgarians tend to believe that Bulgarian was the first major Slavic language to receive the new alphabet and is therefore more pure or otherwise better than other Slavic languages. So Cyril and Methodius Day is an occasion for patriotic expression.

In this wide bowl with its arresting view Turks, Gypsies, Pomaks, and Bulgarians from Yeni Mağalı and surroundings used to assemble every May 24 to celebrate Cyril and Methodius Day with drinking, singing, dancing, and speeches. The school in Yeni Mağalı was named Cyril and Methodius School. "They had the celebration here," Ahmet says, "to mark the togetherness of Bulgarians and Turks." They had it here until 1983, when the authorities began to force Turkish parents to give their newborns Bulgarian names. "Since then we haven't gathered here. And we won't gather here now."

Up and up into the Rhodopes, into the mist, the four of you smelling of damp wool and linen, sweat, and tobacco, your hair and faces moist. At a high clearing you notice that the earth is terraced, with rows of mounds. Above you is a ruined fortification. It was built by the Romans as a lookout; the mounds are ancient graves, the terraces an outwork for defense. Cevat and Ergin crouch behind one and act as if they're holding pikes, bracing for an assault by unknown enemies.

Down again on slippery ground toward the village. You pass by fields, once farmed cooperatively but now broken up into individual plots too small for mechanized farming. A man maneuvers a horse pulling a plow. "You see," Ergin says, "it's like feudalism all over again!"

You pile into a car with hopes of reaching Velingrad to celebrate Cyril and Methodius Day. But first you stop by Batak, a remote village and the site of a famous massacre in 1876. Several thousand Bulgarian villagers were slaughtered by *başıbozuklar* ("broken-heads," irregular troops with faint loyalty to the Ottoman empire) led by Ahmed ağa Barutanlijata, a Pomak. *Başıbozuklar* in this region included Turks, Circassian refugees forced from their Caucasus homes by Russia and resettled by the Ottomans, Crimean Tatars resettled here for similar reasons, Muslim Gypsies, and Pomaks, plundering on their own account and sometimes taking orders from the Ottoman authorities. Bulgarian revolutionary nationalists, encouraged by the Russians and addled by their own enthusiasm, chose this general area for their first uprising. It failed. Particularly distressing was the attitude of the Pomaks, who failed to seize upon their own ethnic Bulgarianness and join the revolution. Instead, Pomak leaders opposed the Bulgarians and set up their own short-lived "Pomak Republic." (History can take odd turns. Initial concern about Pomak intentions had appeared among Russian diplomats ten years before. Misled by the phonetic similarity between Pomak and Poljak—Pole—and worried that Polish nationalist propaganda might have some effect on the Pomaks, they began to meddle in Pomak affairs. This surely constituted a low point in Tsarist diplomacy.) At any rate, the massacres at Batak were quickly embroidered upon and used by European politicians to justify anti-Ottoman policies. They are still used today as shorthand for the special malevolence of "the Turk."

You leave Batak with your Turkish friends and drive to Velingrad, a mostly Bulgarian town with a large Pomak minority. In the last years of Zhivkov, Bulgarian nationalists held angry rallies at Batak and Velingrad, dwelling on memories of the massacres and the abortive uprising of 1876. You take four chairs at a cafe on the town square. A reviewing stand has been set up, with a miked podium and chairs for dignitaries. A crowd gathers. At its edge stand groups of Pomaks, the women wearing knit leggings under knee-skirts or dresses, over these a sweater or jacket and a brightly colored scarf. "These Pomak outfits were forbidden under Zhivkov," Ergin says. "Buses wouldn't stop for you if you wore these clothes. Until fifteen years ago, we too wore more traditional clothes. But not now. The Pomaks are less European than we are."

Most of the gathering crowd appears to be Bulgarian. The mike is tested, a speech given. Tall young girls in majorette outfits appear. The dignitaries on stage rise and sing the Cyril and Methodius song. No one sings along. A band plays Bach's "Jesu, Joy of Man's Desiring," and the majorettes perform a saucy choreography, like deeply subdued Rockettes; each has a baton. "You see," Ergin says, "Rhodope women are very beautiful because we're all mixed together. And the air is clean and rich in oxygen." The girls leave, then reappear in "Spanish" outfits— black skirts, red blouses with short puffy sleeves, artificial red flowers in their hair. And batons. They dance to "Frère Jacques" and the theme from *Can-can*, with interludes of military gesturing and some truly baffling, though languid, movements, as the music slips into Latin lounge tunes.

Thus you celebrate Cyril and Methodius Day in the Bulgarian and Pomak town of Velingrad.

20

YOU ARE LOUNGING with Ergin and some other friends at the disco in Yeni Mağalı when you notice at the next table a broad-shouldered man, unusually tall, speaking in Bulgarian with some other men. Save for him, they all have a rough, somewhat thuggish appearance. Ergin says hello to him in Bulgarian, which is unusual, so you ask in Turkish: Who is that man?

"He's a mathematics teacher at the Cyril and Methodius School. He's been teaching here for eleven years, with two years spent in Algeria. He still doesn't speak any Turkish, though he does speak French. After eleven years, he doesn't speak Turkish."

You're introduced to the man, named Hristo, and you exchange pleasantries in French.

Ergin says: "This man is not a person who can be trusted. He is a sly fox. During the Zhivkov period, he was a nationalist. He was like a Nazi. He didn't seem to dislike the idea of Turks as slaves. I remember talking to him about the name-changing, and he agreed that such a policy shouldn't come from above. He said instead that the ethnic Bulgarians should have a referendum on what should be done with the Turks as far as name-changing went. *They* should have a referendum! Is that democracy, where other people get to vote on what *you* should be? On who you are?"

You turn to Ahmet, a gentle man around thirty with a mature sense of humor. You ask Ahmet: How can you have a man like this here? And he replies, "Well, it's complicated. He—the few people who really believed in the Zhivkov policy are still here, but they have been...isolated. Do you understand?" He smiles. "His wife is the tall, good-looking woman you saw last night. Do you remember? You may have noticed that she is interested in other men." You had noticed.

You invite Hristo outside for a chat. "I was in Algeria, in Annaba, in eighty-five and eighty-six," he says. "At that time, you know, there was a war of words back here in Bulgaria. When I got back here I thought, 'This is politics, but I am a mathematics teacher. Math is not political.'" Hristo gives a weak smile. "In 1989, many of my Turkish friends went to Turkey. I visited them there once. There aren't many people left here now, so life isn't as happy as it used to be. But I have a big lovely house in Plovdiv – my daughter goes to school there – and an apartment here, where my wife and other daughter live."

Back inside, Ahmet asks what Hristo said. "He said his friends all went to Turkey and mathematics isn't political." Ahmet laughs for some time and you raise your glasses to the toast, "Mathematics isn't political."

Hristo joins you. Ahmet and Ergin both joke with him, raising glasses, slapping backs. A butcher called the Arab tells dumb jokes and makes faces. Everybody is very drunk. We laugh. Hristo buys everyone more wine. And as we laugh you whisper in Ahmet's ear: "Ahmet, I still don't understand. This man is a nationalist. He doesn't like Turks. Turks don't like him. So why is he here? Why are we all sitting here like friends? Did you ever consider killing him?"

Ahmet says: "This is not like friends. This is drinking-friends. We cannot kill him because then we would have to leave the village. He can't leave either, because his wife and job are here. So – look at him. Does he really look alive to you? He is not a happy man."

Ahmet has been smiling all this time, while Hristo keeps raising his glass to you, saying, *"A votre santé!"* He suddenly appears to be the loneliest man in the world, and unable to grasp his loneliness, which means that it will never end.

Ahmet has been watching your face and now he looks at you calmly. "Now do you understand?"

21

ONE AFTERNOON YOU SIT at Ergin's home with him, his mother, Ahmet, and various female relatives ranging from infants to Ergin's grandmother. You loll around watching a TV station beamed from Turkey and filled with images of prosperity. What, you ask, is it like seeing all these other ways of life on TV?

"We see how rich places like America and Germany are," Ahmet says pleasantly, "and how poor we are in Bulgaria."

Do you think you had a happier life before you started seeing all this prosperity on television?

"No! No!" Ahmet says, and everyone laughs.

"We're happy here," Ergin's mother adds, smiling. "We just don't have any money."

Ergin's grandmother leans forward with a knowing expression. "True, we don't have any money. But we *do* have the disco. And we can dance." She raises her arms, her hands beside her head, ready to wave winningly.

22

YOU ARE STANDING on a street with Ahmet in the bright light of morning. He is trying to explain what has happened. Once, his ancestors were here under the Ottoman empire. Then the Ottomans left, Bulgaria was founded, and his family became Bulgarian citizens. Later the Bulgarian government tried to take away much of what made him what he is and transform him into a true Bulgarian. Then Communism fell, Bulgaria sought to become part of Europe, and he and his family got their old names back.

But now everyone wants to leave. They want to leave so badly that they no longer really occupy the ground they stand on, because the future lies elsewhere, in Europe and North America, and no one would really want to live in exile from the future. Indeed, in terms of imagination—which has so much to do with identity, and citizenship—one can only live in the future. When the future lies elsewhere, one can't really live. "So—it's a curious thing," Ahmet says. "I feel that we have become exiles in our own country. Time has gone elsewhere, it has taken the land from beneath our feet. So, without moving at all, we have become exiles."

Consider, I pray, and reflect how God in our time has transformed the Occident into the Orient.

For we who were Occidentals have now become Orientals. He who was a Roman or a Frank has in this land been made into a Galilean or a Palestinean. . . . We have already forgotten the places of our birth; already these are unknown to many of us or not mentioned any more. . . . Indeed it is written 'the lion and the ox shall eat straw together.' He who was born a stranger is now as one born here; he who was born an alien has become a native.

—Fulcher of Chartres, *Historia Hierosolymitana* (1127)

God speaks in metaphors to men.

—the Koran, sura 24

Istanbul

1

IN THE DISTRICT called Fatih—once home to Ottoman notables, now less than rich but known for its piety in the not very pious city of Istanbul—someone has written on a wall: *What happened in al-Andalus must not happen in Bosnia.* "What happened in al-Andalus" refers to the gradual expulsion of Muslims from Spain, a process the Spanish call the Reconquest. Muslim armies first landed in Spain in 711; the Reconquest ended in 1492. "Bosnia" refers to the war against the Muslims of Bosnia-Herzegovina in former Yugoslavia, which began in 1990.

2

IN FATIH AND ELSEWHERE some Turks have been attempting to recall the truth of Islam as a guide to their present and future. A few, as one day in the provincial city of Sivas, have even tried murder as a means to revive Islam. Some are attempting to discover the truth of Europeanization, of what they call civilization and modernism. *What happened in Europe must happen here.*

Others pursue more local truths, for example, the truth of vengeance. In the 1960s and 1970s, various groups fought for several different models of truth: Maoist, Stalinist, state-militarist. No one group really triumphed, but this hasn't kept each from attempting to settle accounts, because the demands of honor and the terrors of hatred seem to outlast the more structured compulsions of political ideology. Every few weeks or so, a retired officer or judge is murdered, almost always someone who had worked in a military court or labored in a torture chamber during the years of trouble; or secret police suddenly knock on the door of some leftist safe-house and enter with machine-guns blazing.

(You're riding home with Ömer and Ayşe. Ömer runs through the gears to get his tiny car up the steep hill. At its crest, he shifts again, says, "This was a fascist neighborhood." He points out an apartment building and says that the retired editor of *Cumhuriyet*, a moderate daily newspaper, once lived there. "When he was on his balcony one morning, reading his newspaper, they shot him dead." That was 1975. "Things are better now." A little farther on, Ömer parks next to a high stone wall. Behind the wall lies the headquarters of military intelligence. You're getting out when two men in leather jackets approach from the rear. "Get away!" they say. "You can't park there!" Ayşe looks toward them, she's pregnant, her light dress waves in the breeze. Time slows down, the way time slows when men with guns are approaching you out of the darkness. Ömer tells you, "Get away!" You stay, because Ömer's your friend, you like him very much, and as he tenses up you want suddenly to envelop him and protect him. Ayşe talks to the two plainclothes men—how beautiful and brave she looks—we say hurried good-nights, the little car drives off, the men continue their patrol and you get safely home. Things are better now.)

Yet others pursue nationalist truths: Kurds, Armenians. Actually, the Armenian groups have greatly reduced their terroristic activities since the assassination campaigns of the 1970s and early eighties, which left dozens of Turkish officials dead. Killings by Kurdish nationalists continue, as do killings *of* Kurdish nationalists. Turkey's military men pursue the truth of one unified, Turkish nation.

These and other truths compete in contemporary Turkey. No-one knows which ones will win, or when. Turkey is a democracy.

3

HOW ARE WE to establish the truth? Muslim thinkers have debated this question since Muhammad's time. The Koran, of course, contained the truth, but that wasn't the end of the story. Very early on, Muslims began to argue over whether the Koran was "uncreated" or "created," that is, whether the Koran was the pure utterance of God or a translation, so to speak, of God's words by a human (Muhammad). Broadly speaking, those who believed in the "uncreated" Koran tended to argue for predestination, a literalist approach to scriptural interpretation, a clear distinction between "mass" and "scholarly" Islam, the relative necessity of submission to unattractive rulers, and the preeminence of Arabic (as the only possible language of revelation) and Arabness. Those who maintained the Koran was "created" usually argued for free will, a more "rationalist" (in neo-Platonic and Aristotelian senses) interpretation of scriptural meaning, a fuzzier distinction between mass and scholarly Islam, the possible necessity of revolt against unjust rulers, and the relative unimportance of Arabic and Arabness. Advocates of an uncreated Koran laid the ground for Sunni Islam, characteristically preoccupied with keeping the Muslim community united and stable. They were often Arabs. Advocates of a created Koran eventually found a home within Shiite Islam and were often non-Arabs (many were Persian). The division between Sunni and Shiite continues today. The uncreated versus created debate was revived by Sunni reformers in the 19th century and even appears in Salman Rushdie's modernist Muslim novel *The Satanic Verses*.

This primordial debate over the nature of truth—which has

111

parallels in Christianity and Judaism—appeared again in polemics over language. If a concept is true in one language, can it be translated into another language without altering its meaning? That is, can written truth travel? (The Latin rhetorical term *translatio* sometimes meant "to change place," the Greek *metaphor* meant "change of place"; Greek buses today are labeled *metaphor*.) Some early Muslims were unhappy about the influence of Greek thought on their contemporaries, and argued that, for example, the Arabic word for logic, *mantiq*, because its linguistic root was "speech," implied that foreign (Greek) concepts were trapped in their language of expression and couldn't migrate into other languages (say, Arabic). Those many Muslim thinkers deeply influenced by Greek thought disagreed, maintaining that logic was logic whatever you called it. The dispute was far from trivial. Even today, people argue that the concepts of one culture cannot be moved to, or even understood by, another culture. Can a Muslim be European? Or vice versa?

Muslim controversies regarding the nature of truth began against a backdrop of rapid military expansion of Islam into the non-Arab world. Within a century of Muhammad's death, Muslim rule extended from the Atlantic to the Indian subcontinent, abutting the Franks in Spain, Saharan societies on the south, the Byzantines in Asia Minor, and China to the far northeast. Looking simply at this unprecedented success, one might have formed an idea of truth as historical victory: surely such success could only come with the support of God, and so the truth of Koranic revelation could be seen as proved by its very material success. This is the doctrine of truth as identical with whatever the historical victor believes it to be. For modern Muslims, this dogma has little weight. Today the historical victors are not Muslims.

Things were different in the 8th century. Muslims ruled an empire even greater than that of the Chinese. This did not, however, mean that a huge international ruling class agreed within itself on the nature of truth. The ruling class established by Muhammad's early successors was a military aristocracy, operating from garrison towns, and one proud of its Arabness. Needless to say, in an empire stretching from the Atlantic to the Chinese border the Arab aristocrats were a minority. Moreover, they were divided among themselves by a number of tribal loyalties, supra-tribal (or proto-national, for exam-

112

ple, Syrian) loyalties, and religious differences of opinion. In such confusion, the question of Truth became embodied in a tension between the local and the universal. If something is true for one person, must it be true for all? If something was true for the Arabs, was it true for all peoples? If something is true for one Muslim, is it true for (at least) all Muslims?

Part of Islamic originality lies in Muslims' answers to such questions. The Jews had largely tamed the local versus universal tension by proposing a tribal monotheism: the Jews were God's chosen people, and so the truth of God existed most brilliantly in the life of that particular tribe. Judaism established an ethnic universalism. Christianity, once it had separated itself from Judaic society, was more expansive: God's truth existed for everyone, taught by Christ in Palestine during a brief period but applicable to all persons, in all places, at all times. Islam, first preached by Muhammad to his wife, then to friends and family, and finally to strangers, evolved in opposition to the paganism and worship of multiple local spirits in Muhammad's hometown, Mecca. It was resolutely monotheistic—"There is no God but God"—while retaining a personal element, "and Muhammad is His messenger," because Muhammad heard the Koran from God, via the angel Gabriel, beginning in about 610. Monotheistic Islam could not be tolerant toward pagans. But it was tolerant toward other monotheisms, in two main ways: as fellow worshippers of the universal God and not the local gods; and as receivers of the universal God's wisdom via their respective books (for example, the Old and New Testaments). The Koran views Jews and Christians as legitimate predecessors of Muslims, to be tolerated as fellow monotheists and People of the Book. Thus a certain compromise on the local (Muhammad, the Arabs of Mecca) versus the universal (God, all humans) was made possible by stretching Truth back over time, with Muhammad, the Seal of the Prophets, retaining the last word. Islam then pioneered a monotheism that maintained something could be universally true but also differently true for different peoples. It seems highly unlikely that Islam could have expanded so rapidly without this synthetic and, for its time, amazingly relaxed approach to truth.

Some 1300 years later, the Islamic countries would be at a political, economic, even cultural disadvantage when faced with the West, finding themselves an ill-defined but much discussed grouping of peoples. For the West, Islam was a kind of historical mistake or conceptual error, one which doomed millions to an irrelevant life with respect to universal truth, which Westerners saw as Western. Islam was a *local* mistake. It wasn't even an especially important local mistake. The really important local mistake was Communism. After 1989, one understood, that mistake had been corrected by the inevitable processes of universal human destiny and truth. And so the British essayist Sir Ralf Dahrendorf was able to write: "The First and the Second Worlds are being reunited into something which has no name yet, nor a number: perhaps it will just be the World.... There is only one world left with serious claims to development and hegemony." The American writer Francis Fukuyama could express his regret over the fate of those people who, unlike Westerners, remained "mired in history," as if history were something that sticks to one's shoes. By 1992, the head of the International Monetary Fund, Michel Camdessus, could announce at the fund's annual meeting that "the world has become one." Following the end of the Cold War, he noted, the world underwent a dramatic transformation. "In this transformation, the Fund is a microcosm of the world at large.... Full transformation will take time, but that is a good reason to start immediately, and to take advantage of the dynamism and enthusiasm of the present period to create, irreversibly, the basic structures of a market economy." As if it were up to the Fund to determine, "irreversibly," the fate of the world.

4

NUR KİLİÇ, product manager at Meyna, an Istanbul-based fruit and vegetable firm, believes that Turkish tomatoes are improving. "We are reaching European and U.S. standards on size and color, and packing standards," she says in English. "European shoppers expect tomatoes to be a consistent size and color. You know Dutch tomatoes? Beautiful, so...round, so perfectly round. And consistent."

Kiliç's rise to product manager has not been easy. "I worked twice as hard as my colleagues did, my male colleagues, in order to prove that I can perform as well as they can. Maybe I worked three times as hard." Kiliç is not yet thirty, but she has already seen many changes. "Only in the last five years can a woman go out alone – not everywhere, of course – go out, go to a bar, have a drink, and not feel like she's someone who needs to be protected all the time like a baby."

Her office is in an anonymous corporate high rise and looks out on an anonymous selection of busy freeways and other high rises. It's a great address for a corporation – Meyna dominates much of Turkey's fruit industry – and a depressing one for a human. To work in such an office is the ambition of many Istanbul residents. Nur Kiliç knows that she is a success story. She makes good money; most people in Istanbul do not. Those are the alternatives. "In the seventies, we had a middle class. Now we have an upper middle class and a lower middle class. Yuppies and the upper middle class have a different way of living. They're getting more mechanical. We are becoming a little America. I mean, *mechanical*. In the sixties and seventies, the relations between people were more strong. So of course the mentality, the mores, are changing. People are losing their humanity. They haven't lost it yet, but they are losing it. There's such competition between people, especially in this jungle called Istanbul. The family – we are losing this, too."

It is like the tomato situation. Any Western visitor to Turkey will verify that the tomatoes are better there than in Europe and the United States. They have more flavor. But they come in whimsical sizes and are often dirty. Turkey wants to export its products to Europe – "the fruit market of Europe" has been a political-economic cliché since the sixties – and so it must make them consistently European. Kiliç's company is an industry leader in the production of consistent fruits and vegetables, and she is proud of this accomplishment. Yet she sees that Turks themselves are going the way of all produce. "They're losing their color, their taste – of course, their taste of life."

5

IN THE FALL 1991 ELECTION, all the major parties, left and right, agreed that Turkey should enter Europe and have a free market system. The main candidates packed their staffs with attractive young professionals and technocrats who looked as if they'd been selected for their consistent size and color, if not their taste. For the first time, television advertising played a significant role in campaign strategy. The winner, Süleyman Demirel, was the man who promised the most and explained the least.

Yet Turkey's entry into Europe seems a remote prospect. A November 1991 survey showed that fifty percent of European Community citizens feel there are too many non-EC citizens in Europe. Many of those foreigners, particularly in Germany, are Turks, and some of them have recently been murdered by racist Germans. Yet Turkey's Europeanness has become a basic premise of its own politics. Without this prospect, however amorphous, a Turkish politician would be at a loss to explain how Turkey will ever become prosperous—or, for that matter, to explain why Turks should reckon the disappearance of their middle class and the dramatic polarization of incomes to be a good thing, a necessary step on the road to general well-being. Outside of Europe, there is no compelling vision of historical progress into which a country like Turkey might fit.

And so Turkey is a European country.

6

"TODAY'S TURKEY IS NEITHER a Western nor a Moslem nation; it does not belong to a Christian, socialist, or capitalist community," Niyazi Berkes, a Cypriot Turkish sociologist, wrote in 1975. "It is neither Asian nor European.... The dominant direction of Ottoman history has tilted more toward the west than toward the east. But its adherence to an eastern cultural reference has prevented Turkey's inclusion in the Western world.... Europe has never considered itself as including Turkey, and if we think the contrary, no one but ourselves believes it."

7

A EUROPEAN COUNTRY should be a rational country, orderly and punctual, with perfect circles, equilateral triangles, and straight lines. However, no one culture can lay claim to the straight line. A straight line is universal. Whether one sits contemplating it in Singapore or

Bonn, it is no more nor less straight. The business of laying claim to straight lines, perfect circles, equilateral triangles, and other unnatural oddities is an ancient one. Even the activity of arranging humans geometrically goes back to ancient times, to (at least) Herodotus. But the practice of forcibly arranging humans along straight lines, in conformity with a global vision, required the imagination and power of 19th-century Europeans. By the latter half of that century, after hundreds of years of struggle, several European powers had managed to establish rule over much of the globe. Those areas not directly ruled by European powers were usually governed by people of European ancestry. The immemorial activity of conquest seemed, at last, to be aligning itself into a universal human order.

In 1851, the first universal exposition took place in England, at the Crystal Palace. But it was the French, in 1867, who first applied geometry, in spectacular fashion, to symbolize the new world order. Frédéric Le Play, influenced by the social theorist Saint-Simon, built the Paris universal exposition as an oval (originally planned as a circle), which symbolized the globe, within a rectangle. The oval was divided into wedges like slices of pie. These wedges featured objects of universal interest and significance. At the outer rim of each wedge, corresponding to a pie's crust, lay industry; at the wedge's point was art. In between were clothing, furniture, agricultural products. Within the globe's circumference, everything was arranged mathematically, along straight lines.

Outside the globe, so to speak, the lines bent, though remaining within the exposition's rectangular outer boundary. Various pavilions appeared in a park setting. The French pavilion represented non-universal aspects of France—that is, the French past, without art. The Ottoman empire's pavilion offered a mosque, house, fountain, and a bathhouse (*hamam*). Although these might have been spatially arranged along straight lines, they weren't, because French architectural dogma held that straight lines were not "authentic." Bent lines were authentic, because, while only one line is straight, there are countless ways to bend it.

"Out of timber so crooked as that from which man is made," Immanuel Kant had written some eighty years earlier, "nothing entirely straight can be built." The universal exposition sought to disprove Kant's remark by proposing two kinds of human timber, bent and straight. All humans, once, were bent. By 1867, a portion of humanity, that portion within the geometrical globe, had been straightened. This straightness was the truth of the present and the future, the straightness of people no longer mired in history. As humanity progressed it would inevitably straighten. In fact, at an 1893 exhibition in Chicago peoples of the world were arrayed along a road—a straight line, representing time. This road, according to an observer, showed a "sliding scale of humanity. The Teutonic and Celtic races were placed nearest to the White City [the center of the exhibition]; farther away was the Islamic world, East and West Africa; at the farthest end were the savage races, the African Dahomey and the North American Indian."

8

"TURKS SAY THEY'RE EUROPEANS when they think it's useful to be Europeans," says a young Turkish woman of decidedly mixed parentage. "Nobody really *feels* European. We're just Turks—a mish-mash."

9

TURKEY'S DESIRE TO JOIN Europe could be seen as an effort to change its place of residence on that Chicago street, to leapfrog over the Teutonic and Celtic races and find a home in the White City. In the city of Istanbul, you can find little pieces of this imaginary White City already in place. For example, you might go and sit one nice day in the cafe next to the mosque in Bebek, an affluent neighborhood on the Bosphorus (European side). The mosque's muezzin has an expressive tenor voice; the cafe itself is basic and decorated only by its customers, who enjoy the breeze off the water and drink sugary tea from glasses.

There are no water pipes here, for they would make too premodern and lazy a burbling. Bebek is rich, and the cafe caters to the sons and daughters and young wives of the rich. The boys lounge in their autumn blazers, stylish single-breasted wool jackets with big shoulders. The girls wear tight faded blue jeans torn in all the right places; they are markedly thinner and lighter-skinned than most women in Istanbul. When the mood takes them, these young people may go for a jog along the Bosphorus promenade, looking up occasionally at the many splendid wooden yachts whose prows face toward the Asian side across the water.

Their lives are very far from those of the people who tend goats and live in lean-tos propped against the old city walls. Or those who lost their lives when the garbage dump near which they lived avalanched and buried them. Or the thousands of people who sell glasses of water in the street — or bus tickets, a new pair of socks, one cassette of music, a sweater. The patrons of the cafe in Bebek are in a position to respond to advertisements, such as the one which shows a handsome man holding his head in his hands and staring at an empty teacup. "Today's man," it begins. "He goes around on a 'Harley-Davidson' motorcycle...rides a horse...flies a plane... without stressing his social position, he expresses his individuality by dressing like a man." Like a European man. Most of these young Turks will speak some English or French. They have time on their hands.

But residence in the White City requires money, so maybe we shouldn't dwell on this pretty cafe, because these young people are extremely idle and Istanbul is not an idle city. Maybe we should visit one of their parents — say, Doğan Gündüz. The offices of his advertising agency would look familiar to a Western visitor: plain carpeting, white plasterboard walls, phone and electrical cords strung in unlikely places. The view of Istanbul from his office would be attractive on a clear day, of which there are few in Istanbul because it has ten million people, a lot of cars and buses, and coal-fired boilers. But if there were a clear day Gündüz could look over the Bosphorus to Asia, and might be able to see the Princes' Islands, in the Sea of Marmara, where he and his friends take their yachts in the summer.

"This is Europe!" says Gündüz, an ebullient, sometimes incendiary man in his mid-sixties. "After Atatürk, Turkey became European — mentally, I mean. We are democratic, secular. There's an intelligentsia. We have literature, music. We are not much behind Europe, intellectually speaking."

Gündüz has two posters in his office, one of Atatürk and one of Ernest Hemingway. Mustafa Kemal Atatürk, "father of modern Tur-

119

key," was the man who first tried to make Turkey entirely European. Following World War I, a motley crew of nations decided to carve up the Ottoman heartland—that is, Anatolia, what the Greeks and Romans used to call Asia Minor. Atatürk raised an army, fought brilliantly, and turned Asia Minor into Turkey instead. "To me, what he did was magic," says Gündüz. "Atatürk was a western man—blue eyes, yellow hair. He was from Salonika. He hated religion. He saw what it did, that it was ruining people. He changed everything by decree. He created a new race of Western-thinking people. There was no way out for Turkey. It was the center of the Islamic world. He saw the poverty, the backwardness. It was a miracle that we escaped being occupied after the war."

Most Turks don't have blue eyes and yellow hair, nor do they hate religion. But this didn't stop Atatürk from creating a new race by decree, a race that has been trying to become European ever since. Turkey applied for European Community membership in 1987, was refused, has applied again. Gündüz, whose agency is owned by a French multinational, believes European reticence is due to the Turks who have moved to Europe. "To the European guy on the street, the Turk is a worker. This gives a very bad impression of Turkey. The lowest, most ignorant, most desperate people from the fields rushed to Europe. These people are not educated at all. This is the lowest class of Turkish society." Gündüz says the Turks in Germany have become more fundamentalist over time because they don't understand German culture, and, in any event, Germans don't like them. "You have to find a hanger on which to hang your personality. The only thing they can claim is their religion."

Maybe everybody needs something on which to hang a personality. Gündüz hangs his on EuroTurkishness, the hanger preferred by the highest class of Turkish society, the Istanbul elite. The new Europe is a potential empire of great ambition and dwindling patience. Turks in Germany, of course, are being beaten and even killed by their blue-eyed neighbors. "The unkind truth about the EC," wrote columnist Peter Millar, "is that it aspires to ethno-geographic unity, and the Turks do not fit the bill on either count." This presents Europeans with a tough question: What is the ethnicity of Europe? British journalist Charles Moore explained in *The Spectator* that "Britain is basically English-speaking, Christian, and white. . . . Just as we want to bring Poles and Hungarians and Russians slowly into the EEC, and open markets for their goods, so we should try to open our doors to their people....Muslims and blacks, on the other hand, should be kept out as strictly as at present."

Since most Poles don't speak English, and many black people do, the key characteristics of Europeans—notice that Moore slides nimbly between British and European—must be that they are Christian and white. Turks, in general, are neither. So the EuroTurk in search of a personality hanger in today's Istanbul convinces himself that Europeans are actually secular, tolerant, modern, civilized. And that Atatürk's new race is, too. This means that the entire history of Turks before Atatürk's decrees must be erased from one's mind and heart, a process of education, essentially, or re-education. Atatürk "made Turkey reborn—toward civilization," Gündüz says emphatically. It is late afternoon, soon the lights will go on at Topkapı palace and the Blue Mosque and Hagia Sophia and we'll hear the sundown prayer. "We were an uncivilized people, let's face it."

10

WHAT DO THE CIVILIZED European peoples think of their southern neighbors? Not, it would appear, very much. One poll found that seventy-one percent of French people believed there were "too many Arabs" in France, while about fifty percent found there were too many "blacks." A *Le Monde* writer stated that in the 1980s roughly one hundred Arabs from the Maghreb had been killed in France "simply because they're Maghrebins." In Germany, the number of racially motivated attacks has steadily risen since 1989. In Italy, a Socialist Party politician successfully proposed to parliament that the armed forces be deployed against illegal immigrants. "If the enemy is the immigrant, the clandestine," he said, "if he puts our societies in peril, why not turn to the army to defend the country?" The most generous argument among mainstream European commentators seems to be that racism would not exist if non-European peoples did not exist, and that, therefore, for the sake of social peace, non-European peoples should be kept out of Europe. "To minimise racism at home," *The Economist* editorialized, "many countries need to have racist controls on immigration." Which is in fact the solution to racism adopted by Germany.

This aspect of contemporary European life may seem strange, since the European Community is supposed to be a magnificent coming-together of diverse peoples, peoples who have hated each other over many centuries but now, at last, have recognized the desirability of tolerance and mutual respect. The cultural protocol of the 1992 Maastricht treaty for unification reads: "The Community contributes to the flowering of cultures of member states while respecting their national and regional diversity, all displaying the common cultural heritage." It goes on to emphasize "the improvement of knowledge and diffusion of the culture and history of European peoples" and "the conservation and safeguarding of that cultural patrimony that is of European importance." Two EC advertising slogans convey the spirit: "The ultimate prize is worth it: A Europe where a thousand different faces become a single force"; "The European Community: More is possible when you pursue the same idea."

The premise, then, is diversity, "a thousand different faces"; the purpose is unity. What makes those thousand faces valuable for European purposes is that they might come together into a single face: The European. All efforts will be directed toward making the 340 million citizens of the Community act as "a single force" pursuing "the same idea." History has never before witnessed The European. His or her closest ancestor was Hitler's Aryan, a somewhat different animal. The European exists not as a reality, but as an ideal type, a person no longer mired in history (or diversity): a New Man, to use the old term. To judge from the post-1989 debates on immigration, this New Man will belong to a new race, the European race.

In examining this new man and race, we must consider what they are not as well as what they propose to be. In considering what The European is not, let's look at the case of Turkey. Two distinguished British journalists, in an illuminating book called *Europower*, provide some clues: "Catholic Christendom imbued Europe, including part of what is now called Eastern Europe, with a feeling of unity until the end of the Middle Ages. The earliest pan-European sentiment arose out of reaction to a common enemy with an alien religion—the Muslim Ottoman empire. Today, the same sentiment fuels the objection of many in the EC to the would-be membership of nominally secular but predominantly Muslim Turkey. The fact that all members of the EC have Christian values in common, coupled with presumptions that democracy and free markets are the least bad ways of organising society, are basic to their willingness to accept subservience to some common European law."

Given that a great many citizens of the world today will more or less agree that "democracy and free markets are the least bad ways of organising society," the key factor here distinguishing Europeans must be their "Christian values," later characterized by our authors as "the instincts that Christians have in common." Values or instincts, perhaps it makes no difference. Elsewhere, the authors continue: "Turkey's expectation of, and application for, membership is a source of embarrassment within the Twelve [EC members], and the Commission gave it a polite brush-off in December 1989.... The argument that Turkey is a non-European, Muslim culture gets stronger with every reminder that the next threat to Western security might be a religious not ideological one. The entire 1992 relaunch of the Community is founded upon an assumption of shared values — it is basic to mutual recognition of rules — be they on the environment, cruelty to animals, human rights, or the secular basis of the law. Turkey's instincts don't fit in, and its huge and unpoliceable Asian border makes its inclusion in an area without internal frontiers hard to envisage. 'Never say never' is the EC's current approach to Turkey. 'Never say ever' (while certainly not ruling it out) would be a wise approach in all future association agreements."

The authors', and indeed the EC's, objections to Turkish membership are clearly not based on actual Turkish policies or laws. Turkish law, thanks to Atatürk, is more aggressively secular than Britain's. Rather, the difficulty appears to be that most Turks are Muslims and have different "instincts" than Europeans. Two things are particularly worth noting here. First, the authors of *Europower*, and many other Eurocommentators, proclaim on a Monday that Europe is Christian and on Tuesday that it is secular. They should make up their minds; but they won't, because one day a country of Muslims near Europe may establish a solidly secular society and it would no longer be possible to exclude that country from membership on the basis of its non-secularness, at which point Europe, with its confused identity, would simply switch back to Christianity as a way of excluding

123

the infidel. What "Christian Europe" might mean for Jews remains to be seen.

Second, the notion that Europeans have common "instincts" is a curious one. The thrust of European culture since the war has been toward rationalism, whether conservative or socialist, toward the realization of Enlightenment ideals and the application of rational (or scientific) methods to social organization. What's all this about instincts? Since the ancient Greeks, rationalist tradition has tended to maintain that what distinguishes humans from other animals is that they are not ruled by instinct. Yet suddenly we find that Europeans, otherwise considered by themselves the most rational, scientific, and modern of peoples, are in fact creatures of instinct, and therefore not so much a subgroup of reasoning humanity but rather a species of animal. This brings us rapidly back to the tribal anthropology that was supposed to have died with Hitler, one in which the world's peoples are organized in a natural hierarchy, with whites as lions, blacks as rhinos, and Muslims somewhere in between. A *New York Times* reporter, writing at the end of 1991, noted: "For a long time, Britain, France, Germany and other European countries welcomed cheap labor from the third world, but they have all been restricting immigration since the mid-1970's. Since then, they have also discovered that they face difficulties in integrating non-white foreigners and their children..." These boys and girls, born and raised in Europe, perhaps playing football one afternoon after school: Is the problem that they don't have white instincts? What are white instincts?

Yet it would be a mistake to see European unification as a disguise for some new beast urging white power upon an unwilling globe. The EC did not develop as an opportunity for expression of European instincts, white supremacy, or the worship of Christ. It developed as an institutional structure for assuring peace in Western Europe and wealth for its businesses. The motivation behind the 1952 Treaty of Paris, which laid the groundwork for today's community, "was the conviction that the causes of war lay in economic rivalry and that by substituting economic co-operation for economic rivalry the causes of war would be removed." Those are the words of Lord Cockfield, who is considered the architect of the 1992 single market program. But removing the causes of war was only a step toward something much more interesting and lucrative: economic power.

The 1952 treaty sought, in its words, "to substitute for age old rivalries the merging of their essential interests." Despite terrible grammar, the meaning is clear. "Essential interests" means Western European wealth and power; and Cockfield's "economic co-operation" means eliminating free competition between national companies in favor of supranational entities that, not least because of sheer size, will be able to achieve Western European dominance of global markets. As it says in the Single European Act of 1987, "The Community's aim shall be to strengthen the scientific and technological base of European industry and to encourage it to become more competitive at an international level." In *Europower*, the authors state that "economics is, *au fond*, the driving force behind politics in the modern world." This belief has been basic to assigning rationality to the 1992 project. It is allegedly driven by free market economics, an ideology which gains moral and rational plausibility by asserting that free market policies are radically democratic—anyone who works hard will succeed—and economically rational because they allocate goods efficiently. In practice, EC policies emphasize relatively free movement of goods and services within Europe, and massive government economic regulation and intervention to ensure that Europe will be stronger than everyone outside its borders.

The EC advertisements read: "a single force," pursuing "the same idea." The force is unified Europe; the idea is to assert that force for wealth and power, to make Europe again the center of the meaningful world. Europeans will inhabit the White City all alone. No wonder EC citizenship and immigration have become such tense questions. Aristotle wrote in his *Politics* that the bulk of the "artisan class" were either slaves or "foreigners," and "the best form of state will not admit them to citizenship." As European humanists rightly point out, there is much to be learned, even in the late 20th century, from reading the classics.

11

WELL BEFORE THE yellow-haired, blue-eyed Atatürk decreed a new race, Ottoman reformers had attempted to refit the empire for a Western-dominated world. Such changes occurred both at the practical level—the ambitious Tanzimat reforms—and in ideology. By the early 19th century, it was abundantly clear that Ottoman power was declining militarily, economically, and, so to speak, psychologically. Ottoman possessions like Egypt and Greece were rebelling, successfully, on nationalist grounds; competing imperial powers, notably France, Britain, and Russia, sought to add to their own dominions at Ottoman expense; mercantile powers acquired trading privileges from the empire, thereby lessening the possibilities for Ottoman economic growth. The oldest Mediterranean empire was losing out in the great heyday of imperialism. Unable to compete well militarily or economically, Ottoman emperors tried to compete ideologically, presenting themselves as the leaders of Islam ("Pan-Islamism"). By the end of the century, the emperor had even permitted talk of a unified Turkic race ("Pan-Turkism"). In principle, leadership of the Turkic race would have given Ottoman emperors a territory stretching from Egypt to China. While this idea, given the racial tenor of 19th-century loyalties (and Arab dislike of Ottoman rule), had a longer life than Ottoman Pan-Islamism, it, too, proved insufficient.

Westernization provided yet another possibility for Ottoman renewal. Among other things, Westernization can give a troubled state the theoretical framework for imposing uniformity among its subjects—that is, a method for achieving social solidarity. In the Ottoman empire, a prominent means of displaying social diversity was the donning of distinctive hats. So when the sultan Mahmud II faced down rebellious troops in 1826, his reforming mind turned to hats. By 1829, he had passed a law requiring that all state employees abandon their old hats for the fez. Fezzes were worn by Greek Christians on Ottoman islands in the Mediterranean, and wearing a fez made one, symbolically, a Westernizer.

With time, however, the fez became a symbol of Islam. Almost a century after Mahmud II's legislation, Atatürk tried a hat trick of his own. "Mustafa Kemal proposed to extirpate the fez from Turkish society," write his biographers Vamık Volkan and Norman Itzkowitz in *The Immortal Atatürk*. "He wanted to make his countrymen look properly westernized by giving up their characteristic dress for that of the Europeans. Despite the fact that great suffering had been inflicted upon the Ottoman Empire by the Western world, Mustafa Kemal fervently believed that 'there is only one civilization'—that of the West. He held the practices of Islam in Ottoman times responsible for obstructing civilization's advance among the Turks. When he set out to crush the ways of Islam, he was, in effect, attacking the culture of the people from whom he had sprung and whom he had saved. . . . Determined to change the way the Turks dressed, Mustafa Kemal set out from Ankara [modern Turkey's capital] early on 25 August 1925, accompanied by Nuri, another friend, his two aides-de-camp, and a secretary. He was bound for Kastamonu, north of Ankara, which had been described to him as one of the most conservative districts in Turkey. He was going there to introduce the Turks to the [brimmed] hat and convince them of the need to adopt Western dress. The impact would be equal to that of an American president arriving in New York City dressed as a desert nomad, demanding that everyone follow his example. . . . His suit was of grey linen, but its cut was decidedly Western. He wore a shirt and tie, and in his hand he carried a white Panama hat (without a headband)."

When Atatürk walked among the crowds, he asked them 'Where are your hats?' In Kastamonu he said, 'We must become civilized people from every point of view. We have suffered much. This is because we have failed to understand the world. Our thoughts and our mentality will become civilized from head to toe. . . . Look at the Turkish and Islamic worlds. What great calamity and distress they are in because they have not been able to transform and elevate their thoughts as civilization commands. That is the reason why we have remained backward up to now and sank into the mud of this last calamity. If we have rescued ourselves in the past five or six years, it is because of the alterations in our conceptions. Now we can not stand still. Come what may, we shall go forward, because we must. The nation must certainly know that civilization is such a forceful fire that it burns and destroys those who are heedless of it. We shall take our rightful place in the family of nations in which we find ourselves, and we shall defend it."

On his tour, write Volkan and Itzkowitz, Atatürk was able "to whip crowds into a kind of antiphonal fervor. 'Is it possible for a nation to be civilized without dressing in a civilized manner?' he would cry out, and the crowd would answer, 'Never! Never!' Then he would persist, 'Are you ready to be described as uncivilized?' And again the answer would ring out with even more vigor, 'Never! Never!' The

127

Ghazi [one of Atatürk's nicknames, meaning "frontier warrior" and, historically, "frontier warrior of Islam"] then compared the people to jewels—but jewels covered with mud. 'In order to see the jewel shine, one must get rid of the mud,' he told his audience. Getting rid of the mud, he insisted, involved 'shoes on the feet, trousers over the legs, shirts with neckties under the collar, jackets, and naturally, to complement all of this a headcovering to protect you from the sun.' Then came his most celebrated comment on the revolution in dress. Pointing to his Panama hat, he told the onlookers, 'The name of this is "hat." ' "

Atatürk added, "There are those who say this is not permissible by religious law. Let me say to them, you are very ignorant and heedless, and I want to ask them, if wearing the fez, which is the headgear of the Greeks, is permitted by religious law, why isn't it so with wearing a hat?"

One reason is that the *salah* prayers of Islam required one to touch the ground with one's forehead, and since prayers were normally performed with one's hat on, the hat law—the brimless fezzes were banned on November 25—enforced a peculiar separation of church and the new European-style state. You could submit to one, and then to the other, but not to both at the same time. Atatürk's hat law also meant that all Turkish citizens—most important, the various religious orders with their distinct headgear—would now be indistinguishable.

"When Atatürk returned to Ankara, the welcoming crowds had a surprise for him—they were all wearing Panama hats."

Atatürk soon moved on to another reform: the abandonment of Perso-Arabic characters for the Latin alphabet. In 1928 he announced, "We must free ourselves from these incomprehensible signs that for centuries held our minds in an iron vise.... Now is the time to eradicate the errors of the past." Atatürk was ordering his own end of history, an act he construed as a beginning. The writings of half a millennium would thenceforth be inaccessible to any Turks outside the academy.

Atatürk can still be seen throughout Turkey. He stands, huge and barefoot, dressed in a toga, at the entrance to Istanbul University. He's present in force at the nation's premier Atatürk factory in the Istanbul suburb of Maltepe, a working-class settlement characterized by a major freeway (the old Ankara highway) and a lot of gray, dirty apartment buildings, some smaller residences, some evanescent shops, and, here and there, a hovel. This is the view at which numerous Atatürk statues – field-marshal style, diplomat, civilian, mounted warrior – have gazed over the years.

The statue models of Atatürk haven't changed since 1948, when the "civilian Atatürk" – a stern, big-suited figure that evokes Gary Cooper in *The Fountainhead* – first appeared, a decade after the founder of modern Turkey died, fifty-seven years old, of cirrhosis of the liver. Mehmet İnci started making these Atatürks in the late 1930s. His son Necati has carried on the business since Mehmet's death in 1980. Their Atatürks are all over Turkey, in government offices, plazas, office buildings, factories, even private gardens.

Necati İnci, a vigorous, balding man with a mustache and a tobacco rasp, is optimistic about his business's future. "The leaders of the world – for example, Karl Marx, Lenin, Engels, Mao, or what's his name, Ceauşescu – they're all gone. One leader remains. Atatürk. In all the world one leader remains. *Atatürk*. With each day Atatürk is becoming more important." Many intellectual Turks would contest this view. Atatürk built a state-led, nationalist economy run by a one-party government. He was a military genius, a ruthless politician, and he drank too much. After his death, the Turkish army appointed itself his successor at the tiller of state, overthrowing governments three times since the first true multiparty election, in 1946. The most recent coup was in 1980. Over the next ten years, multiparty politics gradually took hold, and the army's "Kemalism" was entirely absent from the 1991 elections.

But, like any great dead figure, Atatürk can serve many purposes. When he set out to create a new race, he had somehow to reconcile nationalism – necessary to unite Turks against foreign occupation – with the modernizing cosmopolitanism necessary to destroy Ottoman social structures. His solution was characteristically European. Turks, he said, were a splendid and unitary race, stretching from China to the Mediterranean. Atatürk even had a theory that humanity began with the Turks – a proposal that, until recently, was taught to Turkish schoolchildren. As such, Turks were in fact the first Europeans, because Atatürk believed European civilization was the highest achievement of humanity and Turks were the first humans, so. . . İnci sells busts of Chopin and Shakespeare, but not of Süleyman the Magnificent or Mehmet the Lawgiver. In the same way that each European country thinks itself the best, and Europe as better than everywhere else, so Atatürk brought together Turkish nationalism and modern multinationalism. This kind of cosmopolitanism is the privilege of being on top.

Yet it happens that Turkey is not on top. Ottomans were cosmopolitan on their own terms, ruling, for centuries, a fiercely and explicitly multiethnic empire based on universal Islamic principles. Modern Turks are cosmopolitan on other people's terms, those of Europeans, whose own multiethnic polity is markedly less diverse and more ideologically uniform than the Ottomans' ever was.

Anyway, Atatürk certainly was a man of vision, of multiple visions, even if he looks slightly ridiculous when replicated and cast in fiberglass, gazing over the midday traffic on the old Ankara highway. "Washington is America's real leader," Necati İnci says. "George Washington. George Washington is for America what Atatürk is for Turkey."

On the highway below the Atatürks, two Gypsy women pass by steering a donkey cart. In Istanbul, you catch a bus by standing on the side of the highway and hailing the first one you see. To disembark, you just tell the driver to stop. People get off at the strangest places, by an empty lot or on an overpass. The bus leaves before you can figure out where these passengers could possibly be going. In a city of ten million, this mirrors rural habits of transport; in the countryside too, people disembark seemingly at random and wander off to their unseen destinations. One typical Istanbul opinion is that the city has filled up with ignorant farmers who are now neither city nor country. Intellectuals tend to blame "the peasants from Anatolia" for most of the country's problems. Atatürk would have recognized this attitude.

Though at least Atatürk believed his people were jewels, perhaps covered with mud, but jewels nonetheless.

12

ŞÜKRIYE, LIKE TENS of thousands of women who have come from Anatolia to Istanbul, spends her days cleaning up after people who have more money than she does. She always wears a head scarf and, when outdoors, in weather hot or cold, a raincoat. Her outfit communicates piety. "I've been in Istanbul for forty years. I came from Sivas [in Anatolia]. You come to the city because you are young and you want to make money. I've raised four children here—two girls, one boy, and one young boy. Well. . .the city has become very mixed up, very confused." Istanbul's population was still under one million just thirty years ago. "Sivas is a beautiful town. You find everything there: plenty of work, food, fruit, trees. Istanbul is very crowded. Every place you go there are so many people. It's not like it was. There's no peace here now.

"My children like it here in some ways. They were born here. Now they work here—my son works in an automobile shop. But they've been to Sivas on holidays. In four years I'm going back to Sivas. Whether the children will go, I don't know.

"I don't consider myself a European. I'm from Sivas."

13

HERE IS A MAN you see every day but never talk to. Watching him from the kitchen window as you prepare coffee, you are impressed by his consistency. Every day he wears a nice wool blazer, carefully matched, well pressed trousers, a shirt and tie, and polished loafers. No hat. His hair is a medium black shading to gray on top. You watch him enough that you think you can see the gray expanding at the cost of the black. He drives a four-door hatchback. His apartment overlooks the Bosphorus. Sometimes his kids follow him into the parking lot; he pets them, and kisses them goodbye, before driving to work. Every evening at the same time he returns, parks his car, and re-enters his apartment.

14

REMEMBER DINA, travelling between Asia and Europe or vice versa on the *dolmuş* that night: the way it creaked.

Remember eating grilled palamut when the palamut had just come into season and everyone at the waterside restaurants was eating it, the fishermen were out on the Bosphorus in their small boats every day searching for palamut. Remember its luscious taste, the way you loved rolling the word over in your mouth, palamut, palamut.

Remember glass after glass of tea with sugar in the day when it was hot and glasses of raki at night when it was cool.

Remember driving with your friend through Üsküdar one evening during the 1991 campaign, the streets wildly decorated with the various parties' banners. "It's like a holiday!" he said. Turkish elections hadn't always been like holidays; they had also been times of fear and violence. Fear: the police stop you at an impromptu checkpoint, looking for terrorists or at least a few lira from intimidated drivers. (Checkpoints are most frequent before gift-giving holidays.) You watch your friend, a proud, sometimes arrogant man, affluent, well-known both in his own country and abroad, suddenly shake with fear as the police approach.

Remember the markets of Aksaray, with poor Eastern Europeans wandering around, giddy one minute, fearful of robbery the next. The signs said "Polish style," and you wondered: What is Polish style?

Remember listening to the Muslim prayer for the dead when a young friend of yours had just passed away, in another country: and how it touched you. If you forget a dead friend, does he die again? If you forget your ancestors do you lose time, or gain it?

Remember Dina on the drunken boat across the Bosphorus at night, and the boat's creaking.

Remember eating anchovies in cornbread; and the former Roman cistern that's now a restaurant lit only with candles.

Remember. Everything can slip away, like a suicide over the gunwales on a quiet night. If you forget enough then other forces will take over your memory, buy it at a discount. The many people you've met will blend into one person, then disappear; "a thousand different faces become a single force." If you forget enough, then every place you visit will have been the same place, only better or worse. And you will have lost the taste of life.

15

REMEMBER THAT TIME is not the same for all people, that different people think about time differently. In the second century B.C., Polybius wrote the first universal history to mark the rise of Rome. As he saw it, the many times of the past had come together in the single, imperial time of Roman power. "Now in earlier times the world's history has consisted, so to speak, of a series of unrelated episodes, the origins and results of each being as widely separated as their localities, but from this point onwards history becomes an organic whole." Given "the extraordinary spirit of the times in which we live," Polybius wrote, "Fortune has steered almost all the affairs of the world in one direction and forced them to converge upon one and the same goal." A thousand faces, a single force, pursuing the same idea.

In the 19th century, similarly, some people equated time with the progress of civilization, so that more civilized people had, in a sense, more time. In 1867 Mark Twain, watching the meeting of Napoleon III and the Ottoman Sultan Abdülaziz, remarked: "Napoleon III, the representative of the highest modern civilization, progress, and refinement; Abdul Aziz, the representative of a people by nature and training filthy, brutish, ignorant, unprogressive, superstitious—and a government whose Three Graces are Tyranny, Rapacity, Blood. Here in brilliant Paris, under the majestic Arch of Triumph, the First Century greets the Nineteenth!"

Not too much later, the Westernizing Atatürk argued that time had its second birth when Turkey began life as a nation, under his leadership, because he knew that "civilization is such a forceful fire that it burns and destroys those who are heedless of it."

For the EC citizen, time begins both right now, with the birth of the New Europe and New Europeans, and long ago, probably with the Persian Wars (500–449 B.C.). The primordial distinction between Europe and Asia is conventionally traced to these wars, in the course of which Greek forces defeated and expelled the expansionist Persians. The period from 500 B.C. to A.D. 1992 forms a background to the present, a rehearsal period during which the crucial issues of human (or European) life were worked through. In a book on European unification, German sociologist Otto Jacobi asked, "[M]ight I dare list a few examples of European virtue and progressiveness? Rationalism, science, technology and industrial capitalism is one group of European inventions; others include enlightenment, humanism, secularism, tolerance, democracy and the social-welfare state." In other words, everything worthwhile in history and a bit more besides. With all this accomplished, Europe is now in a position to start time afresh, to begin the era sometimes called "post-history" and to count the days according to Eurotime. The rest of the world will presumably cooperate by setting its clocks according to Eurotime, or trying to. Those peoples who fail to do so will be "timeless." If they don't "catch up," if they remain in "undeveloped" or "developing" countries, they may run out of time altogether.

In industrial countries, at least, you can buy time, because, as everyone says, time is money. In New York, for example, you might make in a day what in Pakistan you might make in a month. So you will try to leave Pakistan for New York, and thereby buy time for yourself.

In former Communist countries, time is what you lost when you were still living in a Communist country.

In Turkey, you find still more varieties of time. For example, the time of the Sufi *tarikatlar*, the Muslim mystical orders, with their lineages of spiritual masters stretching back for centuries, back to Muhammad; the time of "fundamentalists," who are not at all sure that modern times are the best of times; and the time of families, who mark time according to their parade of ancestors. Each of these think of time differently, and it isn't at all clear that any of them want to live according to Eurotime, or believe that time is money. They want to live with honor in their own lifetime. Surely every person should be free to do that?

16

"IT BEGAN IN 1755. In the time of the caliph, that is, during the Ottoman caliphate, people from Turkestan, from Asia you might say, came here with the intention of performing the pilgrimage. This area was like an inn. A few weeks they would wait, pitching their tents, while seeking permission from the caliph to make their pilgrimage."

Necmeddin, the head of the Uzbek *tekke* in Istanbul, is telling you the history of his institution. The weather's fine; you sit on a balcony at a small table with him and his wife, drinking tea.

"At one point the sultan, travelling incognito, came by – this is around 1750 – and he saw the tents, water, and food. He asked, 'Who has come here? Where are they from?'

"He was told they'd come from Turkestan, from Asia.

" 'Why have they come here?' he asked.

" 'They want to make the *hadj* to Mecca and Medina,' he was told.

"The sultan stopped for a while and said, 'While you're seeking permission, you should have a place to eat meals. A *tekke* should be built here. You should have a place to stay.'

"So seeing that people were coming every year from Asia and staying here for one or two weeks or a month, the sultan built this *tekke*."

Uzbeks are a Turkic-language-speaking people in former Soviet Central Asia. Though dispersed, most now live in the recently independent republic of Uzbekistan. The Uzbek *tekke* is built mainly of wood, painted white; it has the graceful simplicity typical of pre–19th-century wooden Ottoman structures. It stands at the top of a hill overlooking the Bosphorus, on the Asian side. Two storeys surround a courtyard on three sides, with a fence at the back. A little boy rides his tricycle around the dry fountain in the courtyard's center; sometimes he drives the tricycle right into the fountain's side, then looks pleased and confused.

Generally speaking, a specific Sufi *tekke* will belong to a specific *tarikat*, founded by some inspirational leader. This *tarikat* will usually be named for its founder, who then becomes the first *şeyh* in the *tarikat*'s *silsile*, or "chain" of leaders. A given *tekke* may have its own sub-*silsile*. *Silsile* can mean chain, range, dynasty, pedigree, genealogy. The Uzbek *tekke* in Istanbul has its own *silsile* but the chain was broken early this century, and Necmeddin, fortyish, with the severity and tempestuous humor of a small businessman, is not a *şeyh* (few real *şeyhler* have survived modernism); rather, he runs a small print-shop on a nearby commercial street, producing pamphlets, business cards, announcements, and the like, as well as five-by-seven cards with Sufi sayings on them. In fact, he has these mounted proudly on the wall behind his desk at the office. They provide a calm counterpoint to the clank of the presses in the adjoining room.

The Uzbek *tekke* is part of the Naqshbandi *tarikat*, which now stretches from China and Southeast Asia to Africa and even the United States. The *tarikat* originated in the work of Yusuf al-Hamadani (d. 1140), a famed saint and teacher who instructed his disciples in Bukhara, an ancient Central Asian city on the Silk Road, now in Uzbekistan. Among Hamadani's followers were the poet Ahmad Yesevi, whose legacy would be the influential Yesevi *tarikat*, and later Abdulhaliq al-Ghujdawani (d. 1220). Through visions, Ghujdawani influenced the Naqshbandi founder, Bahauddin al-Naqshband (d. 1389). Naqshband was born near Bukhara in 1318. (His tomb there is today a destination for pilgrims.) According to tradition, a sage visited Naqshband's village when the future *şeyh* was three days old. He received divine knowledge that Naqshband would grow up to be among God's leading servants. The sage adopted young Naqshband as his spiritual son and a remarkable career began. Less than a century later, Mullah Abdullah İlahi, from Simav (like Nâzım Hikmet's hero Sheikh Bedreddin), travelled to Samarkand, near Bukhara, and joined the relatively new Naqshbandi order. İlahi thence returned to the Ottoman realm, to Istanbul, which had been recently (1453) taken from the Byzantines. He established the city's first Naqshbandi *tekke* in a former church. İlahi died in 1490, by which time the *tarikat* had already begun spreading into the Balkans and Anatolia.

Some five hundred years later, at the Uzbek *tekke*, Necmeddin explains that, once the sultan had built the *tekke*, "a *şeyh* of the Naqshbandi came and the *tekke* was devoted to the Naqshbandi rites, and the *dergâh* took on the form of a Naqshbandi *dergâh*." (*Dergâh* is the Persian word for *tekke*.) "The *tekke* was used, for example, as a place to prepare Uzbek pilaf." Pilaf is the Uzbek national dish (*palaw* in Uzbek), eaten on all important occasions and many less important ones. According to the scholar Grace Smith, the early 20th-century sage Küçük Hüseyn Efendi performed, at this very *tekke*, a miracle with pilaf. "Küçük Hüseyn Efendi and a large number of people came to the *tekke* during the period when Istanbul was being occupied by Allied troops after the First World War and the *tekke* was suffering much hardship. Those living in the *tekke* scraped together everything they had to make a pilav for the guests but it only filled part of a pot. Küçük Hüseyn

Efendi came out into the kitchen, looked into the pot, and took out a small portion. He then sprinkled this portion over the remaining rice in the pot and replaced the cover. When the cooking was done, the pilav had filled the pot to overflowing."

The Uzbek *tekke* was also active in politics. During the Russo-Turkish war of 1877 to 1878, for example, the government asked Sufi *şeyhler* to say a prayer for the troops, including the "Victory" chapter of the Koran (sura 48): "If the unbelievers join battle with you, they shall be put to flight. They shall find none to protect or help them. Such were the ways of God in days gone by; and you shall find no change in the ways of God...." As it turned out, the Ottomans lost, and modern Bulgaria received its first taste of semi-independence.

Fifty years later, the Uzbek *tekke* would do its part in helping the revolutionary builders of modern Turkey establish their new state during the 1919–1923 War of Independence. "In the 1920s, when the Turkish Republic was being set up," Necmeddin says, "Şeyh Ata would hide soldiers and important people here in the *dergâh*. This *dergâh* was of great service to the republic. İsmet Paşa hid here." İsmet Paşa was İsmet İnönü, Atatürk's chief lieutenant during the war, later prime minister (twice) and president. He was fleeing the Allies, who had taken over the Ottoman government in Istanbul with the intention of making it a puppet. İnönü hid at the *tekke* on his way to join Atatürk, as did Celâleddin Arif, the last president of the Ottoman Parliament.

This did not mean, however, that the Uzbek *tekke*, or any other, would enjoy protection from the new state. Şeyh Ata was the last real *şeyh* at the *tekke*, for once Atatürk and his comrades had driven the Greeks, Italians, British, etc. from Anatolia and established Turkey, the days of the Sufis were numbered. In 1925, at the same time that he made brimmed hats the official headgear, Atatürk said: "Gentlemen and fellow countrymen, know that the Turkish Republic cannot be a nation of sheikhs, dervishes, and mystics. The truest path is the path of civilization; it is necessary for one to be a man who does what civilization dictates. I could never admit to the civilized Turkish community a primitive people who seek happiness and prosperity by putting their faith in such and such a sheikh, a man opposed to the sparkling light of civilization, which encompasses all science and knowledge. In any case, the lodges must be closed." And so they were.

Or were they? Hadn't you just that morning, nearly seven decades after Atatürk's speech, been sweating your way around Üsküdar, stopping occasionally to cool off in a sea breeze, asking an old man by a mosque, another man carrying groceries, a local girl: Excuse me, do you know where the Uzbek *tekke* is? And hadn't they all known, saying, Oh yes, it's the white building at the top of the hill with a cemetery next to it?

"Turkey became free," Necmeddin explains, "but it wasn't completely free. Dervish ceremonies were prohibited. Of course, the *tarikatlar* still continue, in secret." At this you have to laugh. How secret are they when local people discuss them publicly with passersby? "They are there, certainly, but they can't operate openly. From a legal point of view they remain prohibited, although, practically, everyone is free. Yet legally, as I say, the *tarikatlar* can't practice openly. There is no legal right. But all the *tarikatlar* do exist: Khadiri, Rufai, Djerahi. But in secret, not openly. For the *tarikatlar* there aren't really any problems now, but you have to worship in homes. There is no public organization of the *tekkeler*. And they are not well cared for, they are unkempt."

So the faithful still do gather to perform the distinct Naqshbandi silent *dhikr*, a prayer focussed on the name of God, Allah, which some scholars have compared to the Byzantine "Jesus prayer" chanted by the Orthodox hesychasts. Perhaps people don't sing the *ilahiler*, sacred hymns, as they once did at the Uzbek *tekke*, or perform the special *khatmı khwajagan*, an ancient litany that includes the Koran's first sura ("Praise be to God, Lord of the Universe..."), the 94th ("...Every hardship is followed by ease. Every hardship is followed by ease. When your prayers are ended resume your toil, and seek your Lord with all fervour"), and the 112th ("Say: 'God is One, the Eternal God. He begot none, nor was He begotten. None is equal to Him'"). Perhaps people no longer sing in Uzbek, Chaghatay, or Uygur, as they once did. Necmeddin says he can hardly understand Uzbek, and has never been to pray at Naqshband's tomb in Bukhara, though "Inshallah one day I will visit there." Yet people still believe in "sheikhs, dervishes, and mystics," and contest Atatürk's command that "civilization" is "the truest path."

138

The Arabic word *tariq* means "way." *Sharia* means "the road to the watering-place," and has, of course, been the word for Muslim law. The "law" is in a sense the path one follows to reach the source of life. Sufi Muslims hold that each *tariq* is a small path along the greater *sharia* path travelled by all Muslims. Hence *tariqat* or Turkish *tarikat*. Each mystical order is a small path taken toward the source of life. It was in Mecca that God provided the sacred well of Zamzam. According to Muslim tradition, Abraham abandoned Hagar, the Egyptian bondswoman, and their son, Ismail, in the then-barren valley of Mecca. (According to Genesis, Abraham's wife, Sara, had said to Abraham, "Cast out this slave woman with her son; for the son of this slave woman shall not be heir with my son Isaac.") After two nights and a day alone in the valley, Hagar and Ismail ran out of water. Hagar could not bear to see her son die, so she ran between the hills of Safa and Marwah, crying out to God. "O Thou Bountiful, Thou Full of Grace! Who shall have mercy on us unless Thou hast mercy!" God heard her, and beneath Ismail appeared the sacred well of Zamzam. Muslims making the *hajj* today run between the hills of Safa and Marwah in Mecca.

Each *tarikat* follows its own small path back to the same watering-place. Every Sufi shares the goal. "One person can be Mevlevi, Khadiri, and Rufai," says Necmeddin, listing three *tarikatlar*. "One might be Khadiri and Naqshbandi at the same time, Khadiri and Mevlevi at the same time. You can go to any number of them at the same time. Well—each of these is a subdivision. But all are directed toward Muhammad. I have gone to other *tekkeler*, but I don't like all of them. For example, I went to the Khadiri *tekke* in Tophane [an Istanbul neighborhood]. I only go rarely. The Tophane *tekke* is quite beautiful. You can see Şeyh Mispa."

More and more people, he says, come to the *tekkeler*, including young people. Secular Turks fear the Sufi orders, particularly the Naqshbandi, because there's some evidence that the *tarikatlar* control votes and, therefore, politicians. When the prime minister (later president) had his mother buried next to her Naqshbandi *şeyh* in the 1980s, scandal ensued. Yet the extent, and even more so the nature, of Naqshbandi or other Sufi influence is difficult to determine. Take the issue of veiling women. "For the Naqshbandi total concealment is necessary," Necmeddin explains. "You must be completely covered."

You notice that Necmeddin's lively wife is far from concealed, and her hair stylishly short.

"I'm modern," she says gamely.

Necmeddin smiles. "At this *dergâh*, we see things openly."

He takes you on a tour. You see the huge steel bowl for preparing pilaf, the mounted photos of former *şeyhler*, the inlaid mother-of-pearl box made by a *şeyh*. "The lock still works," Necmeddin says proudly, demonstrating.

He takes you out to the street and around a corner to view the *tekke*'s cemetery. Of course, there's no place better than a cemetery to consider the question of time and how one person might understand it differently from another. Necmeddin takes you to view the Ertegün family tomb, wherein lie Mehmet Cemil Bey, his wife, Ayşe, their son, Munir, and his wife, Hayrunissa. Munir Ertegün was the first ambassador of Turkey to the United States. His son Ahmet would go on to become perhaps the leading producer of rhythm and blues in the United States, handling such artists as Aretha Franklin and Ray Charles. Ahmet Ertegün paid for the restoration of the Uzbek *tekke*, which is why today the buildings are in excellent repair and shine white in the sun.

Also in the cemetery lies Osman Kocaoğlu, a famous Bukharan patriot of the early 20th century. Kocaoğlu had been a great advocate of Pan-Turkism, the belief that meaningful ties linked Turkic-language speakers from China to the Mediterranean—a belief with obvious appeal to Turkic Central Asians, living as they were under the imperial Tsarist boot. Central Asian intellectuals looked to the reforming Ottoman empire as an example and a possible source of assistance. A member of the reformist Union of Holy Bukhara, Kocaoğlu visited Istanbul in 1908. He opposed conscription of Central Asian troops in the First World War—a risky position—and was the first and last president of the Republic of Bukhara, founded in September 1921. Before the end of that year, strains between Bukhara and Soviet Russia led Kocaoğlu to seek Afghan aid. By mid-1922, Turkic Central Asians in Bukhara and nearby regions were in open revolt against the Soviets. Kocaoğlu joined them, then left for Istanbul to head a Committee for the Liberation of Bukhara. He did not return home. Independent Bukhara finally integrated into the Soviet Union in 1924. Kocaoğlu continued his agitations, among other things working on the journal *New Turkistan*, which nurtured Pan-Turkic hopes. (Years later, Kocaoğlu's first cousin Timur would head the U.S.-funded Radio Liberty Uzbek-language service, based in Munich and beaming into Uzbekistan.) Near him lies the body of Dr. Necmettin Ahmet Han Delil, editor of *New Turkistan* and first head of the Overseas Organization of the United Turkistan Nation, a nation that has never actually existed. Not coincidentally, the sacred tomb of Naqshband, nominal founder of the Naqshbandi *tarikat*, is in Bukhara.

For a Sufi, *tarikat* time can bend and sway, backward and forward, from rhythm and blues to a Munich radio station, from this tomb to that tomb, "all leading to Muhammad." The most holy grave next to the Uzbek *tekke* in Istanbul is that of Mir Riza, who died around 1830. On his foot he bore distinctive marks. These he inherited from an ancestor who, over twelve centuries before, had accompanied Muhammad on his flight from Mecca to Medina. The ancestor protected Muhammad from an attacking snake. The marks on the foot were scars from snakebite. Mir Riza is said to have been related by blood to Abu Bakr, the first (632–634) caliph of Islam. Many Sufi *tarikatlar* trace their saintly lines back to Abu Bakr, whom tradition considers a man peculiarly able to understand mysteries and mysterious signs.

Muhammad reportedly once asked Abu Bakr, "Do you remember the day that was no time other than itself?"

Abu Bakr responded, "Yes, O Emissary of God," later explaining to friends that that day was "the day of *mithaq*" – the day on which man is with God for all eternity, or the day when time at last gives way to permanence.

17

FUNDAMENTALIST TIME BEARS some resemblance to *tarikat* time but is also very different. Nilüfer Göle has been studying fundamentalism, or radical Islam, among young people in Istanbul, particularly female university students. In the 1980s, some students began to wear headscarves (never actual veils) to class and to make suggestive remarks about the importance of faith. They isolated themselves, to a degree, from the less pious and attempted to date only boys with similar views on religion. This apparently simple gesture enraged elite opinion. First of all, the girls were wearing scarves *at university*, the very home and training ground of secular modernism, enlightenment, etc. They were bringing Islam to the exact place which took as its mission the elimination of religious superstition. Secondly, they were spreading Islam among the sons and daughters of the elite, the people who would soon enough be running Turkey and, their parents hoped, bringing it into the European Community and a secure place in the future world order of wealth and power. By this gesture, the girls were endangering just about everything that three or four generations of elite Turks had struggled for. The reaction was one of terror, incomprehension, and hatred.

Yet the reaction died down—a ban on religiously significant dress was rescinded. A small minority of girls continues to wear headscarves and rain-or-shine raincoats. A minority of boys continues to seek their hands in marriage. These are the people Göle, a sociologist, studies. "I've tried to show," she says in English interrupted by French, "that through a reading of Islamic movements one can arrive at a different interpretation of modernization movements." For this she has been labeled a "sympathizer," giving aid and comfort to the enemy. The accusation makes her laugh, at least on this pleasant day as she sits in her office at Boğaziçi University, the leading bootcamp for Istanbul's ruling class.

Göle began by divining a difference between modernization and Westernization. "Westernization doesn't mean modern," she says, "nor does modern contradict tradition." In the West, she points out, one can see modernity as the culmination of one's history and, therefore, not divorced from tradition. "For me, as a Turk, 'Western society' means a continuity between modernity and tradition. There is no rupture in one sense; there is a continuity between past and present." So in the West one can become modern in an organic way, so to speak. In Turkey, one doesn't have this option. As Göle says, "Modernization occurs where modernity is absent." After all, where else *would* it occur? Turkey and other countries with Muslim majorities "have lost their traditions. These are societies which are anti-traditional. They don't even know how to change traditions, to reinvent traditions, how to produce modernity out of traditions."

Ottoman and then Turkish reformers tried to produce modernity through Westernization. The 19th-century reformers of the Tanzimat era, and later Atatürk, "tried to get rid of the definition of the civilized man which equated him with the Muslim man. We tried to destroy this identification. Kemal tried to create a definition of Turkishness that was anti-Muslim." This attempt at destroying the past occurred not only at the political, economic, or legal levels: "On the contrary, it's a process of daily life – the way we eat, the way we move, our dress, the way we define the ideal man and woman."

Much of what distinguished Atatürk was the thoroughness with which he sought to Westernize Turkish society. "Perhaps this is the only historical case in which a country decided through political will to have a shift of civilization." Göle laughs slightly. She is tall and thin, tense, with a taste for Western fashion. "I interpret the reforms of Atatürk as an effort to define the civilized man as a Western man. This has had such important repercussions, consequences in our lives that we are still unaware of them.

"This change of civilization was mostly important in terms of women. Because women – I think that, in all these Muslim countries that were involved in this process of modernization, women's status was not a marginal issue. It's directly related with this question of civilization. It is the touchstone of modernization. Because the way we proved our belonging to the Western world was through the visibility of women. The participation in public life of women was the cornerstone of these reforms."

Göle sees a "fundamental asymmetry" between Western and Muslim social organization: "Private spheres do not fit the same conception. 'Private sphere' in the West means 'privacy,' as far as I know, whereas in the Muslim conception the private sphere, *mahrem*, means women's world, women's place. It is sacred. It is the forbidden – forbidden to foreign men. It is basically related with the sexuality of women. It is *not* individualism. I think the basic organization of Muslim society depends on this limitation of women to the foreign man. That's why we speak of segregation of sexes. Women's veiling defines what is interior and what is exterior.

"Atatürk tried to create a heterosocial society and to destroy this homosocial society, which was based on women's segregation – *mahrem, harem*. He tried to push women into society. The visibility of women was the main stake of the Kemalist reforms – more than democracy.

"So secularism and women's visibility were identified, and symbolically we showed to what extent we belonged to Western civilization through this new visibility given to women.

"I will give you an example: the balls that were organized during the first years of the young republic. It was very important, the celebration of the young republic through these balls. The people, men and women, came in their Westernized suits and they didn't know what to do. They were there, they were ready for a very Westernized outlook—but they didn't know what to do. Then Atatürk gave them an order, a very military order, to dance together. That is why I am saying that this is maybe the only country where the will of political men has been so overt to change this civilization—what we call Westernization.

"I think this has had a very deep effect on how we think of *our* culture, *our* identity. Seeing the ideal human being in Western terms shapes our daily conduct. That is why it's very profound."

Profound, yet, as it turns out, inadequate. "We have a tabula rasa. We try to get rid of our past. Because we feel ourselves injured in our identity, because we have not produced civilization, industrial civilization, we have not produced Enlightenment, we are not producing the 'information society.' The void which was left by the Kemalist reforms was never filled. Liberalism is very limited with respect to answering individuals' emotional needs. That is why after the end of socialism we see such a revival of religion. I think the Turkish bourgeoisie has great difficulty in finding a set of values. They have very little to give their children. They give money, and certain kinds of freedom. They do not give their children a sense of place, or of place in time, that is anything but second-rate, semi-Western, inadequate. And so by doing something as mundane as wearing a raincoat when it isn't raining and a headscarf, and being women, at a university, the radical Islamic girls of Boğaziçi and elsewhere struck at the heart of an entire worldview and rejected the tradition of anti-traditionalism—of Westernization.

"This does not mean that the radical Muslims are traditional, or anti-modern. Quite the opposite: Islamic people are in the process of destroying this identification of the West and the civilized man. They are trying to develop new values, new modes of life, new body language.

144

"They are not anti-modern. First of all, they are in urban spaces, in the university—in the spaces, the bastions of modernity. Secondly, they criticize everything traditional. They distinguish themselves from their origin, from their family background—first of all through the social mobility they have achieved." Göle says her foreign colleagues "always associate Islamic movements with a sense of popular uprising. You know, frustrated popular masses coming like barbarians to destroy modernity. But, at least in the university, these are not the most frustrated of Turks at all. They are moving *away* from traditional Islam.

"The raincoat-and-scarf is not traditional. It is militant. They situate themselves with respect to their families as enlightened. They're better educated, they do research, they go back to the sources to understand Islam. Back to the base—the Koran. That is the Utopia for them—Muhammad, the Caliphate. It serves as a source of legitimation.

"But what is happening now is that, through their participation in political Islam, and through education, they are participating more and more *in public life*. Their education leads them into the professions. And so they are leaving the community as well, leaving *mahrem*, leaving this interior, private space through their social practice. They are changing, reforming Islam, even as they claim to be following Islamic precepts and, more than that, that they represent the hard core of Islam. The tension is resolved by reference to their Utopia. It is not completely resolved of course, and the tensions continue, between men and women, and within the Islamic movements themselves."

This process is itself a type of modernization, "a different attempt at modernity, a different conception of modernity." Modernization without Westernization has to do with "how the society produces itself, *innovates* itself," with "the society's creativity." Until recently, radical Turkish university students tended to identify with socialism. In Göle's view, socialism failed because it couldn't innovate itself, because it wasn't creative, or not creative enough. "Socialism was the most loyal son of industrial civilization. Radical Islam is more postmodern. Modern industrial society has already been critiqued by Westerners themselves, by postmodernists and poststructuralists.

145

The Muslim intellectuals use these authors for inspiration. Ivan Illich, [Michel] Foucault. These are very important for Islamic intellectuals.

"I don't know if this will give birth to a new Turkish modernism. Of course this would come about from many factors. In Europe there were always many different factors in modernity. Islam would be just one factor.

"I remember, myself, I saw a woman once in a full *chador*, all covered in black. I felt a twisting in my stomach. I didn't understand why she was in *chador*. But then I see her shoes and her bag, and they were punk. You know the shoes—I don't wear such shoes—with metallic details? It is hard to visualize." It is also a long way from Muhammad and the Caliphate. "These cultures are detraditionalized. You cannot take something that was in the past and bring it back. Because it is dead. It can never exist as if it is not in relation with the Western world. Even at the theological level, these radicals don't really know much about Islam. It is very funny. And now they are criticizing the last bit of tradition we have."

You walk about the leafy precincts of Boğaziçi University. It used to be an American missionary school, Robert College, and stands perched on a hilltop overlooking the Bosphorus. (*Boğaz* is Turkish for Bosphorus; lower-cased it means strait, mountain pass, narrow part, or throat.) Most of the students appear to have sprung full-grown from a Benetton catalog and would be indistinguishable on the campus of UCLA. A strong breeze comes up, stirring a whirlwind of dust on the quad, which doubles as a playing field. Posters advertise upcoming concerts; trees rustle; the girls carry more books than the boys; boys drive up importantly in expensive cars. Some of the girls wear raincoats and headscarves, and with two of them you sit down to chat in an empty room. They will not shake your hand because you are not Muslim and because you're a man—it would violate *mahrem*. They will not give their names, because "you never know how things will turn out, who might be in power some day." They're anticipating an anti-Muslim backlash and would rather not expose themselves to it unnecessarily. They are shy and sometimes giggly.

They approach the conversation formally, discussing answers between themselves and often responding as "we," which sometimes means the representative *we*, "women like us." "We were always Muslims. We did not discover Islam." They're both from provincial

146

families that came to Istanbul. Few people on campus, they say, are religiously in-between, and few of the secular or wealthy students have "converted," though they hope more will. Relations with other students are usually fine, though tensions do arise. "For example," the more serious one says, "club activities and sports. We must follow the *harem* rules, which makes it difficult. But we can make up the credits by taking private classes. I'm taking private *tae kwon do* classes.

"We arrived at the decision to follow Islam beforehand. We didn't decide after coming to university. Some of us follow Islam because of family pressure, but that's a minority. We're not unhappy here. We're happy, because we believe in God and follow His laws.

"We aren't discriminated against much, except for the way we look. People will stare at us, and this can be painful. There's no need to make a fuss over how we dress."

You look at them and can't help but think: *They're so young.*

"We certainly do not feel powerless as women. On the contrary." They're both studying for professions and worry that they will have to violate the *mahrem/harem* rules when they begin work. "I'm studying to be a lawyer, and I won't be able to get a job if I wear *mahrem* clothing."

"One problem is that it's impossible to get an Islamic education here. We have to teach ourselves—that's how we learn about Islam. The state doesn't like Islam, and this is not a very Islamic society. We worry about our children, about the Western influence on them.

"But we are optimistic!" They laugh. "The situation is not *that* bad. There are many things to be optimistic about." Unfortunately, they don't really have any examples.

You meet Ruya at her apartment, where she lives alone. Cigarettes, whiskey, carefully matched furniture. She is strikingly beautiful and always paints her lips a bright red. "The older Muslim intellectuals are very despairing, you know," she says. She lives in a high rise next to other high rises, in a planned urban project. "You learn secularism from grade school on. It's very hard to identify yourself as Muslim."

Ruya is an intellectual who wants to identify herself as Muslim but doesn't know how. For one thing, she likes to drink; also she doesn't want to marry but wants even less to give up sex. Besides, she recently found out that her grandfather was a convert, an Armenian.

147

Apparently his entire family was wiped out at the time when Muslims in eastern Turkey were killing Armenians—this would be around 1915—and he was saved by a Turkish family that went on to raise him as a Muslim. More confusion.

"All of these Muslim kids are from provincial parents. Secularization takes place in the cities. How would you feel coming to Boğaziçi and seeing all these girls in shorts? Fifteen years ago there wasn't a single real Muslim at the university. In the last ten or fifteen years, ex-provincial families have been sending their kids to universities. So just one girl in a scarf—and it's a scandal!"

Ruya was educated in England. Her father made his money doing construction in a provincial city. Now he has a summer home in a village on the Black Sea. The home is among several dozen surrounded by a high wall that separates them from the village. "You should go sometime. You sit on the balcony in a bathing suit, sipping drinks. And outside there's this whole village of Muslims." Ruya became interested in Islam six or seven years ago and was intrigued by the radical young people she found at Boğaziçi: because they didn't drink ("ninety-five percent hadn't tried"), kept to themselves, and had problems with dating and sex. "The Muslim boys often aren't attracted to the girls with their scarves and all. They try to convert the girls who wear jeans so they can fall in love with them." This commonly ends in frustration. The situation isn't too different with the girls. "One girl I know, her family found her a Turk in Belgium. He came back to Turkey and broke off the engagement. Then he returned to Belgium and married a Belgian girl—who then converted."

Ruya laughs her hard laugh. Cynicism comes automatically to her, but not all that gracefully. "I know of not one example of a girl who came from a secularized family and became an observant Muslim. They are all from traditional, provincial backgrounds. Obviously. It's much easier for them to rebel against their families along Muslim lines rather than, for example, through sexual freedom. All this 'radical Islam' among these kids is an easy form of rebellion. People like me, we rebelled against our parents by saying they were too moderate politically. These kids, they're not rebelling against secularism. They're rebelling against their parents. Why do they always say they're 'making a choice'? Because the state always says that fundamentalism is primitive and *conformist*, so they turn around and say they're actually rebelling against the state by *choosing* Islam.

"The Turkish republic urged men and women to mix together. They emphasized that we're all humans. They ignored female sexuality. They said Islam is animalistic, that as humans we can control ourselves. They had the idea that people are asexual. I think it's very drily Puritan to say 'No sex at work.' It's ridiculous to say that you should only think about sex after five o'clock. Islam is a very sexual religion. That's why I like it.

"People can be so sophisticated about other things and so simplistic about Islam. Well. Internally, Islam is secularized and modernized anyway. Secularism, modernization, has totally won. Most people don't know a thing about Islam."

Ruya says "I'm not a typical Turk," but that's what just about every Turk says. None of them is lying.

Once you whiled away a morning at the station, watching the trains come and go and the poor kids stealing. What is fundamentalist time? It doesn't seem to be the past. As Nilüfer Göle said, "You cannot take something that was in the past and bring it back. Because it is dead. It can never exist as if it is not in relation with the Western world." Fundamentalist time doesn't seem to be the future exactly; what will that young student do when she becomes a lawyer? Yet fundamentalist time doesn't seem to be the present, either. There are too many presents, and they move so quickly. In and out the trains go. Four women in raincoats and full-shoulder veils walk through the station. Two black African women walk toward them, and the two groups pass in front of you. The four pious women turn and watch the Africans, who promenade languidly in colorful print dresses. The four women giggle and shake their heads in wonderment.

18

FAMILIES EXPERIENCE TIME DIFFERENTLY. For them, time can be a staircase to the past, each step an ancestor. (Whether the staircase goes up or down is another question.) A person might feel utterly adrift in the present if he or she weren't able to imagine a mother or father, a grandmother, and so on. Families can give one a certain mastery over time, even a mastery over oneself.

Take, for example, the Danishmend family. Supposedly the Danishmend name comes from northern China, but today's Danishmends trace their heritage only as far back as Melik Danishmend, who founded a dynasty in part of Anatolia toward the end of the 11th century. The exploits of Melik Danishmend constitute the main subject of the *Danishmendname*, a classic oral tale of chivalry that survives in its 1360 edition. Melik Danishmend lived a long time and carved out a state that lasted almost a century. He fought against many a Christian Crusader. He even imprisoned the famous Bohemond of Antioch, later freeing him once they'd agreed to ally against the Byzantines and the Seljuk Turks. The *Danishmendname* still makes interesting reading for a Westerner, at once familiar—Muslim literature provided many models for medieval Western chivalric romances—and quite unfamiliar. For example, early on Danishmend, after a day spent in search of infidels, has fallen asleep. Then his horse begins "to whinny and thrash about." Danishmend awakes:

> He saw that a man had risen up in the middle of the plain. It was a horseman with a strange gait, one would have said a male ogre. He looked, saw Melik Danishmend, and cried out to him:
>
> "What man are you then, to be coming on your own two feet to your own tomb? What courage you must have to sit yourself down in this spot when, from dread of me, even the ogres don't pass by here!"
>
> When Melik Danishmend understood these words, he rose up, put on his weapons, mounted his horse, came before the man and prepared to attack him.
>
> "Let's see what kind of courage you have!" he said to him.
>
> Melik Danishmend saw that the man had a cross suspended at his neck and realized that he was an infidel. At once, the man took his lance and rushed upon Melik; Melik repulsed him. He rushed a second time, but could not reach him. He rushed a third time, but could not succeed. Then it was Melik's turn. He drew his sword and swung it down upon the miscreant, but the man repulsed it, he struck again but the man repulsed the blow. They battled with all their weapons but they could not triumph, neither the one nor the other. At nightfall, they separated. The warrior went to the foot of a tree, he dismounted, took down his sack of provisions, put the wine before him, took out a candle, struck a

light and lit the candle. Melik Danishmend himself went near the spring, dismounted, performed his ablutions, said his prayer, then put his horse to pasture and sat all by himself. The warrior started to eat. Seeing that Melik had no provisions, he immediately took his own and approached him:

"Come on, let's eat together," he said to him. But Melik Danishmend didn't touch the food.

"Why don't you eat?" demanded the warrior.

"This food has been touched by wine, I can't eat it," he said.

The warrior asked Danishmend his name. Melik said to him, "I am Melik Ahmed, my surname is Danishmend."

"Why have you come to the land of the Romans?" asked the warrior.

"To conquer the country," responded Melik.

"Why do you want to conquer it?" asked the warrior.

"I have to make this country Muslim," responded Melik.

"You're a devil-worshipper, then?" asked the warrior.

"God preserve me from being a devil-worshipper," said Melik, "I am a Muslim."

"Come on then," the warrior said to him. "and eat something so you won't go hungry, because tomorrow you'll have to fight with me."

Melik Danishmend replied, "If I eat with you, I won't be able to do battle with you, because we will have eaten the evening meal together."

"So eat alone then," the warrior responded.

"It's impossible," replied Melik, "because I would then owe you for your gift and if I combat you tomorrow I should be manifesting my ingratitude."

The warrior was surprised by the beauty of Melik Danishmend's speech and fell in love with his religion. Melik Danishmend then asked him his name.

"I will tell you my name tomorrow," he said...

The next day, Danishmend defeated the warrior, stood upon his chest, drew his sword and prepared to cut off the man's head. Then "Melik Danishmend saw that it was a young man with a face beautiful like the moon and he was overcome by pity. The young man came to, opened his eyes, and heaved a sigh."

"Become Muslim," Melik Danishmend said to him, "and I will set you free!"

"If I become Muslim, will my beloved be with me?" he asked.

151

"Who is your beloved?" asked Melik.

The young man began to weep: "My story is long!" he said.

"All right, become Muslim," said Melik Danishmend, "and whatever your affair may be, with the aid of God the Most High I will bring it to a conclusion."

The young man, named Artuhi, became a Muslim. Having settled between them the nature of the true God, the two friends proceeded to wage war on infidels, of whom there were many. The friends sang: "We make Holy War, we chop off heads/ we brandish our lances and crush the enemy!/ And if God comes to help us/ we will not leave, in the world, one single Heretic!" Danishmend slays a dragon; he reunites Artuhi with his beloved, Efromiya. No wall-flower, Efromiya converts and these "three chiefs" joyfully "abandon their life on the road of the Religion." Following the Turkic epic tradition, Efromiya battles as well as the men. "One by one, 20 Infidels entered the lists, and Efromiya cut off their heads, one after the other."

The Danishmends lost out to the Seljuk Turks in 1178. Some entered the service of the Seljuks, and went on to participate in the Ottoman expansion. According to family tradition, one Mustafa Özbek fought alongside Murat I — grandson of the first Ottoman leader, Osman — during his Albanian campaigns. Mustafa Özbek was a Danishmend, probably a follower of the Bektashi *tarikat*, a learned Muslim, and a *deli* warrior. The Albanian campaigns took decades, as Albania's mountaineers were not easily ruled, and the more *deli* Ottoman warriors tended to be sent to fight them. The important town of Janina, today part of Greece, submitted in 1431, and Mustafa Özbek's descendants became its hereditary muftis. At once religious and juridical, the position of mufti brought considerable power.

For the next four hundred years, Danishmend muftis would interpret Muslim law for the inhabitants of Janina and the surrounding province. It can't have been an easy time. The Albanian national hero, Scanderbeg, fought the Ottomans on and off from the early 1430s until his death in 1468, during which time two crusades, in 1448 and 1464, both failed to dislodge the empire. After Scanderbeg's death, things calmed down and the Ottomans put Albania under direct rule. Imperial control was firm enough in 1536 that France allied with the Ottomans for an invasion of Italy, though this never took place. In the late 18th century, Napoleon considered using the powerful lord of Janina, Ali Paşa, as a pretender to the Ottoman throne – yet another abandoned scheme. Politics became very complex in this period, as both the French and the Russians had imperial designs on Albania and what would become Greece. (The Russians even established the short-lived Septinsular Republic in Ionia.) Ali Paşa played all sides, with great skill, and eventually the Ottomans sent a force against him. Ali Paşa held out in Janina until starvation forced surrender in January 1822. Ali Paşa wrongly expected an imperial pardon. He was executed.

With Ali Paşa gone, Greek nationalists found themselves with a more or less open field. After a period of civil war, the Ottomans sent in Muhammad Ali, their ruler in Egypt and an ethnic Albanian. By 1826, he had broken the Greek revolt. Two years later, however, the Russians were advancing dramatically on the Ottomans from the north and east, and the European powers convinced Muhammad Ali to withdraw from Greece. Negotiations dominated by Russia and Britain brought about the creation of a mini-Greece as an Ottoman tributary. The peace treaty between Russia and the Ottomans in 1829 solidified Greek autonomy and increased Greek territory. The next year, the European powers demanded and got full Greek independence. Janina itself would remain an Ottoman provincial capital until Greece took it during the first Balkan War (1913). The Albanians wanted Janina, but didn't do too well in the second Balkan War, and it remained with Greece over Albanian objections. Today one can find maps of Greater Albania, circulated by Albanians, that include Janina.

The descendants of Mustafa Özbek, however, left Janina around 1830, when the reforming sultan Mahmut II ended the practice of inheriting muftiships. "One thing Mahmut did – he abolished hereditary functions in the provinces." Hasan Basri Danişman sits in his small den. It's afternoon, late summer, and hot. Basri was born in 1924 and so, against his obvious and clearly stated wishes, is no longer young. Despite frequent bouts of writer's block, he hopes to set down the history of his family before going to Switzerland for some difficult surgery. At the moment, he's mid-block, so he has plenty of time to sit down and recall what happened.

"My great-grandfather Şakir Bey was descended from a long line

153

of hereditary muftis of Albania. He may have been the last hereditary mufti of Albania. With the reforms, he decided there was no reason to remain in Albania, so he packed up his luggage and came to Istanbul."

Şakir Bey joined up with the faction that brought about the Tanzimat reforms. He attached himself to the renowned reformer Mustafa Reşit Paşa. "My great-grandfather Şakir Bey became one of the followers of Mustafa Reşit Paşa. He became known as one of the men of Mustafa Reşit Paşa. So when he had his second son, he gave his name to him—Mustafa Reşit. This is why you see in Ottoman history that the Mustafa Reşit of the Tanzimat is called Büyük Mustafa Reşit, the Great Mustafa Reşit, and my grandfather is called Küçük Mustafa Reşit, the Small Mustafa Reşit—the small, if you see what I mean."

Şakir Bey, ex-mufti of Janina, had two sons: Ziya Paşa and the one who became known as Small Mustafa Reşit Paşa. The Danishmend traditions occurred not only along lines of blood and class—Basri himself is a retired UN official—but also along Sufi lines, that is, the *tarikatlar*. Şakir Bey followed the Mevlevis, the so-called Whirling Dervishes with their famous dances and songs. He brought his first son, Ziya, into the Mevlevi order. Mustafa Reşit, however, was born just before his father's death, in 1858, and so was raised by his mother, Neveda—who came from an aristocratic provincial family of Plovdiv (now in Bulgaria). She was of the Bektashi, the same mystical order to which Mustafa Özbek likely belonged back in the 15th century, and the same Sufi order still active in Bulgaria's Deli Orman. "I know," Basri says, "that when my grand-uncle, Ziya Paşa, had his musical soirées and gatherings with all the musicians and so on and so forth, if my grandfather was in Istanbul at that time he would be there. But it wasn't for the spiritual side but the musical side." For Basri's grandfather, Mustafa Reşit, had, under his mother's influence, become a Bektashi.

"The Mevlevi concept of things was that the best way to commune with God was to approach him through anything and everything that contained beauty. And that was why they were always connected with the fine arts. Their concept was that the finest poetry was mystical poetry connected with their order. And that is also why they practiced music in their ceremonies. Dancing was included in

154

that because it helped them commune with the infinite, with God, you see. You approach God through anything that is perfect, that is beautiful, so that for instance among the Turks—at one period there was a great number of Turks who practiced gardening. If you produced a beautiful rose you were in communion with God. And so if you were a good gardener you were as much in communion with God as was a good poet or musician or whatever, you see.

"The Bektashis, on the other hand, were not like that at all. They were connected with the military establishment and the administrative establishment of the empire. So they were the doers. Because of the very nature of the order. In their structure, it was again a mystical approach to the infinite, to God, but through different levels. You could not reach the highest level of understanding unless you went through different stages of development. It was only step by step that one could attain the highest levels of the structure—which is common with the Masons, too. So, in this one family, we have the example of the great-grandfather coming from Albania and joining the reform movement in Turkey. And himself a Mevlevi, he brings up his eldest son as a Mevlevi. And he has a second son, after whose birth he dies very soon, and his second son is brought up by the mother, who is a Bektashi." The Bektashis are unusual among Sufi orders in admitting women as active members.

Mustafa Reşit's mother was buried near the Merdüven Köy Bektashi *tekke* on Istanbul's Asian side, as was Reşit himself. "My grandfather was buried with her in the Bektashi *tekke*. He was a patron of the Merdüven Köy *tekke*. When he reached a high level in the administration he became a patron of the *tekke*. And the *baba* eventually thanked him for all the help, material and spiritual, that he had given. We have so many friends who say, 'Oh, my grandfather was Bektashi.' "

Which isn't to say that the Danishmends were anti-Western, spouting arcane poetry in the face of oncoming industrialization. "My father and his brothers were mostly educated abroad, especially when my grandfather [Mustafa Reşit] was abroad as ambassador in Rome. They were educated in French as my grandfather was educated in French. The boys took their baccalaureates in Rome, were taught by French tutors, with a brief stop at boarding school in Switzerland."

In fact, some Danishmends were Western enough to become

155

Masons, if that is indeed a token of Westernization. Many eminent Ottomans, especially if they had Bektashi roots, became Freemasons. Bektashis generally have been open to new spiritual and social influences. Moreover, Basri says, the Masons gave the Bektashis "ideas about how to reorganize and modernize the organization of their sect. They even adopted some of the Masonic practices. The secret signals used by the Freemasons were actually adopted by the Bektashis." Finally, Masonic membership gave reformist Ottomans a valuable clandestine link to Europe, one they would use to help undermine the tottering imperial regime in the late 19th and early 20th centuries. Even today, upwardly mobile Turks covet Masonic membership as a step toward prosperity and social power.

"While my father, Ziya, traveled in the West he became a Mason. A lot of the Young Turks who had been exiled into Europe under Sultan Abdülhamid became Masons, though the Masons were not directly connected to the Bektashis.

"During the late 19th century, each [foreign] country in Istanbul had its own postal system. A lot of the Young Turks were able to smuggle their information in and out via these postal systems. Masonry was very useful, as they were able to take advantage of their Masonic connections.

"The Turkish Masons mainly had links with the French lodge. My father, because of his background and education, was connected to the French Masons. But he was not so happy with them. One thing my father said he could not bear about the French lodge was its atheism. You know, the French skepticism; and it was anti-clerical.

"Then my father happened to discover Scottish Masonry. He was pleased to discover that the Scottish Masons were not anti-clerical. Also they were not anti-monarchist, whereas the French were Republicans. And this attracted him, because he was himself not anti-monarchical. This is why all the members of the British royal family are still Masons.

"Anyway, after he joined the Scottish Masons, he returned to Rome. My grandfather, as ambassador, used to receive everybody there at these big lunches. It was at one of these lunches that my father made secret signals toward my grandfather—the sort of signals one learns as a Mason. My grandfather said, 'Ziya, I want you to come see me in my study.' They went up to the study. My grandfather shut the door behind him, then embraced my father.

" 'Son,' he said, 'I'm so glad that you've become a Bektashi!' And my father replied, 'But father, I thought you were a Mason!' "

Basri laughs. It's an old family story. "Not only did Atatürk, when he had the chance, ban the Sufi lodges, he also banned the Masons. He had learned the lesson of how Abdülhamid's reign had been undermined by the Freemasons."

In his passionate desire to bring Turkey into the dominant European civilization, and under his control, Atatürk not only banned the Sufi *tarikatlar* and the Masons, he tried to banish the eminent families as well, families like the Danishmends. Perhaps he understood that families have, among other things, their own ideas about time and how time works. For families, time gets much of its significance from their presence in it. Many people may recall World War II, for example, as a turning point in socio-political organization; but some will remember it most, in their hearts, as the event in which their parents perished, or their uncle was wounded, or the family house was destroyed by bombs. For families, time begins when their ancestral memories begin, it lasts as long as those memories last. Atatürk wanted time to begin anew with the founding of Turkey. Family time should give way to the new time of nation-states and universal civilization; the ancestors should be forgotten. Some old families were forbidden to use their names. The Danishmends had to change their name to Danişman, Turkish for "information," the name Basri still uses.

The younger Danishmends, however, have reverted to the old name. And Basri has sat in his study writing down the family history so that other Danishmends will know something about their ancestors even after Basri himself has run out of time.

19

OFTEN, EMPIRES FORCE PEOPLE in or near them to conform to an imperial idea of time. The empire says: Either you're living according to our time, or you're not really living at all.

Nevertheless, other times—Sufi time, fundamentalist time, family time—exist alongside imperial time. In some cases, they have outlasted empires.

Probably the greatest Muslim thinker about time was Abu Ali ibn Sina, known in the West as Avicenna. Born in 980 near Bukhara, his father a Persian from Khorasan, Avicenna was a passionate genius with an immoderate, nearly unquenchable thirst for wine, sex, and ideas. "In all beings, therefore, love is either the cause of their being, or being and love are identical in them," he wrote. "It is thus evident that no being is devoid of love." Certainly not Avicenna. His love for ideas drove him to study Aristotle with extraordinary zeal; his synthesis of classical Greek philosophy with monotheism laid the basis for similar work by Averröes and St. Thomas Aquinas after him. His philosophical and medical books were read enthusiastically in the West well into the Renaissance, and are studied in Persian-speaking lands to this day.

Avicenna's work has stood the test of time, and time was among his main preoccupations. "The key to Avicenna's synthesis," writes the scholar L. E. Goodman, "was his conceptualization of this world and everything in it as contingent in itself, but necessary with reference to its causes, leading back ultimately to the First Cause, the Necessary Being, whose timeless existence eternally authors the finite and determinate reality that we know." In other words, he was a romantic rationalist in search of immortality: "For the access of the mind to pure rational concepts is taken by Ibn Sina, as it was taken by Plato, as clear proof of immortality."

The human soul, Avicenna wrote, "is distinguished from all other spirits by its perfect rationality, its comprehensive and articulate intellectuality; and its object, throughout life, is to purge the sensory and grasp the conceptual. God gave it a power specific to it, the like of which no other spirit shares: the power of reason. Reason is the tongue of the angels..."

Yet Avicenna was an earthly, even earthy man, living in Central Asia and Persia from 980 to 1037 of our era, addicted to love, addicted to reason, attentive to the precious individuality of each human being. He was addicted to the beauty of the soul, wanting to preserve for each one of us something that would be at once unique and eternal: "Suppose your being to have just begun. You are of sound and capable intelligence, but your bodily parts are so disposed that you cannot see them or touch your limbs or organs; they are separated from one another and suspended for the moment in thin air. You would find that you were conscious of nothing but your own reality.

"By what means would you be conscious of your self at that moment, or at the moment just before or after it? What would it be in you that had such awareness? Do you find any of your sensory faculties that could play this role? Or would it be your mind, a power quite other than the senses or anything connected to them?...[Y]our consciousness at this moment is unmediated, and it follows that you can be conscious of your self without reliance upon any other power or the intervention of any other faculty.... Does it occur to you to ask whether the vehicle of your awareness is not the skin you can see with your own eyes? It is not. Even if you shed your skin and acquired another, you would still be you..."

Do you see? And that part of yourself that is your soul continues on, through love and reason, through time: "[O]ne sees in one's own rational self a being akin to the very eternity and rationality of the heavenly bodies.... As a result one yearns to apprehend all the levels of their hierarchy, one is aroused to enter into relation with them and to share in their exaltedness, and so one ever humbles oneself and meditates steadfastly, praying and fasting constantly, thereby attaining abundant reward. For it is the human soul that receives a reward, since it survives the perishing of the body and is unmolested by the passage of time."

Avicenna's tale of the timeless, bodiless soul is known to philosophers as the Floating Man argument. One can float on a boat, or in thin air; let's float a while longer, like Nâzım Hikmet dreaming his way out of prison to join Sheikh Bedreddin in the Mad Forest. Avicenna was a big advocate of the East, so let us float eastward, away from Istanbul, out of imperial Eurotime, across new borders. By plane to Trebizonde, a rushed, commercial town on the Black Sea, site of the Byzantines' last stand. Up a steep valley, small tea plantations clinging to the side, and higher still into a place like the Bernese Oberland, isolated houses, swards of summer pasture glimpsed through trees. At last over the crest and onto the Anatolian plateau, rugged and barren, scarce fodder, little streams with wispy trees planted alongside them in rows. An immense stone castle atop a cliff.

You're nearing the border. Through Erzurum, with its shops

159

selling truck parts, its outlying garrisons, lots filled with tanks pa-
tiently waiting for some new battle. (With the Kurds this time? The
Armenians?) Go farther east: a jagged valley with orange cliffs, cool
mountains forested with pine, desolate rangeland, into Kars, the last
town in Turkey. Keep going along a rutted road East. Whose land is
this?

Go to the high stone walls of Ani, walk beneath the faded image
of a lion, into a vast open city without people, just you and a young
Turkish man, a nationalist. ("It's something in your soul," he says. He
hates Istanbul, because it's so dirty and crowded and heartless, and
yet he swears he'll leave Kars for the big city "the second I can save
enough money.") The ruins of a caravansary, monasteries, churches,
and mosques. Ani is first mentioned as a fortress in the 5th century
B.C. It was, for the most part, an Armenian capital, profitably set on
the trade route between Persia and the Black Sea. Ani had its first
heyday under the Bagratid king Gagik I, from 990 to 1020 — during
Avicenna's lifetime — when it housed the Armenian Catholicos. The
sultan Alp Arslan (*arslan* means "lion") conquered Ani in 1064, then
sold it to the Muslim Shaddadids. They were related by marriage to
their Christian predecessors the Bagratids, so both religions lived together. The Georgian king David II conquered it in 1124 and continued the exceptional policy of religious tolerance. By the 14th
century Ani was a ruin.

Hurry, the sun is going down. To a vaulted Armenian church,
peeling pictures of saints, scenes of torture. To a 13th-century Seljuk
mosque, in the pure, tranquil style of that period. Climb together up
worn stone steps to the top of the minaret. Soon a war will begin near
here, just over those mountains. You are above a cliff, on the edge of
Ani and the edge of Turkey, looking down to the Arpa-Çay river.
There is a ruined monastery bored into the cliff. "That's where we
used to take girls," the nationalist says, smiling. Look across the river,
take it all in before the light goes and you run out of time. A sere
steppe, a garrison, a watchtower, some barbed wire: Armenia, or the
former Soviet Union, or something. Whose empire is this?

Climb down the minaret, the sun has set; stumble over the remains of houses. A howling rises across the gorge.

"What are those, dogs?"

"Wolves," he says, smiling again.

The truth is also an allegory of Empire.

—Rudyard Kipling, "Naboth"
(1886)

Uzbekistan

1

YOU TRAVEL IN UZBEKISTAN under false pretenses. You purchased your visa in Istanbul through bribery from a man who explained, "There is no law in Uzbekistan. You can do anything you want, as long as you have money and know whom to give it to. Because there is no law, you have great freedom." No law, perhaps, but there is politics. The bribe only got you a visa to the capital, Tashkent. Your trip to Uzbekistan begins with an illegal act and continues to be illegal. At the airport you are required to state where you will be staying. You lie, of course. You continue lying for weeks on end.

You cannot stay in a hotel or take a domestic flight, because if you were to do these things someone would ask for your passport. They would realize that you are travelling illegally—your visa is only for Tashkent, yet you wander throughout the country—and so they would have to report you or face the consequences of having disobeyed the rules.

No one would wish to face such consequences. An American friend was through here last year, under the same "post-Communist" regime, and he was arrested by plainclothes "policemen." (He was smarter than the average visitor, and knew who the two men were. They were part of the vast and unnameable group known as Them, the people who enforce the rules. He knew who they were and so when they began to harass him he, an ex-military man, hit first, a last gesture of freedom.)

Given the circumstances, you travel incognito. You don't always give your real name or your true country of origin. You prefer shade to sunlight, quiet to noise, back streets to boulevards, the rear of the bus to the front. You are like a roving question mark. Your strongest weapon is a certain confidence: Perhaps (you try to suggest in small, speechless ways) if one were to ask the question one would not like the reply? In this society, most people don't ask questions. As a rule, curiosity will not get them anywhere they want to be.

Given the circumstances, you need friends. The official route – government interpreters, prearranged interviews, surveillance, meetings with officials – holds no interest for you, any more than you would care to visit Detroit with a patriotic Mickey Mouse, his face stitched into a grin, as your only companion. So you need friends. They will do everything for you, buy train and bus tickets, apply bribes, shelter you in their homes, tell you whom to speak with and, more importantly, whom to avoid, fix meetings, feed you, protect you. You are utterly dependent on them. Connected one to the next by family, friendship, professional or political ties, they form an alternative to the official network. They move you about the country like troubling merchandise or an unwieldy piece of contraband.

The nature of these friends needs clarification. They fall into three main groups: those who want you to discover the truth about their lives (few in number); those who are generous (just about everyone); those who fear you. This third group overlaps the second. For once people shake your hand, they become in some way tainted by your lack, in the official view, of innocence. Once that's done, they have started down a road they should have avoided. They have become, however slightly or benignly, co-conspirators in a dubious enterprise: your attempt to learn. The only way they can back out is to go to the police. But that has its risks – unless, of course, the police are part of the family, for the police live here too – because the only thing to talk about with the police would be the fact that they made the mistake of talking to you in the first place. Furthermore, if they were to talk to the police they would likely face the consequences of having betrayed a friendship (whatever connection brought you, the contraband, to their door). Ties of family and friendship are, in Uzbekistan, far more lasting and serious than politics. Betraying them is a crime, *the* crime—a real crime in a country hemmed about with rules concerning false crimes like insulting the president or aiding a traveller who doesn't have a visa. By official standards, most Uzbeks are criminals. But most won't have to pay a price, if they are careful, except that they will have to continue to live in this official society, and that is a high enough price. As for the parallel society of family and friends, there both crimes and punishments are more serious. Everyone knows that the crime of betrayal will be avenged, sooner or later, and probably not in a pleasant way. This holds the society together.

And you take advantage of it. Really, you have no choice, under the circumstances. You're not happy about it, week after week of sneaking around. Merely by existing here you have become someone new, or rather a character whose identity must shift with its audience. Anxiety infuses your life, not so much because you fear for yourself, though you do, but because you fear for your friends, whose hands are dirty because they have touched you. You will leave. They won't.

2

IN *NATURE AROUND US*, a book for children published in 1988, one picture shows Vladimir Ilyich Lenin with several Russian and Uzbek youngsters, all smiling and full of energy. The book, in Uzbek, is a language training tool with certain ambitions beyond language instruction. In the back, the publishers have provided a series of questions that teachers can use to initiate discussion. For the picture of Lenin with the children, the questions run as follows: "Who is this picture depicting? Is V. I. Lenin in good spirits? Why are the children so happy?"

3

JON MARIANICH MALINEVSKI is a short, slight, clean-shaven man who lives in a small apartment on Gagarin Street with his wife and daughter in the European part of Tashkent. He's had several heart attacks and has just emerged once again from the hospital. Having reached his seventy-seventh year, Marianich finds his wife and daughter—especially his daughter, Vicky, with her nervous manner, her plucked eyebrows and green eyeshadow—doting on him as he pads around the apartment.

Marianich is best known for his years as an English instructor and for being founder and head of the Tashkent Museum of the International Workers' Movement, later renamed the International Peace Museum, and often referred to as the Museum of International Communism—possibly the only museum of its kind in the world, certainly the only one in Central Asia. Now closed, it may yet reopen. Marianich says there are plans to relocate it in a bigger space.

Vicky brings tea and cakes to the tiny study. Marianich slumps into a low chair. We're having one of those unseasonably cool, overcast Tashkent days. "Initially, the emphasis of the museum was on contacting those groups working underground against fascist regimes such as those in Paraguay, Uruguay, and so on. They supplied us with many unique materials produced underground—leaflets, badges, photographs, resolutions of underground meetings. We would contact the United Nations regarding violations of human rights, writing to the UN in support of intervention on behalf of the oppressed. And the UN was always supportive of our work. All of these countries now have democratic governments."

Marianich speaks a lovely, careful, delicate English. His family moved to England from Ukraine when he was a little boy. His father had agitated against the tsar, helping to found the Social Democratic Party of Ukraine; he suffered imprisonment, and escaped to England. After Ukraine declared independence in 1918, he became its first ambassador to Britain. This job didn't last long. (Ukraine was officially Soviet by 1922.) "My father found himself unemployed in the United Kingdom." Between 1920 and 1921, Marianich and his younger brother lodged at the Fellowship for Reconciliation dormitory in Whitechapel, London. "We were at Toynbee Hall, sort of a boarding house for various wanderers. Tagore stayed there too!" Marianich's family evidently made the best of a difficult situation.

"Then Lenin asked my father to start a charity [the Ukraine Cooperation Association] to help relieve the famine. I was six. I helped as best I could, as did my brother, who was four." The early interwar period had much to offer someone intrigued by politics and class struggle, even a six-year-old. The family lived in Essex, in Leigh-On-Sea. Marianich's strongest early memories are of 1926, the year of the miners' strike. "I was a witness to it. I have a violet pin in the shape of a miner's hat. Every member of my family was presented with such a pin. My father gave part of his wages to the strikers. He contacted the miners in order to adopt a child. She was a Welsh girl. Her name was Hannah Moat, from Caerphilly, in the Rhondda. She was ten or eleven years old. We sheltered her, then sent her home once the strike was over.

"I remember being at a rally in Trafalgar Square to free Sacco and Vanzetti. That would have been around 1926. [Sacco and Vanzetti were anarchists arrested in 1920 for the murder of a paymaster and his guard in South Braintree, Massachusetts. They were executed on August 22, 1927.] And I met George Bernard Shaw. We were at a boarding house in Antibes that year. Shaw was celebrating his seventieth birthday. He had the table next to ours! He treated everyone to a big fish."

The Ukraine Cooperation Association lasted until 1930, when the Marianich family returned to Ukraine. "We were expecting support," Marianich says. Vicky sits on the edge of her chair, glancing at you but mainly watching her father. How many times has she heard these stories? "Instead my father was humiliated, persecuted, and we all suffered terribly. In 1934 he went to Moscow. He tried to plead his case.... In 1937 he was arrested again. A few months later he was sentenced to ten years in prison without the right to correspond. We know now what Stalin meant by that. We never heard from him again.

"Then my mother and brother were taken away to serve five years in the labor camps. I was out of the house that time. I came home the next day. They were gone. My brother was killed, at the age of twenty-one. He was the most talented of us. He wrote brilliant poems in English. The last one he wrote... imagine, it was dedicated to the French Revolution. He was most talented in math and physics.

"My mother spent her five years in the camps. Already the war had begun when, from what I can make out, the doctors realized she only had a few days left. They released her. I never saw her. She died while trying to make her way home.

"During much of this period I was in Moscow. Once I went to

Lubyanka [prison]. I was interrogated for seven hours. It was all just another torture. I had been hoping I would see my mother again, and my dad.

"I had been studying at the Law Institute, but I was expelled. I had no home. I had been interested in international law. I knew things were turning, that they had to be turning for the better. In 1937 to 1938, I went to employment agencies in Moscow, but they all turned me away, saying 'You're from England, go away.' Five times I fainted in the streets of Moscow, without a penny in my pocket. I had some friends in Moscow, but I didn't want them to contact me, given who I was. Eventually I found work on a construction site, digging foundations. I begged for work; I begged. I worked there for one year. I begged to be allowed into the military, but they wouldn't let me in. Then I managed to get back into the Law Institute, where I met Olga. I graduated in 1941.

"So that's why I couldn't go to Spain [to fight in the Spanish Civil War]. Though I did go to a bookshop and I found a copy of the British *Daily Worker*. I got the address for the British Battalion in Spain, and sent fifteen parcels. I got an appreciative letter back from the commissar.

"Later the situation improved; Stalin died. But until then we were always afraid we might be arrested at any time."

Jon and Olga moved to Semipalatinsk, where Jon took a job as counsel to the Republican Chinese government, that is, the Kuomintang. "I helped arrange a banquet to celebrate the victory over the Japanese. We raised our glass to Chiang K'ai-Shek." Later they relocated to Andizhan, thence to Tashkent. Marianich started planning his international communism museum in 1967, opening it in 1970. "We have contacted one hundred twenty-five centers all over the world. Ninety-one sent materials to us. Sixty-four have sent visitors to see our museum."

Shifts in emphasis at Marianich's museum closely followed shifts in the Communist Party line. In the mid-1980s, the museum switched its attention from clandestine Communist movements to peace issues. "I wrote to the women at Greenham Common, in solidarity with them, and to tell them about the peace-loving people of Uzbekistan. I found addresses of peace groups, people opposing nuclear holocaust. I got badges, pins, leaflets, and posters from all over the world. We had, by this time, stopped collecting social material, except for material concerning the 1984 miners' strike [in Britain]. The fascist governments had fallen, and there wasn't much of interest going on anymore.

"Later, when one had changed one's mind in connection with the new political thinking, we began to collect material on the women's movement, especially from the U.K., U.S., and Canada. Then, with the emergence of new all-world values, we collected material on peoples in danger of becoming extinct—from the Amazon, Eskimos. And naturally we focussed on ecologic matters. So many people and institutions, so much world support for what we've been doing, on behalf of the people. And this is *all by correspondence*. This is what I call 'citizen's diplomacy.' We are all brethren on one planet. Brothers and sisters. We have to love each other, help each other, understand each other.

"I have written to Islam Karimov, our current president, about these matters and the museum. And they said he liked that letter very much."

You go to the living room for more tea, wine, and cakes. Jon has grown tired and says little, Olga is uncomfortable with English. Vicky sits at your left, dispensing tea from a samovar along with a raspberry wine she has made. The question loitering inside you—Why would someone whose father, brother, and mother were destroyed by the Party, whom the Party threw onto Moscow's streets to die, remain loyal?—never comes out. "I'm afraid there isn't much food," Vicky says with a nervous smile. "Everything has become so dear. I don't think I'll be making raspberry wine again, only cherry and grape wine."

You drink to understanding among the world's peoples. Jon shouldn't have wine but he downs one small glass and Olga smiles lovingly as she watches him. Without a breeze the room feels muggy. The wine tastes sweet and fresh.

"It is still funny to hear Uzbekistan referred to as a country," Vicky says. "We never had to know Uzbek. . . . We always spoke Russian, and everyone here knows Russian. Suddenly we're supposed to learn Uzbek. We *did* go around with our noses in the air." She gestures with a finger, pushing up the tip of her nose.

167

"You can't say that this experience means Communism is wrong. We had a Soviet system. That's not the same thing as the *idea* of Communism. *That* hasn't yet been decided. Two people take clay: one makes a beautiful sculpture, the other doesn't. Really, there was nothing here before the revolution. The literacy rate was two percent. No industrial development at all. Now, there's such nationalism. An American astronomer came and said he was surprised to see all the signs in Uzbek, and some in English." For decades, virtually all signs in Uzbekistan were in Russian. "This is what's happening now. Isn't it strange?"

"Well," you say, "a lot of Uzbeks just hate Russians."

"You've noticed that? So many have left in the last ten years. Eventually, people will realize how the revolution helped Uzbekistan. It was backward before.

"Russia may come back. She can be very strong, very brave. But also very weak."

Vicky has left her job to study Eastern philosophy—not Central Asian philosophy, but Indian philosophy. "I am trying to make sense of life." She is also trying to show she isn't one of the "bad Russians."

"I went to a shop and I said '*Rahmat*' [Uzbek for 'thank you']. And he said, 'Thank you for saying *rahmat*.' In Russian, of course. It was delightful. Even if you just know a little, they are pleased. If you just show that you care."

4

A YOUNG RUSSIAN WOMAN, tall and composed, Inna has been involving herself in "joint ventures"—the phrase has acquired talismanic importance since the Soviet collapse—with Pakistanis seeking to get in on the ground floor of the tourism industry in independent Uzbekistan. "The present situation for Russians is difficult to explain in a few words. The Uzbeks...it isn't expressed openly. They don't throw stones at us in the streets. But you sense it everywhere—this hatred. In taxis, on the bus, in stores. They simply hate us. They wish we would go away."

5

THE QUESTION OF WHAT RUSSIANS are doing in Asia has preoccupied Russians more or less since the birth of Russia itself. Eastern
Slavs settled northern Ukraine in the 9th century. The traditional date
for the founding of "Russia" is 862. By 882, Oleg had established a
strong state with its capital at Kiev. A century later, Vladimir I accepted Orthodox Christianity. Kievan Russia broke up into principalities in 1054 and was destroyed in 1237 to 1240 by Mongols and Tatars.
The latter proceeded to dominate the Russians until 1480, when Ivan
III, grand duke of Moscow, refused to pay further tribute. Russians
know the 1240 to 1480 period as the "Tatar (or Mongol) yoke," and appear never to have forgiven Asians for humiliating them. They also
appear to have developed a strong sense of mission. Under Ivan III's
successor, Basil III, some Russians came to imagine themselves as the
army of God and Moscow as the Third Rome. (Constantinople was
the Second Rome until the Ottomans took it in 1453.) As the monk
Philotheus wrote in 1510, "Know then, a pious Tsar, that all the Orthodox Christian realms have converged in thy single empire. Thou
art the only Tsar of the Christians in all the universe.... Observe and
hear, o Tsar, that all Christian empires have converged in this single
one, that two Romes have fallen, but the third stands, and no fourth
can ever be." Basil's successor, Ivan the Terrible, began Russia's conquest of Siberia, and Russians continued expanding their territory
into Asia until Gorbachev withdrew Soviet troops from Afghanistan.
That makes nearly five hundred years of steady imperialism.

Leaving Siberia aside, Russia's expansion into Asia led mainly
straight east and south. Ivan the Terrible took Kazan in 1552, Astra-
khan in 1556, thus subduing Russia's immediate Muslim neighbors.
The Russians tried to convert their conquests to Christianity, with
very mixed results. The ideology of Russian expansion in this period
focussed on "retaking" Constantinople, known as Tsargrad. The Orthodox peoples of the Balkans were imagined as lost brothers struggling beneath the Ottoman yoke. Russia intended to free them. The
Ottomans, meanwhile, were themselves expanding into the lands
north and east of the Black Sea. Matters inevitably came to a head,
preliminarily during the Russo-Ottoman War of 1676 to 1681, then under Peter the Great (1682–1725), a leader of astounding intelligence

and drive and a heavy drinker. Peter pushed Russia's frontiers to the Black Sea and even adventured into Persia.

Peter also pursued "Westernization," or the imitation of European norms. As imitations, Peter's measures partook of a tradition as old as Muscovite Russia. In fashion, for example, Ivan III had imitated the Tatar and Mongol khans, and later the Italians. A certain Russification under Basil and Ivan the Terrible eased into widespread imitation of the Persian style in the late 16th and early 17th centuries (also the fashion then in Ottoman Istanbul). In the following period, just before Peter's consolidation of power, Polish and Eastern European styles competed with Greek and some Western European fashions in setting the tone at court. Clearly the Russians had some trouble deciding what to wear. This understandable insecurity would be exacerbated dramatically by Peter, who posed the dilemma along West versus East lines. Peter believed that Russia must become "European," and famously demonstrated his zeal by cutting the beards off his nobles and ordering them to wear Western clothes. (He later *taxed* beards.) He believed in the European idea of Enlightened Despotism and transformed Russia without pity. As the 19th-century historian Mikhail Pogodin wrote: "Yes, Peter the Great did much for Russia. One looks and one does not believe it, one keeps adding and one cannot reach the sum. We cannot open our eyes, cannot make a move, cannot turn in any direction without encountering him everywhere, at home, in the streets, in church, in school, in court, in the regiment, at a promenade—it is always he, always he, every day, every minute, at every step!"

After Peter, Russia continued to make war against Asians, conquering the Little Kazakh Horde in 1731, the Middle Kazakh Horde in 1740, taking the Crimean Khanate in 1783. To the question of Russian identity, Peter had given his answer: Russians are Europeans, or rather will be. Logically, of course, if one has to make a given people become X, then they must not have been X beforehand. So, as Westernization proceeded steadily through the 18th century, an undetermined non-Western Russianness also percolated away. The two met forcibly in the 19th century. While many influences were at work, from a Central Asian perspective the most compelling question was whether or not Russians were, in fact, Asians. Russians began to torture themselves over this question (and still do). Not by chance, the issue became most pressing during the period, roughly 1839 to 1922, when Russia pushed itself to take over all of Central Asia.

For a reasonable Russian nationalist of the time, Asianness had to be denied because the Mongols had been so horrible. "The splitting up of Russia into many principalities and the discord among its princes," wrote the extremely influential historian Nikolai Karamzin (1766–1826), "laid the ground for the triumph of the descendants of Genghis Khan and for our long-lasting calamities." The Mongols and Tatars delayed Russia's great destiny. Yet the Russians still "did their best to catch up with Europe in the matter of enlightenment, in which Russia had been left behind as a result of two centuries of the Mongol yoke."

One perceives a certain vain self-pity, and insecurity, in Karamzin. A Russian sense of inferiority vis-à-vis Europe both tempers and undermines his nationalism. "Peter the Great, who *united* us with Europe and showed us the benefits of enlightenment, did not for long humiliate the national pride of the Russians. We looked at Europe, so to speak, and at one glance we assimilated the fruits of her long labors. . . . Our state institutions rival in wisdom the institutions of states that have been enlightened for several centuries. Our civility, the tone of our society, our taste astonish the foreigners who come to Russia with a false notion of a people who were considered barbarians at the beginning of the eighteenth century. Those who envy the Russians say that we have only a very high degree of *imitativeness*. But is this not a sign of admirable development of the soul?"

In the 19th century, the Slavophile movement answered Karamzin's question with an ear-splitting No. The Slavophiles proposed the familiar Russian dream of conquering Istanbul (Tsargrad), but in terms often more ethnic than Orthodox Christian, and with an emphasis on Slavic identity as anti-Western. The seeds sown by Peter germinated into resentment. Slavophile Konstantin Leontev wrote: "A Russia in possession of Tsargrad will bring fresh life to Muscovite Russia, for Muscovite Russia originally issued from Tsargrad; it would be more cultured, that is, more authentic than Petrine Russia; it would be less rational and less utilitarian, that is, less revolutionary; it will outlast the *Petersburg* Russia [that is, Peter the Great's legacy]. And the sooner Petersburg becomes something in the nature of a Baltic Sebastopol or a Baltic Odessa, the better it will be, I maintain, not only for us but probably also for so-called humanity, for would it not be horrible and downright injurious to think that Moses ascended Mount Sinai, that the Hellenes built their graceful acropolises, the Romans waged their Punic wars, Alexander, that handsome genius, crossed the Granicus in a plumed helmet and fought at Arbela, that the apostles preached, the martyrs agonized, the poets sang, the artists painted, and knights shown in tournaments — *only in order that the French, German, or Russian bourgeois in his ugly and comic* clothes should thrive 'individually and collectively' on the ruins of all this magnificent past?" Leontev worried that out of the "suffering depths" of "universal history...merely a mouse crawls out! A self-satisfied caricature of the people of former days is born, the *average rational European*, in his comic clothes that even the ideal mirror of art cannot reflect, with a small and self-deluded mind, with his creepy, practical good will!"

Anti-Western, Slavophile or Pan-Slav sentiments eventually reached an odd culmination in Russian identification with Asia, as in Alexander Blok's famous lines, "We're Scythians and Asians too, from coasts/ That breed squint eyes, bespeaking greed," or Sergei Esenin's 20th-century advice, "Let us be Asians, let us stink, let us scratch our buttocks shamelessly in sight of everyone. Even so, we don't have such a putrid smell as they [Europeans] have inside.... Only an invasion of barbarians like us can save and reshape them."

Clearly, Slavophiles did not hold up a pleasant, nurturing image of Asia. Rather, they saw in it a source of dark and virile energy. Nazis later praised their own special German "barbarism" for similar reasons, and indeed one strand of 19th-century Russian thought entertained visions of a Shangri-La in the mountains south and east of Uzbekistan whence the first people, the Aryans, had come, and to which the Russians (as Aryan representatives) were destined to return. Yet another group, called Easterners, advocated a Russian invasion of China; its most delirious champion, Prince Ukhtomsky, wrote simply, "Asia — we have always belonged to it. We have lived its life and felt its interests. Through us the Orient has gradually arrived at consciousness of itself, at a superior life.... This great and mysterious Orient is ready to become ours."

Westernizers also believed Asia a source of dark energy, only they thought that was the problem, not the solution. As the critic Belinsky wrote to Gogol, anxiously: "Advocate of the knout, apostle of ignorance, champion of obscurantism and reactionary mysticism, eulogist of Tatar customs—what are you doing? Look at what is beneath your feet: you are standing on the brink of an abyss." Or Konstantin Kavelin in a letter to Dostoevsky, urging Russians to live according to Christian truth: "This will not turn us into Europeans, but we shall cease being Orientals and shall become in fact what we are by nature—Russians." To Westernizers, Asianness was a name for what Russians needed to overcome within themselves.

Meanwhile, beyond the vivid rhetoric of Slavophilism and its crazier variants, the Russians continued taking over Central Asia. Westernizers and Slavophiles disagreed on many things; but they were commonly able to agree on the decency and goodness of Russian imperial advancement. Interestingly, the progressive expansion itself seems to have occurred in something of an intellectual vacuum. Prince Gorchakov wrote in 1864 of his nation going "from annexation to annexation... not knowing where to stop," and the following year Russia's interior minister noted in his diary, "General Chernyaev took Tashkent, nobody knows why and for what purpose."

Perhaps there really was no reason, beyond insecurity and vanity. Commercial justifications were feeble at best, the desire of Russian peasants for land an ambiguous argument. The scholar Milan Hauner defines *Aziatchina* as "an ambivalent Russian term meaning the almost unlimited capacity among Russians to identify themselves with Asia while showing their contempt for the Asian peoples and civilizations as utterly barbaric." The Russian drive to the East, or *Stremlenie na vostok*, made the ambivalence in *Aziatchina* acute. Yet the results on the ground were plain: slaughter, an empire.

Perhaps there was no reason. Not every Russian thrilled at the news in 1881 that General Skobelev had taken the fortress of Gök-Tepe, now in Turkmenistan. The massacre involved had been horrifying. The general explained to a visitor: "'Do you know Mr. Marvin,' said Skobeleff, 'but you must not publish this, or I shall be called a barbarian by the Peace Society—that I hold it as a principle in Asia that the duration of peace is in direct proportion to the slaughter you inflict upon the enemy. The harder you hit them the longer they will be quiet afterwards. We killed nearly 20,000 Turcomans at Geok-Tepé. The survivors will not soon forget the lesson.'" Skobelev's biographer,

Madame Novikoff, explains in *Skobeleff and the Slavonic Cause* (1883), "War is horrible at the best, and the [enemy], who themselves have been so ruthless in torturing, massacring, and enslaving their neighbours for generation after generation, would probably be the last to complain that upon them in turn had fallen a frightful retribution."

Evidently some need existed to justify Gök-Tepe. This Fyodor Dostoevsky set out to do in an 1881 essay, "Geok-Tepé. What Is Asia to Us?": "[O]ne has to admit that, of late, many people began to adopt a hostile attitude toward our aggressive policy in Asia.... Generally speaking, our whole Russian Asia, including Siberia, still exists to Russia merely in the form of some kind of an appendix in which European Russia has no desire to take any interest. 'We are Europe,'—it is implied.—'What is our business in Asia!'...What is the need of the future seizure of Asia? What's our business there?"

Dostoevsky, of course, has an answer. "This is necessary because Russia is not only in Europe but also in Asia; because the Russian is not only a European but also an Asiatic. Moreover, Asia, perhaps, holds out greater promises to us than Europe. In our future destinies Asia is, perhaps, our main outlet!...

"We must banish the slavish fear that Europe will call us Asiatic barbarians, and that it will be said that we are more Asiatics than Europeans. This fear that Europe might regard us as Asiatics has been haunting us for almost two centuries. It has particularly increased during the present nineteenth century, reaching almost the point of panic.... This erroneous fright of ours, this mistaken view of ourselves solely as Europeans, and not Asiatics—which we have never ceased to be—this shame and this faulty opinion have cost us a good deal in the course of the last two centuries, and the price we have had to pay has consisted of the loss of our spiritual independence, of our unsuccessful policies in Europe, and finally of money—God only knows how much money—which we spent in order to prove to Europe that we were Europeans and not Asiatics."

However, Russia's failure in Europe extended not so much from her Asianness as from her special Russian "idea." "Under no circumstances will they [Europeans] believe that we can in truth, on an equal basis with them, participate in the future destinies of their civilization. They consider us alien to their civilization; they regard us as strangers and impostors. They take us for thieves who stole from them their enlightenment and who disguised themselves in their garbs. Turks and Semites are spiritually closer to them than we, Aryans. All this has a very important reason: we carry to mankind an altogether different idea than they—that's the reason."

Dostoevsky doesn't explain what this idea is. But he makes it clear that, whatever the idea may be, it will be greatly improved, perhaps even discovered, in the course of conquering Asia. "[W]hen we turn to Asia, with our new vision of her, in Russia there may occur something akin to what happened in Europe when America was discovered. Since, in truth, to us Asia is like the then undiscovered America. With our aspiration for Asia, our spirit and forces will be regenerated. The moment we become independent, we shall find what to do, whereas during the two centuries with Europe we lost the habit of any work; we became chatterers and idlers. . . . In Europe we were hangers-on and slaves, whereas we shall go to Asia as masters. In Europe we were Asiatics, whereas in Asia we, too, are Europeans. Our civilizing mission in Asia will bribe our spirit and drive us thither. It is only necessary that the movement should start. . . . But the main thing is that our civilizing mission in Asia will be understood and learned by us from the very first steps,—this cannot be doubted. It will lift our spirit; it will convey to us dignity and self-consciousness, which at present we either lack altogether or possess in a trifling degree."

And finally, Dostoevsky writes, Russia's conquest of Asia will earn Europe's respect; and so "let me exclaim once more: 'Long live the Geok-Tepé victory! Long live Skobelev and his good soldiers!' "

6

TASHKENT TV CARRIES an advertisement for videocassette players. In the first scene, a Russian man nods with confidence at his television, then the camera pans to show his wife and children watching a second television. What luxury! In the second scene, a man is shivering, covered by a blanket. Then he turns on the TV, which carries images of a beach—suddenly he's warm, he throws off the blanket and dons sunglasses. In the final scene, the same man is looking at his TV when a blonde woman appears onscreen. She looks at him, makes a kiss. You see the man lean back, stunned and happy, with lipstick on his cheek.

7

TASHKENT HAS AN EXCELLENT subway system—the V. I. Lenin Tashkent Metropolitan Subway, as the signs call it, opened in 1978. A train for whatever direction comes every five minutes. The Lenin Station has been renamed Liberty Square Station; Komsomol is now Youth; October Revolution is Central Boulevard. These stations have an odd feel, because all the reliefs of Lenin leading the people are still there, the hammers and sickles, the slogan "We Are Building Socialism" (at Central Boulevard Station). It feels as if you're performing a play on the wrong set. Fortunately, these are just train stations, and so the queasy sensation of being perched at the same time in two quite different, mutually hostile historical epochs only lasts five minutes at most. Unless you work in the station.

8

LIKE THE TSARISTS BEFORE THEM, the Soviets had their own version of a "civilizing mission." Not surprisingly, given that they had overthrown Tsarism, the Soviets initially argued that Asian rebellions against imperial Russia were a good thing, and that, as the scholar S. S. Dmitriev put it, for "the peoples of Central Asia," Tsarist Russia was "the prison of peoples." By the mid-1940s, however, the need to keep Asia firmly within Soviet Russia's own prison, and the resurgence of Russian patriotism in the face of German invasion, led to an about-face. In 1954 Dmitriev himself added to his book a section on "the progressive consequences of the annexation of Central Asia to Russia." Marx and Engels could be quoted in support of either position. In 1959 one Dzhamgerchinov wrote: "The founders of scientific Communism already in the 1850's stressed the progressive significance of annexation to Russia." Even Central Asian sources were drafted into use, for example the Uzbek poet Furkat (1858–1909), who wrote: "O youth! The priceless light of Russian wisdom/ Has overshadowed the traditions of past years."

The basic concept of Soviet imperialism was "friendship." Russia, the "elder brother" of Soviet historiography, had brought the "fraternal" peoples of Asia into a new era. A "correct understanding," A. V. Piaskovsky noted in 1955, "of what happened in the past (particularly in the territories of Central Asia and Kazakhstan) can facilitate an even greater strengthening of the friendship among the peoples of the U.S.S.R. — one of the basic motive forces of the Soviet state, one of the most important sources of the might and invincibility of the U.S.S.R." Events once perceived as "conquest" now became "friendship." Wrote one historian: "At first the Buriats [in Siberia] were afraid of the Russians, especially the Cossacks. . . . But after a few decades, the Buriats, because of more and more frequent clashes with the Russians . . . began little by little to associate with them, even to establish a mutual friendship." A Kazakh historian described the nature of Tsarist imperialism this way: "The ravaged and starving Kazakhs constantly approached the Russian fortified lines, seeking to subject themselves to Russia."

The "strengthening of the friendship" among Soviet peoples mainly involved strengthening Russia's image as a country that could do no wrong, whether Tsarist or Soviet. The enforced use of Russian (and of the Cyrillic alphabet for Asian languages) would bring everyone together; the sending of skilled Russian colonists would both impress and gladden the hearts of the natives. In the 1960s, Nikita Khrushchev argued that Soviet ethnic groups would engage in a "flowering," then a "drawing closer together," and finally "unity" or "fusion." In 1971, Leonid Brezhnev announced a whole new concept, "a new historical community of people — The Soviet People." No one ever knew quite what the new Soviet People was supposed to be. One non-Russian thought it an "abstract veil under which the Russian chauvinist backbone conceals itself." Russians, however, seemingly accepted the idea, partly because they believed that "Soviet" did just mean "Russians-plus-others."

At any rate, nationalistic activity among all the supposedly drawing-together Soviet peoples increased during the seventies and eighties. One influential Russian nationalist wrote in a *samizdat* journal of "the strengthening of Russian ethnic culture and tradition in the spirit of the Slavophiles and Dostoevsky, and the assertion of Russia's originality and greatness." By the time Gorbachev came to power, an intellectual nationalism was well established among Russians and non-Russians.

Gorbachev wanted to keep the Soviet Union intact, but under the circumstances this meant going to the border regions and trying to pull his unwieldy country in one direction this day, another the next. In Vladivostok, he emphasized Russia's Asianness, later writing, "The Soviet Union is an Asian, as well as a European country." Gorbachev did not explain what Russia's Asianness was, though he did expound, in the city whose name means "Lord of the East," upon "those trailblazers who laid the road to the Pacific Ocean" and "the valor, industry, and steadfastness of the people who settled and defended this land." These people, of course, were Tsarist Russian colonists. As for Europe, Gorbachev emphasized the idea of "Europe – our common house." Gorbachev had no trouble defining Russia's Europeanness: "Europe, 'from the Atlantic to the Urals,' is a cultural-historical entity united by the common heritage of the Renaissance and the Enlightenment, of the great philosophical and social teachings of the nineteenth and twentieth centuries."

As it happened, within a few years the Soviet Union had collapsed, and five centuries of patient, stubborn empire-building simply ended.

10

IT'S NIGHT, you lie in your bunk on a train crossing the steppe. Outside the towns drift. Unable to sleep, you watch their lights. These are new towns, built in the Soviet period around chemical, metallurgical, and agroindustrial factories – towns populated mainly by Russians. Now these towns, their factories, and the Russians who live in them have become outdated. No more Soviet Five Year Plans will be coming along to give them a place in the world. Though they themselves have not changed, rebelled, or misbehaved in any way, the economic and political landscape surrounding them has altered irrevocably. Though these towns and the people in them can still work, given enough fuel and materials, suddenly no one wants them. They have been cut adrift, and only the lights at night glitter to demonstrate they're there at all.

11

THE STREET YOU LIVE ON in Tashkent is shaded by grape arbors, and since temperatures can reach over 100 degrees Fahrenheit everyone's understandably grateful that in summer the vines give leaf and make it possible to sit comfortably outside even in mid-day. Coming from the broad sweltering avenues of Tashkent into the leafy tunnel of the street is like coming into a restful home poised between inside and outside. *Mahalla*: from Arabic, it can mean "street, corner, district," or "ward in a city or town." Its ancestor *mahal* simply means "place," as in the Bulgarian village Yeni Mağalı, "New Place." In Uzbek, *mahalla* means everything. You will probably be born, live, and die in the same *mahalla*. You'll play with the other kids in your *mahalla*. Later, they'll form the core of your circle of friends. People do marry across *mahallalar*, though usually they don't wander too far. The woman comes to live in the man's *mahalla*. A new couple will parade through the district, preceded by musicians. A huge feast will be held, with endless mounds of pilaf. The wife will regularly return to visit her own *mahalla*, where her husband will always be something of a stranger.

Each *mahalla* is its own world, a refuge, and a place with its own rules. "If your daughter marries a man from another city, that is a tragedy," a man on your street explains. "If a man comes to the *mahalla* from Samarkand, for example, no matter if he spends his whole life here, he will still be called 'the man from Samarkand.' " When you die, a table will be set up outside your home, and people will come from the *mahalla* to share the grief of your relatives. This lasts twenty days. When such a table is set up, your neighbors can't pass without stopping, having pilaf pressed on them. *Majburi*: it is obligatory. A person without a *mahalla* is hard to imagine. Such a person would be *mahalsiz*, "groundless, ill-founded, out of place; insignificant."

In the *mahalla* you feel safe. The street is narrow: a connected row of brown-rose, two-storey houses with small gardens between the facade and the street. Before each door is a bench, where you

179

while away the day and the evening. Across the street are larger gardens. Ideally, as at your home, the garden will be filled with fruit trees. You have mulberries, pomegranates, pears, apricots, apples, three kinds of cherry, squashes, and tomatoes—*pomidori* in Uzbek, from Italian "golden apples." (Originally a New World plant, the first tomatoes in Italy were golden and thought to be poisonous. They're a staple of the Uzbek diet.) Some people keep sheep in their gardens, even a cow.

The street where you live in Tashkent is populated entirely by Uzbeks. Historically, Russians have not wanted to live with Uzbeks and vice versa. Tashkent has an "Asian side" and a "European side." Russians in Tashkent tend to live in apartment blocks and are far less likely to have gardens; thus, now, they have less food than do Uzbeks. They also have fewer friends. Though only about eight percent of Uzbekistan's population of twenty million, Russians rarely know Uzbek. Until 1989, they were the occupiers, usually better educated and wealthier than Uzbeks. Since 1989 or 1990, they have been the unloved detritus of colonial rule, a desperate species of expatriate or exile, *mahalsiz*.

The best times on your street are early morning and night. In the morning, the young wives of each household emerge to hose down the street. The youngest wife occupies the bottom of the household hierarchy. On the female side, above her are the less-young wives, with the mother-in-law above them and, possibly, a grandmother-in-law. One way for the youngest wife to demonstrate her rectitude is to hose down the street around sunup. The earlier, the better. The young wives compete. The first to water her patch of street wins. You can tell a lot from when households have their piece of street watered.

Of course, the youngest wives also have their own powers, because they are reproducing the family—which is, after all, the main point—and because one day they will be mothers-in-law themselves.

During the day, the young wives control the *mahalla*. Their children play in the street, which resembles nothing so much as a chaotic playground. Kids come by with wheelbarrows to collect food scraps with which to feed their animals. Bad kids come by and shake the fruit trees, grabbing their booty and running away. During infrequent rests, the young wives visit with each other, slumping a bit on the benches because of the heat and constant work.

At night, you sit on the benches or in the garden under the fruit trees, eating whatever's ripe, drinking tea from shallow bowls, talking with your *mahalla* friends. Eventually, the children go to bed and you can hear the leaves flutter and shake, you drink your tea and talk and life is sweet.

11

YOU SIT WITH NASRUDDIN at home, watching television. President Karimov is visiting South Korea. Later he'll move on to Indonesia, Malaysia—the centralized, authoritarian, free market quasi-democracies of East Asia. The government hasn't yet been able to agree on an entirely new national anthem, so, for the moment, you hear the old Soviet anthem with new words. Karimov looks uncomfortable as he watches the honor guards pass by. He speaks expansively of an Asian way, of modern government on an Asian model, which apparently means a free market democracy that places more emphasis on social stability and government leadership than is the case in the West: democracy without conflicts or argument. "Blind men," Nasruddin says, "always find each other in the dark."

You have also seen, many times, footage of Karimov visiting Saudi Arabia. There he stresses the ties between Muslim countries, the joy he feels now that Uzbeks can worship freely.

Then he's in Turkey, where he dilates upon the ancient and indissoluble ties among Turks of the world and how they must all help each other. He takes a moment to point out that Turkey has seen fit to repress radical Islam, and he sees no reason why Uzbekistan should be any different.

Then he appears in Kazakhstan, where we find that nothing could be more precious to Uzbeks than making common cause with their Central Asian brothers and sisters.

Then, back home, he denigrates the West, particularly the U.S., for attempting to impose conditions on free Uzbekistan. This was not quite the line he took when James Baker visited, but then James Baker isn't U.S. secretary of state anymore, isn't even in power.

It's as if Karimov, like Gorbachev before him, is trying to triangulate the location of his country by looking outside it—or trying to find a center to something that exists mainly in parts. Historically, two views of Uzbekistan present themselves. One could see Uzbekistan as forever on the margins of empires. Alexander the Great, in his mad push to the East, reached a northeastern limit in Uzbekistan, as had the Persians before him. From the opposite direction, the Chinese empire could reach no farther west than the easternmost reaches of Uzbekistan, and really not even that far. Pushing up from Persia, urban Islam got no farther north than the great cities of Bukhara and Samarkand, with the exception of Muslim Khazan straight east of Moscow. As for the Russians, the historian George Lantzeff once wrote, "One of the most spectacular aspects of Russian history is the unique, enormous and continous expansion of Russia" – but even the Russian empire at its height considered Central Asia marginal, and would, of course, lose it.

One could also see Uzbekistan as forever at the center of the world – a vision sometimes preferred by Uzbeks. This view honors Alisher Nawaii (1441-1501) as the national poet and Tamerlane as founder of the Uzbek state (1320?-1405), even though neither Nawaii nor Tamerlane were Uzbek. (The Uzbeks proper invaded from the north at the end of the 15th century.) Influential religious figures, such as the Sufi şeyh Naqshband and Avicenna, both from Bukhara, are promoted as exemplars of the Uzbek contribution to world civilization and Uzbekistan's status as a spiritual and intellectual heartland. (Again, neither was ethnically Uzbek.) The properly Uzbek empire of the Shaybanids did, in the 16th century, extend into Persia and Afghanistan, only to split into khanates after 1598. An imaginative version of Turkic history places the Uzbeks at center stage, sending their warriors forth to conquer the world, their merchants trading from Europe to China – though, once again, relatively few Uzbeks fought among the great wandering Turkic tribes, and the Silk Road had already entered its precipitous decline by the time of the Uzbek invasion.

President Karimov, his uneasy world centered in Uzbekistan and specifically Tashkent, plays all these themes, portraying his country as suffering marginalized victim one day, cradle of humanity the next; at once Turkic, Muslim, Asian, and modern. One wants to put all those terms in quotation marks, for of course no one can agree what they mean. And, indeed, no one can really say where or what Uzbekistan is, not even the Uzbeks themselves.

12

AN UZBEK FRIEND spent one and a half years in Moldavia and the Ukraine as part of his compulsory military service. He found these places revolting. "I saw women, with blond hair, holding babies while smoking in the street. Boys and girls would kiss in the street. When I got back to Tashkent I looked at the women and thought: Oh, they are so beautiful! Their eyes, their hair. After the Russian women, every one of them was an angel."

13

OFTEN YOU SPEND YOUR EVENINGS in the garden with Nasruddin, sitting on the *kravat*, a wooden platform raised a few feet above the ground, about six feet square, with a low railing on three sides. The sour cherry trees droop, heavy with fruit, so that you can rise up on your knees, pluck a few cherries, share them around; you chew, spit out the pits, the juice stains your fingers red. Sometimes Nasruddin's only child, Bil, will trundle out in his gravity-defying way—he's around two—and demand his father's attention. Nasruddin will ask Bil difficult, playful questions, Bil will attempt to answer; Bil will quickly tire of the questions and point meaningfully toward the tree; Nasruddin will laugh, stand up, pick some cherries and give them to Bil. While Bil eats, you can talk. When Bil finishes eating, it's not so easy. He does various things to get his father's attention. He goes over to a trellis, hangs from a bar, and shouts "Papa!" He makes warlike moves with a stick. Sometimes he just walks over to Nasruddin and hits him. This is probably Bil's least wise strategy for getting Nasruddin's attention. But even here Nasruddin is gentle. He's absolutely stupefied with love for his son. Often he says, gazing at Bil, "I think children are the wisdom of life"—sometimes "the happiness of life," even "the meaning of life." Usually, after a fair amount of back and forth, Nasruddin takes Bil by the hand and walks him through the little orchard to the bench in front of their house – the house where you live in your Tashkent *mahalla* – and attempts to deposit his son with Mahmuda, his wife, who sits there chatting with the neighbors, dressed like every other woman on your street in a brightly colored, long, flowing silk *atlas*.

Nasruddin and Mahmuda married here in the orchard. Once the prospective match had been examined and provisionally approved by their respective families, Nasruddin and Mahmuda met on three occasions to talk. "I liked her. She's funny," Nasruddin says. "You have to learn how to love." You've seen a video of the ceremonies. First, an enormous nighttime party at her parents' house, where the women of her family and her brothers, in particular, say goodbye, dance, and drink a great deal. A professional emcee tells jokes and pays tribute to Mahmuda's mother. Her father and his friends spend most of their time sitting on the street, monitoring who comes and goes. The next day, it's off to city hall. Nasruddin wears a Western suit – still his only suit – while Mahmuda wears a white Western wedding dress. From city hall they proceed to Nasruddin's *mahalla*, to this orchard, where they sit stiffly at the head table in their wedding outfits, backs against the garage door, while the younger people drink and dance beneath the trees. Older men of note occupy the table at the entrance to Nasruddin's house; inside, women prepare food. Mahmuda's dowry consists principally of a wall of cabinets filled with teapots, crystal, and crockery. Taking up one side of the living room, they face a similar but smaller set of cabinets and display cases – Nasruddin's mother's dowry.

Mahmuda doesn't always want to take care of Bil. He can be a demanding child and is somewhat spoiled. He doesn't like other children to touch his toys, or even to touch their own toys once he has borrowed them; and he rarely suffers punishment. The only unambiguous crime he commits is to strike his mother – at which point the entire weight of patriarchal authority, not just Nasruddin's but that of whatever men happen to be around, descends upon his tiny self with absolutely implacable gravity.

Mahmuda doesn't always want to look after Bil in the evenings, but Nasruddin insists, because there is so much for him and you to talk about, sitting on the *kravat* eating sour cherries. He worries for his country. The Aral Sea, in Uzbekistan's northwest corner, has lost a third or more of its water. The water of the rivers that feed it has been drained off for irrigation. Soviet agricultural policy dictated that most of Uzbekistan's suitable land be devoted to cotton. The fields were drenched with pesticides. Perhaps a quarter of these lands have become so severely salinized that they can barely produce cotton. Such a disastrous policy has consequences. Animals become weak, foals disfigured; people acquire diseases they've never heard of before; hot winds blow away the topsoil, rivers silt up, mud flows; drinking water becomes poisonous. Between 1965 and 1986, the infant mortality rate near the Aral Sea increased by nearly half.

As we sit on the *kravat* in mid-summer it should be dry and hot; instead it is cool and humid. The day was punctuated by torrents of rain. Our little orchard is still soaking wet. The grapes are sick, and many of the apricot leaves have four holes in them. Even in bright sun there may be a shower. Children love the rain because they can play in the many puddles that form on our sheltered street. "Everything has changed," Nasruddin says. "We get aches we can't explain. Everyone is complaining about these aches. We didn't get aches like this before. Suddenly old people will die, many of them, for no reason. There have been many deaths this week." When you expect warmth, you find only cold. People will feel listless, then have a sudden rush of energy they don't know what to do with; and just as suddenly they will be drained.

"Stones appeared in a yard," Nasruddin says, "and no one knew where they came from. Lately, things have been suddenly catching fire. The Uzbekistan Academy of Sciences wrote a report on it."

Nasruddin has to go now to see his grandmother. She has been terribly ill, her abdomen swollen for weeks. Doctors have come and gone, but they can't diagnose her illness. So she lies in bed, receiving visitors. She has begun refusing food and takes water or tea only occasionally. Nasruddin stayed with her during some of his student years, and she also helped him with money. "Her only wish was to help other people. She has always thought just of others, not of herself." She had barely known her first husband before he went off to fight in the Second World War. She never saw him again, nor did she ever hear news of his death. She waited for years and years hoping he would return. She bore a child not long after he left—Nasruddin's mother. She raised the girl and waited. Nasruddin says she had loved

185

her husband very much. Eventually she remarried. Her new husband, a policeman, was a strong, kind, straightforward man. "Once he found a packet filled with money. He searched and searched for the owner, and eventually found him. He gave back the money. People laughed at him. They couldn't believe he'd returned the money. He was probably the only really honest policeman in Uzbekistan." He has been dead for years now, and Nasruddin must go and be at his maternal grandmother's side. His mother has been there twenty-four hours a day, for weeks. "She did so much for me, and now I thought, at last, I could serve her. We had her new house almost fixed up. I wanted her to live in comfort in her old age. Now I worry I won't be able to give any more service to her." He picks up an umbrella at the house then walks off beneath the grape arbors.

14

ONE WOMAN YOU KNOW was at work late one day when she suddenly realized that her workplace was an *ağurjoy*, "heavy place." She turned on the faucet, and no water came out. She heard laughter. She went to open the door but it wouldn't budge. She went back to her chair and began to sleep. Then, suddenly, she remembered to recite chapters from the Koran. She recited and recited and gradually came to her senses. When she had finished the door opened.

She spoke to others about the event and later brought a *mullah* to say prayers and preside over the sacrificing of an animal. The *mullah* read chapters of the Koran but had to stop many times as the force of the place was overwhelming. He became drenched with sweat. But he continued and no further incidents have been reported.

Much of what happens in this world is due to magic, *duwa*. If you find yourself in the grip of *duwa* you must consult a *damle*, someone who understands *duwa* and knows how to neutralize its power. You find a *damle* by asking your friends or otherwise making discreet inquiries in the *mahalla*. (You might also consult a *falbin*, or fortune-teller, who might be a *damle* as well.) Bad *duwa* is called *ıssık-sowuk duwa*, "hot-cold *duwa*."

There is, of course, good *duwa*. In 1991, in the Ferghana valley, a woman appeared who could remove devils from your body. You

186

would give her a piece of white cloth, three rubles, and your address. At home, you would go about your usual life, except at night. Then you would leave your window cracked open, put a bowl of water mixed with sugar and a plate of flour next to your mattress. You would lie down on the mattress leaving part of your hand in the flour. You had to sleep alone. After two or three days, old people would appear to you. You would then recite: "*Bismillah al-Rahman al-Rahim.*" And the devils would leave.

A local *mullah* opposed this woman, and her career was brief. He said she was trading in *issik-sowuk duwa*, that she was an agent of Satan. None of her remedies needed to be followed. It was enough, he said, simply to recite "*Bismillah al-Rahman al-Rahim,*" for that is the anti-Satan formula recognized by Islam.

In his most mundane form, Satan travels as a normal person, identifiable only by his or her eyes: eyes have power, and Satanic power is revealed by the eyes. Such normal people use their power when jealous. "I don't dress Bil in too-nice clothes," Nasruddin says, "because people might become jealous and cause the eye to touch him. Never forget the power of eyes. Also, they might become jealous because Bil has such white skin."

15

MOHAMMED SALIH IS AN unusually tall, very handsome man around forty, and when you meet him—he enters the room with the easy confidence of a thoughtful businessman—he's dressed entirely in pristine white. He smokes foreign cigarettes stuck in a holder. He has just quit parliament.

Mohammed Salih leads the Erk party, the only legal opposition party of any size. Erk puts out a weekly newspaper which is the only legal opposition newspaper of any size. He has left parliament because he was attempting to speak there about what the government ought to do and his microphone was cut off. So he deposited his parliamentarian's card on his desk.

"It was the last way remaining to me to fight against the established regime of dictatorship. Over the last two years, I have demanded, on behalf of the opposition, that the government fulfill its promises of radical reform. But they do nothing. On the contrary, they have begun to work to strengthen the former system. All the same, this system won't work. The totalitarian system worked for seventy or eighty years. But now it won't work. Such a system has, historically, run out of time.

"We have emerged from this system, but we haven't gone *to* anything. We are living in a system without a system."

The government, he says, has used the militia to keep itself in power; and indeed there have been regular arrests and beatings of Erk members and other dissidents. "But that government which survives by force cannot survive long. People are becoming more opposed to the government, mainly because of the economy, and it has wasted the stability of the period that followed independence. We in the opposition understand very well that stability is necessary for reform. For the last three years we have tried to ensure stability, refraining from holding big meetings. But, as it turns out, this stability wasn't used to provide a space for reform. On the contrary. So the government has lost its chance to use stability. We are not at all sure now that stability will continue."

Erk is working on a new constitution and an alternative economic plan, as well as building its own party structures. Conditions are less than ideal. The government printing house – the only printing house – reduced Erk's newspaper's press run from one hundred thousand to twelve thousand. And now Erk's leader has left parliament, which most people still call the supreme soviet. A majority voted to accept his resignation.

"I won't go back until there's a new parliament. I didn't decide to be leader of the opposition, but events take you to such places. I never liked politics or politicians. I was just a poet. There are such periods in each country, when poets become involved in politics. Independence, liberty, are among the ideas most dear to poets. A man should do something in his life. This is a rule of life. Writing poems was once my aim in life. Now this is my life-activity."

Meanwhile, the government is creating its own opposition parties so that it can eliminate the existing opposition while preserving the appearance of democracy. And it is increasing repression. Salih looks impressively calm in his crisp white clothes, gesturing with his cigarette holder.

"If the government reforms, such a tightening of control won't be needed. Such a repressive system will only increase instability. They're doing their best to increase stability, but they are destroying stability. The government should give the people economic and political freedom. If it doesn't, its life will be very short. If it does, then perhaps its life will be prolonged. This would be better for everyone. We don't want to throw President Karimov away. I talk to him all the time. But then, many people talk to him. Maybe their influence is greater than mine. The national and provincial chiefs—of course, all ex-Communists, like the president, only under a new party name—they're making obstacles to the new laws. The president can't enforce the laws by himself. Maybe, yes, he knows this. But if he eliminates these people, what will he have left? He's afraid of the system he leads. The old Communists still rule. I am very sympathetic to him."

The government uses the fear of Islamic fundamentalism to make itself more attractive to foreign governments and the ex-Communist bureaucracy. Salih believes fundamentalism will become a problem only if the government makes it one. "The Islamic activists are not aiming at political power now. But they certainly have such a potential. If there aren't reforms, some Muslims may turn to politics. But as for now there is no fundamentalist leader or program. Fundamentalism is not politically important, not shaped or ripened. If a strong man appears with a strong program, then his party could become powerful.

"Islam is our holy religion. Of course its role is very great. This is natural. In our opinion, Islam shouldn't be political. Islam is higher than any party. To draw it down would mean to curse God."

By chance one afternoon you meet Babur Shakhirov and take off in his car to find the other leading Uzbek opposition figure, Abdurahim Pulatov. One of the many distinctive things about Babur is his driving. He reserves one hand for cigarettes. The other hand takes care of steering, gesturing, adjusting the radio, and anything else that might come up. As for Babur's face, it is turned toward you as he explains the intricacies of Uzbek politics. The road, other cars, and pedestrians are left to take care of themselves.

Pulatov is not at the hospital anymore. He was beaten a few weeks ago by unidentified men. They cracked his head open. Last night the lights went out at the hospital. Pulatov's bodyguards hustled him from bed and into hiding.

We drive here and there. Babur, fleshy and sweating in his baseball cap and unkempt clothes—highly unusual attire for an Uzbek man—strides up to closed doors, knocks importantly, fires questions. Babur's favorite moniker is "Uzbekistan's first dissident." He spent ten years in jail under the old regime, then two more in Brooklyn as a political exile. He seems much more Brooklynite than Uzbek. He acts like a free man, as if he can do whatever he likes: park on the sidewalk, smoke in the elevator, order things that aren't on the menu.

This would be obnoxious in Brooklyn but in Tashkent it's electrifying—because no one in ex-Soviet Uzbekistan is free, not even Babur, certainly not Abdurahim Pulatov, whom we eventually find sprawled on a sofa in a sanatorium, his head wrapped in bandages. We chat for a while. Pulatov insists that the Western countries, ex-Soviet commonwealth members, and so on should pressure the Karimov government to quit repressing its own citizens. He insists that fundamentalism is not a problem but rather a spectre raised by Karimov to quiet Westerners spooked by Islam. At one point, Pulatov could stir thousands with fiery speeches about the evil of Communism and the necessity of unity—his organization is Birlik, "unity." Now he's on the run, weakened by his wounds. The sanatorium's chief stops by to say Pulatov can't stay. A nurse takes his blood pressure. Pulatov looks up at you and Babur from beneath his bandages.

You depart, and Babur takes you to his apartment where you eat a lot and drink even more. You meet his family, show his daughter where Brooklyn is on a map. Babur says he's organizing a national parliament, or rather a shadow parliament, the Milli Majlis, which will unite all the opposition groups and bring about the downfall of the neo-Communist regime. More drinking, and laughter. Babur likes a party.

Soon all of this will be history. The next morning Pulatov will flee to Moscow, then to Baku, Turkey, even visit the United States. The government will pass a law mandating that foreigners who do journalistic work on a tourist visa can be imprisoned for up to three years. In a few months, Pulatov's brother, Abdumannob, will be kidnapped · in neighboring Kyrgyzstan while attending a human rights conference and brought to Tashkent to be tried on grounds of insulting the presidency. A few months after that, Mohammed Salih the handsome poet and leader of the moderate opposition, who doesn't even want to get rid of the president of a government that rejects him, will find his party crushed, his newspaper eliminated, his offices sealed. He will be jailed twice, charged with crimes against the state. One day his Erk companions will inform him that he is due to be arrested again, this time for good, and at three the next morning he will slip away, travel by car to Kazakhstan, thence to Baku, Turkey, the United States. His wife and two small children will also flee, travelling for days around Uzbekistan to confuse the authorities then dashing over the border into Turkmenistan. Religious leaders will go underground or be jailed. People will begin simply to disappear.

And Babur—he will be beaten by unidentified men and later thrown in jail. In a 1993 Helsinki Watch report, "Human Rights in Uzbekistan," you will read the following: Babur "is a former people's deputy of the USSR and is founder and chairman of the organizational committee of the Milli Majlis, a political coalition forum.... He spent ten years in Soviet camps beginning around 1970 on charges of treason and involvement with anti-Soviet propaganda and agitation. Mr. Shokirov was re-arrested in Tashkent on August 14 or 15, 1992. Although allegedly he has been charged with violating Article 60 of the criminal code, there has been no formal confirmation or explanation of the charges." Article 60 concerned "anti-Soviet propaganda and agitation," but the Karimov government changed "Soviet" to "government."

The report continues: "His apartment was reportedly ransacked by law enforcement officials after he was detained.... According to family members interviewed by Helsinki Watch, Mr. Shokirov has been denied access to legal counsel and, with one exception, to family members since his arrest."

16

DURING THE SOVIET PERIOD, Uzbek TV-watchers saw many programs the message of which was that everyone in the world speaks Russian. They'd see film of school children in India or Africa speaking

Russian, in Canada, everywhere. Now they see soap operas from Mexico. "The Rich Also Cry" has been phenomenally popular.

The Turkish government decided to broadcast into Uzbekistan. It has its own channel, Eurasia, which broadcasts in Turkish, a language that Central Asians don't understand. But the production values are relatively high, and the channel includes shows featuring scantily clad Turkish women singers. Turkey trumpets itself as a model for Central Asian nations because it is richer than they are, with a free market system and democracy. Turkey's prime minister has declared repeatedly his eagerness to bring civilization, progress, and democracy to his long-suffering fellow ethnic Turks, an activity for which Western governments have given their thanks.

One afternoon you sit at home in Tashkent watching Turkish TV. Mahmuda comes in, sits down, and stares at the TV. "Do you understand it?" she asks.

"Some of it. They're talking about Bosnia."

Mahmuda looks at you, at the TV, back at you.

"I don't understand it. What are they speaking?"

"It's Turkish."

17

ALTHOUGH MOST OF THE TIME you and Nasruddin sit on the *kravat* in the garden when you want to talk, sometimes you go deeper into the garden and squat next to the tomatoes and squashes, especially when Fakhriddin visits—because when Fakhriddin visits you're likely to talk politics. If you sit on the *kravat*, male neighbors will feel free to come over and chat. Out by the tomatoes nobody will bother you, unless Mahmuda gets so fed up with minding Bil that she brings him nearby and sends him up the stairs to the back of the garden.

Fakhriddin and Nasruddin are best friends, better educated than most Uzbeks, and they have made the dubious decision to involve themselves in politics. Fakhriddin is more active, Nasruddin more reflective. Nasruddin's main political activity right now is helping you, a risky enough proposition for himself and his family. (A similar action two years ago brought him a visit from the KGB.)

Tonight, next to the squashes, we discuss the possibility of war.

"If it weren't for these little gardens," Fakhriddin says, "there would have been war in Uzbekistan a long time ago." The gardens allow Uzbeks to keep from going hungry and from being dependent on wages. Since 1990, the post-Communist government has passed privatization laws; but lower-level bureaucrats, whether in agriculture, manufacturing, or trade, have been reluctant to implement them, so most people still receive their wages from the state. Controlling the possibility of employment—or rather, the possibility of unemployment—is an excellent way to control political dissent. If you oppose the government, you lose your job, without much hope of finding another. Inflation simply raises the stakes. It also makes your garden even more important. Nasruddin earns enough selling his cherries to pay the rent. (The government keeps rents low.) Besides, Uzbeks are not highly urbanized. Eighty percent live in the countryside, and the ideal Uzbek way of life takes place in a village. In this, Uzbeks distinguish themselves from Kazakhs. "If an Uzbek gets some money, he will buy land for more fruit trees," Nasruddin says. "If a Kazakh gets some money, he'll buy horses." In cities, the village becomes the *mahalla*.

Identification with one's village or *mahalla* survived Communism. In fact, it was one of the main ways in which Uzbekness withstood decades of centralization, the transition to wage earning, state appropriation of private land, and Russian ethnic prejudice. The garden you're sitting in, along with every garden up and down your street, was illegal for years. The government wanted to build a high rise on this land and the local residents simply refused, bulldozing the land at their own expense to clear plots, planting trees, and daring officials to stop them. Which they never did, as Uzbek officials knew quite well who would win a contest between a determined *mahalla* and the state. The Uzbek *mahallalar* stood for decades like minifortresses against nearly every aspect of Communism and Russian imperialism, from intermarriage to land tenure laws. There's even an Uzbek word for it: *mahallaçilik*, "being-in-a-*mahalla*ness," which could be inadequately translated as "localism."

However, *mahallaçilik* has its problems. The very social structure that preserved Uzbekness may be the undoing of democratic society, which presupposes a certain respect for, and loyalty to, the state—while many Uzbeks have spent the past sixty years cultivating precisely the opposite, substituting fierce loyalty to the *mahalla*. The fear of war in Uzbekistan derives not so much from foreign affairs as from internal disunity. "If one *mahalla* goes against another *mahalla*, there would be chaos," Fakhriddin says, standing next to the tomato plants and smoking a cigarette. "You cannot imagine what it would be like. Block against block. This could occur at a national level. If one region fights another—say if Ferghana [an intensely farmed basin east of Tashkent] rebelled against Tashkent—the war would be horrible. It used to be that Uzbeks were united against the center, against Moscow. Now they are not united against anything, or each region is united, separately, against Tashkent. The government can't enforce its laws in a province if the provincial government doesn't cooperate—and they don't." The post-Communist government deals harshly with political dissent in part because dissent strikes the Communist mind as inherently repugnant, but more because the government knows how feeble its hold on real power is, and how much greater is the hold of *mahallaçilik*.

The cementing of *mahallaçilik* extends partly from Communist policy. The Communists wished to keep as many Uzbeks as possible working the land. They provided cheap labor—Uzbek agriculture is dramatically under-mechanized, and schoolchildren were drafted en masse for unpaid cotton picking each year, spending months in the fields. As peasants, the Uzbeks could (or so the government imagined) be more easily controlled. When possible, Moscow wanted to restrict skilled labor to Russians, both as an outlet for Russian workers and as a strategy for colonization. This complemented the broad program which posited the Russian people, specifically Russian men, as the vanguard of the united Soviet peoples, the "elder brother." Finally, the government wanted to prevent an uncontrolled rush of peasants into the cities. So to move into any city you needed state permission, and that wasn't easy to get. If you were caught living in a city without permission, you might face severe penalties. The Communists kept Uzbeks in their villages and in the *mahalla*, to which Uzbeks responded by making the *mahalla* a place where Russian Communists feared to go.

Mahallaçilik may also have roots in the Uzbek past. Modern Uzbekistan wasn't really a state until Russian Communists made it one. Prior to that, the land area of contemporary Uzbekistan had been united only under Tamerlane, whose political career began in 1360. Tamerlane was himself building on the work of Genghis Khan (1165?–1227), who had conquered the whole of Central Asia, organized it into an empire, and divided it four ways among his sons, with one of them as his imperial heir. Genghis, besides being an unsurpassable warrior, had a talent for hiring good administrators. Turkic and Persian political traditions blended with the Mongolian (and some Chinese) in a fairly stable synthesis which was further refined by Genghis's sons. It was a historical moment when the cultures of steppe nomads and those of settled farmers and urban traders formed a dynamic whole. After Genghis's death, the empire continued to expand, stretching at its height from Russia to Iran, from Afghanistan to Korea. However, once Genghis's third successor as great khan, Möngke, died in 1259, the empire collapsed, with Kubla Khan taking China, where he began the Yüan dynasty, and parts of Mongolia. The remaining territory was divided up among several khans who warred against each other. The area of Uzbekistan fell under the Chaghatay khans, who split it into eastern and western khanates. Despite this fragmentation of political power and the straying of China (Kubla Khan and his successors found the Chinese difficult to assimilate), the synthesis of political culture continued, and several aspects of Central Asian life today were first solidified: the predominance of Turkic languages, general acceptance of Islam, and the distinctive mix of primarily Turkic and Mongolian elements with Persian and, to some extent, Chinese.

Into this world, the scholar Beatrice Forbes Manz writes, Tamerlane "catapulted with overwhelming force. Aspiring first to lead his tribe, next to control the Ulus Chaghatay [successor state to the western Chaghatay khanate], then to maintain his precarious position of leadership and finally to conquer most of the known world, Temur [Tamerlane] pursued power with an awesome singleness of purpose." He fought constantly until 1405 when, though too weak to walk, he set out to conquer China only to die along the way. Perhaps his greatest advantage was that he began his career in what is now Uzbekistan, near the city of Samarkand, a region that, while not militarily formidable, was centrally located for expansion south into Iran, west via northern Iran toward the Ottoman empire, northwest to Golden Horde territory and thence to Russia, east along the Silk Road to China. Through constant warfare, Tamerlane succeeded in keeping the Turko-Mongolian synthesis alive into the 15th century. The synthesis depended, above all, on a series of dynamic oppositions: between nomads and sedentary peoples, between tribal and non-tribal groups, and between tribal regions and an imperial center, embodied by Tamerlane as it had been by Genghis Khan.

For today's Uzbekistan, the most important aspect of 14th-century politics was that the tribes had no particular need for central leadership. The Turko-Mongolian synthesis had, thanks to Genghis Khan, some need for the *idea* of a central power, but in practice the local tribes concentrated on their own succession struggles. This didn't lead to isolationism – too often associated, by modern writers, with tribes. On the contrary, someone wishing to be a tribal leader would normally seek help outside the tribe. Tribal leaders were no strangers to foreign policy or the subtleties of diplomatic negotiation. Tamerlane managed to take the idea of central power and make it stick for a few decades. But no one after him, not even the tsars, would pull off the same trick. And, after the Shaybanids in 1598, there would never again be a single ruler of the land now called Uzbekistan until the 1930s. This didn't mean that Uzbekistan was chaotic, not at all. Compared to any European region of comparable size, it was downright placid. It simply means that Uzbekistan has a tradition of *mahallaçilik* extending over some six centuries.

And *mahallaçilik* today worries the president of Uzbekistan, and Fakhriddin and Nasruddin as you sit smoking cigarettes next to the tomato and squash plants in your own *mahalla*, screened from the street by shrubs. "The president always speaks of *tinçlik*," Fakhriddin says. *Tinçlik* means "quietness" or "peace." "This is because he fears chaos and the power of *mahallaçilik*. He says, 'First *tinçlik*, then food, then democracy.' He's in a difficult position. But he shouldn't always try to channel the people. He tries to channel them, like Stalin did."

As it happens, the only real source of practical *tinçlik* (and even of food) for many Uzbeks is precisely the *mahalla*.

18

HOW COULD ONE HOPE to hold Uzbekistan together? In seeking a principle for unity, early 20th-century Central Asian and other Turkic peoples under Tsarist control explored the notion of Pan-Turkism, or rather three overlapping ideologies: Pan-Turanianism, Pan-Turkism, and Turkism. Simply put, Pan-Turanianism concentrated on "Turan," imagined as a land north of Persia, centered more or less in today's Uzbekistan, and arcing toward China on one side, Anatolia and Europe on the other. The Turan concept rested on a free interpretation of the Persian epic *Avesta*, the story of three brothers from whom the human race descended: Tura (Turanians), Arya (Aryans, i.e., Persians or Iranians), and Sayrima (Westerners). In principle, Pan-Turanianism could include such long-ago nomadic peoples as the Finns, Hungarians, and Estonians. (It enjoyed a vogue in Hungary earlier this century.) Pan-Turkism was intellectually and geopolitically more focussed. It sought to unify all people who could conceivably be racially Turkic. Pan-Turkists tended to invoke the Central Asian legend which maintained that the Turks were descended from a white she-wolf named Zena; they used pictures of a *bozkurt*, "steppe-wolf," as their symbol. (This leaves aside yet another genealogy that relates the Turks to Noah.) Turkists concentrated more on the Ottoman lands and specific Turkish nationalism.

In 1918, M. A. Czaplicka presciently wrote: "It may be argued that there is something in the political atmosphere of our century which makes people revert, as it were, to past ages." For Czaplicka, "It is pretty certain that the several Turkic nations which the author has had the opportunity of meeting in Asia would be surprised if any one proposed to unite them in one local group on the ground of some remote tradition." As he says, "Throughout its whole history, except perhaps for a period between the fourteenth and seventeenth centuries, Central Asia has been the scene of the mingling of various cultural and political influences." Yet Czaplicka slightly missed the point, for there is something attractive about asserting one's bonds with other people—especially when one is being trampled by foreign powers, and even more when asserting those bonds might make one huge and powerful rather than weak and defenseless. "But to speak of the Osmanlis [Ottomans] and the Turanian Turks as a racial and cultural unity would be by a stroke of the pen, or by means of a propagandist pamphlet, to wipe away all the invasions, migrations, massacres, and fusions which for twenty centuries have played havoc with that part of the world." It seems never to have occurred to

Czaplicka that a chance to wipe away all the massacres of twenty centuries was part of what made Pan-Turkism so alluring.

The full Pan-Turkist vision originally appeared to non-Turks such as the Pole Konstanty Borzecki (1826–1876), who believed modern civilization had its origins in the Turkic past, and the Hungarian Arminius Vambery, who wrote in 1871, "Anatolians, Azerbaydjanes, Turkomans, Ozbegs [Uzbeks], Kirghis, and Tartars are the respective members out of which a mighty Turkish Colossus might have arisen, certainly better capable of measuring itself with its great northern competitor [Russia] than Turkey such as we see it in the present day." Within Central Asia, the earliest and most important Turkic advocate of Pan-Turkism was a Crimean Tatar, Ismail Gasprinsky (1851–1914). Through his influential journal *Tercüman* ("Interpreter"), begun in 1883, Gasprinsky tirelessly argued that the Turks in Russia had to unite, learn to speak the same language (a variant of Gasprinsky's Turkish) while cleansing it of Persian, Russian, and Arabic words, and somehow link up with their co-ethnics in the Ottoman Empire. The notion gained support among rebellious Tatars and Azerbaijanis. In 1905, several events conspired to make Pan-Turkism seem faintly practical. Russia had just been defeated by Japan—an *Asian* power, the Asians noted—and the tsar had proclaimed both a constitution and a parliament. A first congress of "Russian Muslims" took place in August, formulating demands for Muslim unity. To avoid secret police, the attendees gathered on a river ship, saying they were going for a pleasure cruise, and so the first congress was known as "the Congress on the Waters." A second congress took place in January 1906, a third in August the same year. Gasprinsky sat on the presiding committees of all three. The Russian government, naturally, was alarmed, particularly after forty-nine thousand Volga Tatar Christians reconverted to Islam. The government put controls on Muslim schools, held conferences on what to do, and, as the historian Riasanovsky says, "the representation of Central Asia [in the parliament] was entirely eliminated on the ground of backwardness."

Despite all this, Gasprinsky didn't hate Russians. Like any Central Asian intellectual outside strictly Muslim circles, his understanding of intellectual and political life had been colored by Russian ideas. Indeed, his youthful experience of intellectual Pan-Slavism probably did much to help him form a notion of Pan-Turkism. (Pan-Slavism itself opposed and took ideas from Pan-Germanism.) Early on, Gasprinsky appealed to the Russians to "give us the possibility to learn. You, great brothers, give us knowledge." The later, forlorn statement of another Pan-Turkist—"It was dangerous for us to encourage the Russians to approach in the guise of a big brother, creep into our hearts, give us decorations and uniforms, make love to us in order to betray us"—proved true. But such things are not always easy to predict.

In any event, the three Muslim congresses featured constant infighting between those who wanted national autonomy for their separate groups—a version of *mahallaçilik*—and those who wanted a central Muslim government. In the end, they achieved little. Tsarist repression had already begun in 1906 and would worsen. Pan-Turkist intellectuals sought refuge with the Ottomans. Gasprinsky and his relative Yusuf Akçura left the Tsarist world and joined the Young Turks, who had already tasted Pan-Turkism and were ready for more. Their leading Pan-Turkist (and Pan-Turanian) ideologue was Ziya Gökalp (1876–1924), who wrote in a 1911 poem, "For the Turks, Fatherland means neither Turkey or Turkestan; Fatherland is a large and eternal country—Turan!"

At the outbreak of World War I, Gökalp had a poem ready: "The land of the enemy shall be devastated,/ Turkey shall be enlarged and become Turan." His Tatar colleague Akçura supported him: "Pan-Turanism is chiefly an enemy of Russia....The European powers who are in conflict with Russia will support the Pan-Turanian plans of Turkey." Gökalp's ideal had a certain vibrancy:

> They listen to the Occident, and the Occident
> Lends its ear to the voice of their glory.
> They let their heart speak, they let their heart cry,
> But never, never do they forget, these children of Oğuz Khan,
> This land called Turan, and the very name of Turan.
> And you, enemies of the Turks, turn your eyes on these books,
> Learn who were Farabi and Ulugh Bek.
> Do not forget the origin of Avicenna
> And do not forget heroic Attila.

The Young Turks saw matters similarly, and announced: "The ideal of our nation and our people leads us toward the destruction of our Muscovite enemy, in order to obtain thereby a natural frontier to our Empire, which should include and unite all branches of our race."

Such dreams never came true, but they had power. At least, they had enough power that European governments tried to use them to advantage. The Germans, as Ottoman allies, helped disseminate Pan-Turkist and particularly Pan-Islamist propaganda, hoping among other things to stir colonial Muslims against Russia, Britain, and France. The Bolsheviks, promising to give autonomy under their regime, were not above inciting Central Asian groups on nationalist grounds against the tsar.

But in the world war and the Russian civil war that followed it, most of the powers involved were willing to promise anything to anybody. The confusion among Pan-Turanianism, Pan-Turkism, Turkism, Pan-Islam, and the many active nationalisms, large and small, didn't help. The Pan-Turkists themselves had divergent ideas on what they were doing. Some associated Pan-Turkism with modernization. A Tatar Pan-Turk said in 1907 that his goals were "Turkism, Islamism, and Europeanism." An émigré group with Pan-Turkic sympathies, based in Europe, appealed to "today's standard-bearers of Western civilization—Germany, Austria, and Hungary" in 1915: "We Turko-Tatars, bearers of culture up to the present time, believe that Western culture, with the help of the Turko-Tatars, will conquer Russian-Byzantine culture in all Asia." At the huge conference of "Russian Muslims" held in Moscow in 1917—between the February Revolution and the Bolshevik Revolution—one speaker emphasized Turkness: "We are Turks, and the sons of Turks, and we should be proud to be so." Another promoted Islam: "The time is near when all Moslems will rise in defense of their faith and civilization and will initiate the struggle against the Europeans, who continue to regard themselves as the rulers of the universe." The chief problem at the conference, however, was that too many people wanted to have their own little states.

Both Lenin and Stalin understood how valuable this division was to them. They feared Pan-Turkism and Pan-Islam. Localism was a godsend. Stalin caused a manifesto to be published: "Moslems of Russia, Kirghiz and Sarts of Central Asia and Siberia, Turks and Tatars of Transcaucasia, Chechens and mountaineers of the Caucasus—all those whose mosques and prayer houses were destroyed, whose beliefs and customs were trampled under foot by the tsars and oppressors of Russia...from now on your customs and beliefs, your national and cultural institutions, are declared free and inviolable. Organize your national life freely and unhindered. You now have the right to do it. Know that your rights, exactly as the rights of all the peoples of Russia, are now protected by the entire might of the revolution and its organs...." The mixed appeal to Islamic belief and localism was perfectly balanced.

By 1920, the Soviets had crushed most localist Central Asian opposition, and felt it best to redirect Islamic feeling against outside powers. The Third International sponsored a Peoples of the East conference in Baku, at which International president Grigori Zinoviev explained: "The Communist International turns today to the peoples of the East and says to them: Brothers, we summon you to a Holy War first of all against British Imperialism." Within three years, most of the remaining Central Asian leaders—religious, Pan-Turkic, nationalist, micro-nationalist, reformist, even Communist—had disappeared or been executed.

Despite this, the Soviets continued to be obsessed by the threats of Pan-Turkism and Pan-Islam, which they tended to confuse. By 1935, the term Turkestan was forbidden for use in historical publications. The next year, two Central Asian professors attempted to say something nice about Turkic contributions; they were accused of being Pan-Turkists (and nationalists) and disappeared. In 1952, *Pravda* railed against Pan-Turkism, as did the head of the Uzbek Communist Party. A 1954 conference had on its list of five topics "The reactionary contents of Pan-Islamism and Pan-Turkism." That same year, one Smirnov wrote: "The task confronting Soviet investigators of Islam is...unmasking the contemporary role of Islam as a support for the exploiter classes and the colonial regime, disclosing the reactionary, anti-popular essence of the ideology of Pan-Islamism and Pan-Turkism, used primarily by the American imperialists to enslave the peoples of the East." A 1963 Georgian work linked Pan-Turkism to Turkish imperialism, whereas a 1972 work in Kazakh tarred Pan-Turkists with having aided the Nazis.

Pan-Turkism did continue its active life in Turkey, usually in far-right, anti-communist circles. After World War II, the old magazine *Bozkurt* reappeared with its striking motto, "The Turkish race above any other race!" In 1950, the editor of another journal defined the Pan-Turkist: "A Turk who believes in the superiority of the Turkish race, respecting its national past and ready to sacrifice himself for the ideals of Turkdom, especially in the fight against Moscow, the implacable enemy." By the 1960s, Pan-Turkists had a party, the National Action Party, with seats in parliament and an addled leader, Alparslan Türkeş. Türkeş believed that "Turan, that is the union of the Turks, means the union of not only the Asiatic Turks, but of all the Turks. . . ." Türkeş was known to his detractors as "the skull man" because he apparently believed he could identify true Turks by the bumps on their skulls. He remains a minor political force today.

And – who knows? – perhaps Pan-Turkism will revive in Central Asia. "The Soviets created Pan-Turkism and Pan-Islam in order to give names to their own fear. And they wanted to divide people here. Many people began to say they weren't Turks, and academics argued that Uzbeks aren't really Turks," says Uzbek scholar Ibrahim Rakul one afternoon in Tashkent. "Today Turks understand that only Turks will help Turks. *Türkçilik* [Turkishness, also the word often used by Pan-Turkists] means first of all unity of language, then unity of ideology, then the actual work of unity. The state now is interested in these ideas. The history we were taught before was all lies."

19

THE FUNDAMENTAL FORM of Central Asian literature is the *dastan*, an epic poem, recited orally, celebrating the deeds of an *alp*, or people's champion. "The Alp endures many trials and tribulations," writes the scholar H. B. Paksoy, "which ultimately are shared by a supporting cast. His problems are nearly always aggravated by one or more traitors, who although a problem to the Alp, can never stop his ineluctable progress toward victory. His success is celebrated by a *toy*, or lavish feast. Traitors and enemies are dealt with, frequently paying with their lives for their treachery, but more often left to roam the earth in search of some kind of reconciliation with their consciences and with God. . . . Dastan characteristically refers to historical events; it is a repository of historical memory, a record of the events and customs of its creators and their descendants. The dastan travels with Central Asians, and, like its immediate owners, it is not bothered with borders. . . . The dastan is the collective pride of tribes, confederations of tribes and even larger units. It serves as a kind of birth certificate, national anthem and proof of citizenship all rolled into one. . . . Dastans are intended to be both didactic and emotive."

Some of the great "mother *dastans*," such as *Alpamıs* and *Dede Korkut*, have been recited since pre-Islamic times; others — for example, *Chora Batır*, which relates the fight of Khazan Tatars against Russians — are more recent. Although Soviet scholars once praised the *dastanlar*, calling *Alpamıs* "the liberty song of Central Asian national fighting against the alien invaders," beginning in the 1950s they changed their minds and, for example, found *Alpamıs* "impregnated with the poison of feudalism and reaction, breathing Muslim fanaticism and preaching hatred towards foreigners." Officialdom strained its every resource to eliminate all written copies of *Chora Batır*.

In 1981, the Uzbek writer Mammaduli Mahmudov published a short new *dastan* called *The Immortal Cliffs*. The *dastan* had two time frames: in the initial period, two heroes bring their tribe from Central Asia into the Jizzakh mountains to escape Genghis Khan; in the second period, the late 19th century, one of their descendants, Buranbek, battles successfully against the Russians. He studies the life and teachings of Tamerlane, in particular, and applies the lessons learned to fighting the tsar. Among other things, Mahmudov emphasized in *The Immortal Cliffs* that the Arabs who brought Islam were no better than the Russians were centuries later, and that all Turkish peoples should unite in order to gain freedom.

While the Soviet authorities may or may not have welcomed Mahmudov's critique of the Arab invasion and of Islam, they certainly did not appreciate the rest of *The Immortal Cliffs*. Mahmudov was criticized for "a lack of true ideological content, inattention in defining the world view, and deviation from a clear-cut class position in evaluating some historical events and individuals." He apologized, blaming himself for "rating my creative potentials higher than I should have done," affirming his "affection" for the Russian people and gratitude for all they'd done to aid their Central Asian brothers and sisters. The authorities were afraid, not only of Mahmudov but of other Central Asian writers who had begun to dwell, however elliptically, on the themes of Central Asian unity and Russian imperialism. In his short story "The Kiowah Sun" (1981), Davran Khurshid offered a pointed historical parable about the struggle of some American Indians against "white" people. Uzbeks refer to Russians as *ak kulaklar*, "white-ears." In "The Sun Is Also Fire" (1980), Alisher Ibadinov had his *alp*, Teginbek, oppose the Arab invasion and Islamization. Teginbek says, "I will mobilize all Turks into action. Let us steadfastly hold onto the fortress. No peace for those who sell or seize the homeland!" When Teginbek decides to burn a traitor who has advocated Islam and the Arab language, he asks her, "Why have you lost the tongue of our parents and praised God in another language? After all, who goes hunting after two animals and who is born by two mothers? The mother tongue and motherland they are, after all, the heart. Can there be two hearts?"

Such unsubtle messages enjoyed a vogue among Central Asian intellectuals, not only in Uzbekistan, and still do. And whatever hardships Mammaduli Mahmudov suffered after publishing *The Immortal Cliffs*, he doesn't suffer them anymore. Rather he sits in his spacious office at the Turkic Cultural Center in Tashkent. He chainsmokes Marlboros, floats flamboyant ideas, and affects the air of a colorfully menacing genius. On his wall hangs a large painting of mountains at dusk. At their base are the lights of a village, and a river.

"This is where we were born. There are two hundred and fifty million Turks, in all religions—Jews, Buddhists, Hindus, the Fire religion, Christian. The mountains represent all the different Turkish groups. Uzbeks are not a 'nation.' All Turks came from the Uzbek Turks. There is no Uzbek nationality. We are the original Turks.

"Everybody is afraid of Turkish unification, because with it the Turks might become powerful. The Arabs and Persians were never friends of the Turks, even though they were Muslim. The only friends of the Turkish people are the Turks themselves."

(As Mahmudov speaks you remember a similar proverb: "The Kurd has no friends.")

Mahmudov takes a dim view of Islam and the possibility of Turkic peoples uniting on the basis of their common religion. "The Shiites, the Sunnis, they have tried to unite all Muslims. But it's impossible to unite Muslims. Besides, Islam is not our religion. The Arabs invaded. We fought them for three hundred years. This is my idea; others don't like it. Before the Arabs, we had seven alphabets. The

Arabs acted like the Russians. They enforced the use of their language, destroyed our monuments.

"So now we don't know our pre-Arab culture. They destroyed our past, our books. They made people accept Islam. When the Russians came, they used Arab policy. They changed the alphabet. It was KGB policy not to put clever men in leadership positions. There was a special order. They killed the clever ones. When the clever ones died, the country became like a headless body.

"After Tamerlane, because of religion Turkestan was divided into three khanates. Islam, to me, shouldn't play a great role. In the first place, there should be a Turkic nation. So religion shouldn't be involved. If it is, we will be divided into different khanates."

Divide-and-rule had, of course, been a useful Russian strategy for over a century. "The Russians, especially, divided Turkestan into many nations. After dividing, they began to rule. The idea goes back to Peter the Great. Peter the Great said, in his [apocryphal] will, 'Always make war between Sunnis and Shiites, always make war between Persians and Turks. They must fight each other. Otherwise they might become strong and threaten Russia.' Now all of the world tries to put Arabs and Kurds against the Turks. Europe puts Bulgarian Turks against Bulgarians.

"When Germany unified, Turks felt themselves happy. All nations should unify and be what they want. I will be glad if the Angles and Saxons unify, if the Jews unify. We must create a Turkic nation again. When Russia, Belarus, and Ukraine made moves toward unity, they showed their real face: They wanted to create a *Slavic* nation. I immediately called Karimov, and Akayev [Kyrgyzstan president], Niyazov [Turkmenistan president], Nazarbayev [Kazakhstan president]. I got no response."

On one hand, Mahmudov may not have got a response because his ideas seem so easily to cross the line from reasonableness into idiocy. "The American Indians are also ex-Turks. And the Japanese, Chinese, Mongols, and Bulgarians. One thousand years ago, Turks went from the mountains to Turkey. They invaded the Caucasus, Iran. They all came from the same parents. There were also Turks around the Mediterranean. The Trojans were Turks."

On the other hand, he may not have got a response because there is something deeply compelling about Pan-Turkism, something

205

emotionally obvious and powerful—a principle of pride and unity in a Central Asia nearly empty of anything, beyond nationalism and the struggle for power, that could be honored as a principle. "The Turks are awakening," he says. "The 21st century will be the Turkish century. The U.S. and former U.S.S.R. are afraid of two things—Muslims and Turks. But we will possess their world throne one day." Mahmudov's cultural center is giving Turkish lessons. He has joined a group advocating Turkic unity that has branches all over Central Asia. He's the chief of an organizing committee seeking to create a single language for all Turks. "Our main idea is to explain the identity of Turks to Turks." Mahmudov keeps in contact with Alparslan Türkeş, the Turkish colonel, politician, and phrenologist. Mahmudov's only difference with Türkeş, he says, is that the latter wants to combine his cultural politics with Islam.

"We have bought a building and a hotel. In the near future, we will have our own newspaper." Mahmudov is a laughable, frightening figure, because he's selling something that ex–Communists, Islamic revivalists, and democrats alike don't have and may perhaps need: a glorious romance of the past for people whose past was stolen long ago and whose future remains up for grabs.

20

NASRUDDIN'S FATHER, A PROFESSOR, stands in the hallway in creased slacks and a clean, freshly pressed shirt. Is that a hint of cologne in the air? Normally a most casual dresser around the house, a short man with slippery eyeglasses and a prosperous belly, he looks both uncomfortable and proud of himself.

"I'm going to a *gap* with my college schoolmates," he explains. His mother laughs mischievously: "Ah-ah! Going to a *gap*!"

From *gapirmok*, "to speak," *gap* is the word for parties, but parties of a very specific sort. *Gaplar* normally take place once a month. The rounds of *gaplar* cement the urban Uzbek social world. Each tier of social advancement brings with it a new *gap*. First, and most important, is the *mahalla* schoolmates' *gap*. There will, depending on one's circumstances, be a university schoolmates' *gap*, a professional-training *gap*, workplace *gap*, wife's schoolmates/friends-from-the-old-neighborhood *gap*. *Gap* can also mean "gossip." The hosting of a *gap* will rotate among a given group's members, with much pressure brought to bear on the host to acquit himself or herself well. One spends one's entire life working these rounds of *gaplar*.

Ah, the warm night, the prospect of a *gap*. The professor emerges, stands at the top of the front steps to test the air. His mother sits on the bench gazing at him. He strides with confident idleness down the steps and into the street, where he stands again, greeting passersby with dignity. The night, the *gap*! How splendid, clean, well-fed and well-pressed he looks! And he strolls off.

Late the next morning, you will find him sprawled uncomfortably in the dining room, comporting himself like an accumulation of fluids all out of balance. How was the *gap* last night? Words form within him but somehow never make it to the outside world. He'll spend the rest of the day alternating between naps on the floor and puttering walks outside, trying to sweat out his hangover beneath the cherry trees, which are already past their prime, and the apple trees, whose fruit hasn't yet ripened.

21

"DON'T EVER FORGET," Nasruddin says, "that we were conquered. That's the most important thing to remember."

22

THE MOST RETROGRADE and horrifying (Soviet view) and most honorable (emerging Uzbek view) revolt against Communist rule was the Basmachi movement. *Basmachi* means "bandit." Originally applied by the rebels' detractors, the term was taken up by many supporters, as were the terms *mujahiddin* and, for the leaders, *korbaşılar*, "lords."

The ground for the Basmachi war of 1918 to 1922 was well prepared in Uzbekistan and surroundings by constant famine, the abysmal rule of a handful of washed-up colonialists followed by the worse despotism of the Tashkent Soviet, economic collapse, general anarchy, a wildly divided Central Asian opposition, and the bloody revolt of 1916. Although the 1916 events were triggered by a first-time order for conscription of Muslims, fighting soon managed to take on an anti-Russian and anti-infidel cast. A Soviet estimate puts the loss of life in Russian Turkestan between 1914 and 1918 at one million, mainly due to the 1916 revolt.

With the October 1917 Revolution, the situation worsened. The Bolsheviks had less confidence in Central Asians than had the Tsarists, and they announced at a congress of Turkestan Soviets in November that "the inclusion of the Mussulmans in the organs of the Higher Revolutionary Power appears at present moment unacceptable." Central Asians hoping for a Communist deliverance had to rethink matters. A *mullah*-dominated Muslim conference held in November in Tashkent, concurrently with the Bolshevik congress, proposed coalition with the Bolsheviks—which the Bolsheviks quickly rejected in favor of an all-European administration. The Soviet theory was simple: since there was no Muslim proletariat (Tsarist policy had kept proletarian work in Christian hands), there could hardly be a Muslim Soviet. Overnight, the petty colonialists of Tashkent, most of them Russians, were transformed into "the proletariat," and they proceeded to rule in the name of Communism.

Desperate Muslim leaders convened in December 1917 in Kokand, in the Ferghana valley, and proclaimed a Provisional Government of Turkestan. As Mustafa Chokayev, its president, later wrote: "The Russians, who had done nothing for us, politically or culturally, in half a century, had yet managed to destroy all our old national structure and customs. The tribal regime was on the eve of complete break-up. Persons of authority had disappeared, with none to replace them, so when the revolution broke out we folk of Turkestan were unable to create anything solid. All the efforts of a few Turkestani intellectuals were directed to the hurried creation of some sort of centre. . . ." The Kokand government appealed to Moscow for help against Tashkent, to which Stalin replied that if they didn't like the Tashkent Soviet they should overthrow it. The opposite happened. The Tashkent Bolsheviks, commanding starved European prisoners of war, took Kokand in February 1918, sacked it, and burned it to the ground, leaving thousands dead.

This was enough to inspire local *korbaşılar* to take up arms. As

Chokayev wrote, they were mainly motivated by "the instinct of self-preservation," with little ideology beyond Muslim faith, hatred of Russians, and localism. The Ferghana valley *korbaşılar* organized a rural government, leaving the cities to the Russians. They collected taxes, administered law, issued visas. The Bolsheviks sent forces against the Basmachi, with little success – and in any case the Bolsheviks were already facing opposition within ethnic European ranks. Conditions degenerated to such a degree that in 1919 a "Peasant Army" of starving Russians joined the Basmachi. By October 1919, a Russian-Muslim Provisional Ferghana Government had formed.

Meanwhile, the Moscow Bolsheviks reasoned that the time was ripe for some internationalist Pan-Islamic Bolshevism, the kind of ideological hybrid weirdly common at the time. They appealed to Central Asian Muslims to join the fight against British imperialism and infidels in general. This drove a wedge between the Basmachis and their Russian peasant comrades. A second Bolshevik propaganda offensive, promising gentleness, further weakened the Ferghana government. The spruced-up Tashkent Soviet appealed to the Basmachis: "To those who are styled robbers but are actually innocent, poor labouring classes: You are ignorant of the political status of the world and what revolution has done to drive away this ignorance." A similar, if less condescending, appeal to the Peasant Army led it, along with some Basmachis, to give up in January 1920.

Many Basmachis remained under arms, however, and the irritated Bolsheviks resorted to fierce repression. The Ferghana Basmachis regrouped and proclaimed yet another government, this time of the whole of Turkestan. The Basmachi did rather well in 1920, limiting themselves to guerrilla warfare, taking and losing towns with equal speed. Meanwhile, the emirate of Bukhara, controlling a large territory west and south of Tashkent, was gradually being undermined. The emir himself had little grasp of the situation; the Bukhara Central Asians were frantically divided; and by August 1920 the Bolsheviks had succeeded in taking the city itself. The emir fled into the mountains, from where he wrote to the British king, whom he addressed as "brother." He asked for £100,000, twenty thousand rifles, thirty guns, and ten airplanes. "These things may kindly be dispatched to me quickly with my above-mentioned officials, and this will make me happy." The emir received nothing. The new Bukharan government proclaimed: "Brothers, crush all the adherents of the old regime, and join the ranks of the Bukharan Red Army! Foment trouble!"

The emir's loyalists in the northern mountains of what is now Tajikistan fomented some trouble themselves. The Red Army marched against them, with considerable success, but committed such atrocities along the way that the Red Bukharans began to lose their edge and regret having been Soviet tools. They entered into negotiations with the Basmachi, who hated the Red Bukharans as petty, weak-kneed modernists. The Soviets changed tactics, again appealing to Pan-Islam by sending Enver Paşa, former Ottoman minister of war, who had lost a power struggle to Atatürk and had been freelancing since 1918. Enver surprised the Soviets, however, by defecting and taking part of the Red Bukharan government with him. He attempted to unite the emir's supporters with the Ferghana valley Basmachi and others. They fought well, though often against each other as well as against the Red Army. They were, however, outmanned and outgunned, even though the Bolsheviks' casualties between 1920 and 1923 have been estimated at 327,000. The Red Army kept up a steady campaign, and by fall 1922 Enver Paşa was dead. The Basmachi fighters, especially the emir's loyal defender, Ibrahim Bek, continued the fight, but the overall war was lost. Ibrahim Bek, uniformly described as tireless and fanatical, battled on until 1931, when he was captured and then executed in Tashkent.

The story of this long war against the Soviets, undertaken sometimes in the name of localism, sometimes for Islam, sometimes for Turkestan, would henceforth be kept from Central Asians, mentioned briefly as a rear guard action by backward lunatics. Even this judgment would, after the 1930s, be suppressed, to a point where the Basmachi War was hardly mentioned at all.

23

THIS TUESDAY AFTERNOON the heat has become nearly unbearable. You sit on the *kravat*, reading, hoping for a breeze. Nasruddin's paternal grandmother sleeps upstairs, as she does every afternoon. Nasruddin is away at his maternal grandmother's house. Her health shows no signs of improving. He's been laying concrete these last few days and painting, preparing her house for the twenty-day mourning period he's afraid is not far off. The condition of his maternal grandmother seems to color everything he does. He desperately wants her to live, but what can he do? Comfort his mother, who has been at her side for so long, who never comes home anymore, who has hardly been eating and is beginning to show signs of collapse herself as she attends her mother, the only immediate relative she has apart from one aunt. Nasruddin lays concrete, paints the walls: renders service. When he comes home he must report to everyone on her condition – everyone except his paternal grandmother, whom no one wants to upset unnecessarily. She's either eighty-four or eighty-five; she knows only the year she was born, not the date. As a young woman she wore the *paranca*, the black outfit that covers the entire body, with a horsehair mesh over the face. She still has hers, folded away. Now she wears thin silk shifts and you can see how tiny she is, how seemingly fragile. She bore fourteen children, seven of whom lived to adulthood. Little Bil is her main interest and amusement, though she's not strong enough to play with him. She just watches, calls his name, laughs.

At 3:30, music starts a few gardens away. The air is already thick with the smell of pilaf being cooked. The band plays fast, classical Uzbek music though with a set of drums and a cymbal. Two lovely adolescent girls dance together in the orchard next door, their hands tracing patterns gently in the air. The young wife of their household walks out, in a bright red-and-green *atlas*, toward the orchard, starts and retreats three steps when a cat crosses in front of her. This is a Russian superstition that has jumped cultures. The cat moves on. She enters the orchard and looks at the laughing girls. The little purple plants in your *mahalla* have just bloomed. Soon the large apples will be ripe enough to eat. (The small ones, less sweet, already litter the ground.) This morning we ate the first jam made from a species of tiny, sour berry. In another hour or two, a newly married couple will walk down the street, preceded by a band featuring an extremely long horn that makes a distinctive honking screech and a woodwind riffing elaborately. Relatives and friends will walk behind the couple.

Nasruddin's paternal grandmother emerges suddenly from the house. "*Toy boladı!*" she shouts happily to no one in particular.

"There's going to be a celebration!" The word *toy* for "celebration" lands nicely on an Anglophone's ear. Grandmother maneuvers toward the bench, laughing her "oh! oh!" laugh and chuckling in its wake.

24

THE DREAM OF MANY an Uzbek boy and girl: to visit Shohimardon. The name means "brave Shah," but to schoolchildren it means a ferris wheel, other carnival rides, children they don't know, nearly undivided parental attention, sweet treats, peacocks on leashes, and a stuffed toy leopard. It means pictures taken by raffish boy entrepreneurs, taken in front of a backdrop of California mountains or of Indian movie stars. Shohimardon means drunken men, and responsible women buying packets of rice and spices to prepare pilaf on open platforms next to flowing streams. The luckiest children will stay at summer camps upstream from the town, go hiking, sing songs, perform calisthenics, and grapple with the rare spectacle of dozens of Uzbek boys and girls dressed only in shorts and T-shirts, leaping about in pure alpine air and drinking clean water from the rivers, streams, and rivulets that rush down from snowy peaks.

You reach Shohimardon by bus from the Ferghana valley, at the rim of which you cross the border of Kyrgyzstan. You and Nasruddin affect a look of heat prostration—you've already secured the confidence of your fellow passengers—and the border guards wave the bus through without checking passports. "I hope one day all borders will be as easy as this," Nasruddin says. Shohimardon is surrounded by Kyrgyzstan, except for the roadway that connects it to Uzbekistan. The Uzbeks traded some pastureland nearby for Shohimardon, whose population is mainly Uzbek.

You and Nasruddin do not linger among the carnival rides and candy sellers; rather, you head for the Hamza Museum, on a bluff overlooking Shohimardon. The last of four children, Hamza Hakimzade Niyazı was born in 1889 in the Ferghana valley city of Kokand (home of the two-month republic of 1917–18). He died in 1929, in Shohimardon, murdered by a group of villagers. His father, Ibn Yamin Niyazoğlu, was a doctor. Having learned Uzbek and Persian as a young boy, Hamza attended a Muslim school, or *madrassa*, beginning in 1899 – his eldest brother, Israel, had taught in a *madrassa*. The family fortunes declined, and Hamza went to work in a cotton mill owned by a rich local, Sadiq Bey. At night, he studied more Western subjects, including Russian, under a man named Arlov. He briefly attempted to finish his studies of the Koran and Arabic in Bukhara, but he hadn't enough money. In 1911, Hamza opened his own school in Kokand, writing his own textbooks and affronting the clergy with the non-Muslim content of his teachings. His marriage the next year to a Russian woman, Aksinya Uvarova, did not improve his standing with the Uzbek clergy. In 1913, he made the *hadj*, reaching Mecca by way of Afghanistan and India, thence by ship to Arabia. He returned via Syria, Lebanon, Istanbul, and Odessa. The journey took a year.

By 1915, he had relocated from Kokand to Margelan, in the Ferghana valley, at the foot of the Kyrgyz mountains. He began to train teachers and publish poetry, though he'd been writing verse since his late teens. Between 1915 and 1917 seven volumes of his poetry appeared, as did short stories, plays, and teaching materials. His pedagogical work attracted the attention of Uzbek *jadid* ("renewal") reformers who were active at the time. The anti-Tsarist rebellions of 1916 and the February 1917 revolution radicalized Hamza. He organized meetings and demonstrations and soon had to flee into Chinese Turkestan. He returned in 1918 after the Bolsheviks secured power. During the civil war, Hamza toured the Ferghana valley and other Central Asian areas with his drama troupe, Red East. Western theater was new to Uzbek audiences and made for effective propaganda. In 1920, Hamza was among the few bold Uzbeks to join the Communist Party.

As Soviet control solidified in the early 1920s, Hamza travelled through much of Uzbekistan establishing schools, putting on skits and plays, advocating the liberation of women from *mahrem* and the veil, propagandizing for the new Soviet era, and distancing himself from the *jadid* reformers, whose days were, by this time, easily numbered. The *jadid*ists weren't especially Communist – sometimes they were resolutely anti-Communist – and they were, for the most part, nationalist. Having observed Tsarist imperialism for many decades, they tended to be cool toward Soviet empire-building. Hamza was not. He discerned in it the future. He joined, and for a time headed,

213

the Society of Atheists. In 1926 the Soviet government named him National Poet. In August 1928 he moved to Shohimardon, armed with the first Five Year Plan.

To reach the Hamza Museum in Shohimardon, you depart from a somewhat untended esplanade favored by rambunctious children, weary parents, and boys giving their peacocks a rest from the rigors of souvenir photo-taking. You then climb up a long, steep staircase. Older visitors huff and puff and complain about the heat. At one of the rest stops along the climb an elderly man begs. For a ruble he recites a prayer and blesses you.

The Uzbek Soviet government constructed the first Hamza Museum in 1952. On May 18, 1989, it inaugurated the present museum and the esplanade below, built at a cost of over two million rubles, to mark the centennary of Hamza's birth. A young woman takes you through the two-storey complex. She shows you a life-size diorama of one of Hamza's homes, including the original carpet and a mortar and pestle. You see a period cartoon illustrating how a poor man was exploited by the local lords, rich men, and so on; a poster showing "Long Live Soviets," the title of a Hamza poem, on a flag; an order from Tsar Nicholas II permitting the peasants to work only eight hours each day rather than twelve; a 1917 photo of Uzbek revolutionaries hanging from scaffolds. "They were poor peasants and workers," the young woman says, "and they raised their hands against the king." Hamza appears in a photograph from 1919, taken as he toured Uzbek territory rallying the Red Army during the civil war; he carries a violin case. You see vivid woodcuts of Red forces (in red) crushing their opponents (in black).

You see photos of women wearing *parancalar*, faces invisible behind the fine horsehair grilles. "Because they were beautiful," the young woman says, "they had to conceal their faces." More photos: of Nurhan, the first Uzbek actress, who performed without a veil and was killed by her brothers at age sixteen; another woman, a propagandist, killed; a third, Tursanay, killed by her husband. Hamza wrote a poem for her. You see photos of these mutilated corpses, their faces smashed in, and photos of Uzbek women from Hamza's troupes, grinning, standing proudly, affecting the stagey expressions of their characters. "The problem was that the Uzbek women

214

were so pretty," your guide says, smiling. "Don't you think they're beautiful?"

The light outside the museum is blinding and your lungs struggle with the thin air. Looking north, toward the Ferghana valley, you see a stone flume on the mountainside, coming down a canyon to your left. Hamza had this flume built to water a garden, straight across the gorge from where you stand; later it would be a Young Pioneer camp. Hamza opened a school in Shohimardon, organized a collective, and built a teahouse; it stood in the park at the base of the staircase, directly below you. He also built a power station to make use of the rushing waters. On the eighth of March, 1928, Hamza held a big meeting for women in front of the teahouse. Twenty-three of them took off their *parancalar*, making a pile of black fabric and horsehair. A group of pious villagers then organized. On March 19 they called to Hamza, invited him to come behind the teahouse. There they murdered him with knives and stoned him to disfigure his corpse. They threw his body into a crevice beneath the flume and the new garden. After three days, the body was found and buried in the garden. Ten years later, Hamza's corpse was moved from the garden to its present tomb, next to the museum. According to the Hamza museum's director, the actual killers fled Shohimardon, but sixty people were arrested and five shot. Shohimardon became a symbol of the Soviet struggle against Islam. The government renamed Shohimardon "Hamzaabad," a name that never took. The biographies of his killers would gradually be amended so that they included not only Muslim clerics but also lackeys of imperialism, bourgeois nationalists, reactionaries, and obscurantists. The state drama theater in Tashkent would be named for him, the Hamza Prize first awarded in 1964. He would be praised as the founder of Soviet Uzbek literature and the pioneer of socialist realism in Uzbek, although he'd been dead some years before socialist realism became doctrine. The Uzbek writer Hamid Alimjan would build much of his notable career on a poem called "Shohimardon," which he wrote to commemorate Hamza.

Hamza's impressive roofed tomb is surrounded on three sides by iron bars, with a stone wall at its head. Above the tomb is a line from one of his poems: "We will create new life/ in our own time./ Then we will live/ forever." Coins, tossed by visitors, litter the tomb.

The statue of Hamza has him wearing a skullcap. "You see," Nasruddin says, "he was a *Muslim*. He wrote mystical poems, Sufi poems." The museum director says that Hamza wrote Muslim poetry all his life, but that it wasn't published until 1989, when the Soviet hold on cultural expression had sufficiently weakened. Directly in front of the museum, on the bluff's edge, stands a small amphitheater, scaffolding, and a brick construction. You drink water from a pipe, wash your face and hands. The construction is a tomb of Ali, cousin of Muhammad, key figure for all Muslims though particularly for Shiites. One story has it that Hamza was killed while on his way to convert this shrine into a Communist museum. Also nearby stands a Communist war monument, which is slated for destruction once the Ali shrine has been rebuilt.

"Ali was one of the first to accept Islam," the museum director, a native of Shohimardon, says. "People at first laughed at Muhammad. Only Ali and Fatima [Ali's wife and Muhammad's daughter] believed him. After Muhammad's death, Ali was the last of four kings. This is his tomb. There were many legends about Ali. It's said he was buried surrounded by mountains where two rivers meet—as here. There are seven places of this description in the Muslim world. Nobody knows where Ali is really buried. The tomb was a ruin by 1951. Now we are rebuilding it. We began in 1992."

"Shohimardon": "the brave king," or "shah" (a Persian word), or, perhaps most accurately, "caliph." The village was named for Muhammad's cousin and that is the name that has stuck. "In Hamza's time," the museum director says, "there were seven mosques in Shohimardon. They were all destroyed. Now, a new one is being built. There are six *mahallalar* in Shohimardon, and eventually each will have its own mosque."

You and Nasruddin go to have pilaf with the museum director and some other men. The heavy meal, the required toasts with vodka, and the heat make this multiple shrine of Shohimardon below you in its defile, with its carnival rides, peacocks, and tinny music—they make it shimmer and split. Russians haven't been coming here so much since the events in nearby Osh. In mid-1990, Kyrgyz and Uzbeks battled each other for days, supposedly over land. The writer Marat Akchurin, a Tatar from Tashkent, had the misfortune then to be in the Kyrgyz capital, Frunze (now Bishkek), "which used to be shady and green, [but] now looked like an active volcano at the moment of eruption. At a bus station where I came to find a seat for Tashkent, crowds of enraged Kirghiz youths were commandeering buses to go to the Osh province and destroy Uzbeks. The general hysteria was inflamed by reports that Kirghiz babies had been thrown onto bonfires by Uzbek crowds in Uzgen. It was clear that new and terrible anti-Uzbek violence had broken out in two city markets with casualties on both sides.

"In the city centre," Akchurin continues, "several young men, evidently hurrying from one mêlée to another, said they were students at the local polytechnic institute. I asked them to explain what was going on, and one, half-smiling, answered that they were 'sick of living in the most Soviet among all the Soviet republics, which looked more like a Disneyland than a normal State.' 'And what do Uzbeks have to do with it?' I asked, rashly. 'They are too fertile. And they need more and more living space,' one of them answered studiedly.

" 'Wait a minute—who is he?' the third one cried out, growing pale. 'I'm a journalist from Moscow,' I said as calmly as possible and put down my bag, ready to defend myself. I at once found myself in a situation where two big men were holding my arms, and a third was pounding me with his fists, after which all three of them had five more minutes' fun laying into me with their feet."

The men around you at lunch say that most of the people coming to Shohimardon since the Osh events have been Uzbeks, though the valley is surrounded by Kyrgyzstan. These days, local Uzbeks are concerned about a plan to build an elaborate ski lift from near Shohimardon to the high lake that feeds it. The project has two sponsors: a Kyrgyz chemical plant and a Kyrgyz metal-casting plant. They anticipate greater tourism revenues. The locals anticipate too many visitors and water pollution. The clear mountain waters are one of Shohimardon's biggest draws and, along with pristine air and wild beauty, the pride of its residents. Uzbek tourism workers have allegedly been replaced with Kyrgyz workers. Half the lake belongs to Kyrgyzstan, half to Uzbekistan.

"I don't think there will be a war over this," says the museum director.

"No, there won't," says a local man. "We're all Muslims. And if the water becomes dirty, the Kyrgyz downstream will also suffer."

After lunch you wander with Nasruddin up behind the museum to a cemetery. In 1921, near the graveyard, twenty-four Red Army soldiers were killed by Central Asian rebels who had been hiding in the mountains. The besieged soldiers ran out of ammunition and were massacred. The doomed monument next to the shrine of Ali commemorates this event. The graveyard itself is surrounded by a wire fence, which has bits of fabric tied to it, as do the bushes and trees. You walk with Nasruddin, admiring the view, when he says he will catch up in a moment. He goes off to some decorated shrubs, kneels, prays with his hands together, open before him, their palms to the sky. And you scramble downward toward the village.

The next morning is clear and cool, you walk at sunrise up the valley, up a narrow road toward the lake called Kopkurbon. The road meanders past small youth camps, sanatoria, and holiday sites. On the steep slopes you see huts here and there, patches of pasture or even some tilled land. Occasionally you pass a spring or a tree decorated with fluttering cloth offerings. "Don't walk so fast," says Nasruddin, in a scolding mood. "Go slowly and look around you. See how beautiful it is? How can anyone say God doesn't exist when they see this?"

After a few kilometers you reach a touristic outpost at the canyon's head. Above you rises a dizzying wall of talus and boulders, bisected by a cable from which hang tiny enclosed cabins. The lift isn't working this early, so you make your way up a random path, crisscrossing over icy rivulets that emerge unpredictably from the jumble. "Kopkurbon" means something like "many (*kop*) victims"; *kurbon* is also the word for "sacrifice," as in animal sacrifice. An earthquake in 1821 killed some ninety-five percent of the valley's residents. The Uzbeks slowly repopulated the valley. (Kyrgyz, according to local Uzbeks, only appeared in the last twenty years with the growth of tourism.) Beneath the stones lie hundreds of bodies, *kop kurbon*. When the earthquake ended, this wall of talus and boulders stopped up the streams and created a lake. All along your path, the shrubs and small trees are covered with ribbons and strings. You watch their fluttering and hear the burbling of streams as you pant upward.

At the crest you see this dark blue impenetrable lake, cupped among the mountains; and you sit together beside it. A rowboat floats tethered to a post. "How can anyone say God does not exist?" Nasruddin looks at you. High on one slope, goats knock stones loose; villagers let their goats wander in summer. From the far end of the lake you hear whistling, a jaunty tune with tremblings of melancholy.

Too soon, other visitors appear and you leave, back down the unstable slope, where Nasruddin pauses once more to pray.

25

NASRUDDIN'S GRANDMOTHER DIED at five this morning. She hadn't taken food for a month. Of six brothers and two sisters, only one sister remains. "Do you know what my grandmother's deathbed advice to her was?" Nasruddin asks as you sit on the *kravat* under the sour cherry tree. "She said, 'Take it easy. Don't worry so much.' The corpse washer said she was a saint. The corpse washer comes in a full *paranca*, an old woman. She looked at my grandmother and said, 'She is an angel. I have only seen such a woman once before in my life.' "

Nasruddin says: "Uzbeks live with their parents. Parents are wise, they have seen a lot. My father can remember the war, when women would prostitute themselves for bread. This was a time when prostitutes would be stoned to death. But nobody touched them, because they knew that life had forced them to do this. Parents can give you advice. When they are gone, you will need advice and try to go to them but they're not there. And you don't know what to do."

26

WHEN YOU ARE in the countryside, entering or leaving someone's home, meeting a friend, greeting a guest, or just hanging around the *mahalla*, you must practice an elaborate politeness. At the least, *salaam aleikum* and *waleikum asalaam* are exchanged, as you hold your right hand at the base of your ribcage and bow slightly. You do this even when riding a horse or donkey, bicycle or motorcycle, even, if circumstances permit, when in a car. Outside of busy city streets, you greet every single person between adolescence and death who comes closer than, say, thirty feet in the countryside or fifteen in the urban *mahalla*. On any given day, walking up and down the street in your *mahalla*, you will greet dozens of people; the number goes up in the country. These are only the most basic greetings. More substantial encounters involve a lengthy call and response to establish family health and general well being before other subjects can be broached. Women's patterns differ slightly, in that two women will greet each other by placing their right hands on each other's left shoulders. Men sometimes shake hands, especially in the cities or at gatherings. If as a man you encounter a group of men from the village or *mahalla*, you may well shake hands with every one of them, particularly when you are the senior person or a guest. Upon entering or leaving a room as a group, each man vies to let the others pass first, to outdo his companions in humility.

Everywhere you go, you pray. When you pass a cemetery or an ancient tomb, you pray, holding your hands open before you then passing them over your face as if to wipe it clean. Before meals, or any kind of meeting, you pray. The only exceptions are strictly business meetings or meetings with non-Muslims. When a new guest arrives, you pray again to welcome him. If you have been discussing matters out on the *kravat* at night, when the discussion ends you make the motion of prayer before leaving. You do the same thing at the end of any meal, when passing any holy site, or indeed at any moment when you feel yourself being touched by anything outside your own mortality.

27

COULD ISLAM UNIFY Central Asians, or at least Uzbeks? The tsars recognized in organized Islam—the *mullahs* and *imams*, the lower schools and the *madrassas*, the stable blend of customary and *shariat* law—a natural ally, and had, with exceptions, supported it. Back in 1788, Catherine the Great created an Assembly of Muftis. *Mullahs* were exempt from taxes, and the income-producing properties of religious institutions, the *waqf*, were protected. As classic colonizers, the Russians wanted more than anything a quiescent native population. They allowed and even encouraged official Islam, particularly against the Sufi *tarikatlar*—above all, against the widespread Naqshbandi *tarikat*. A *tarikat* is less susceptible to the appeal of a bureaucratic life and the material blandishments of this world. And, indeed, the revolts against Tsarist rule that invoked Islam were almost always linked to the *tarikatlar*.

The Soviets were a new and quite 20th-century species of imperialist. Although, of course, the Bolsheviks frequently used Islam to rally Muslims against momentary enemies—a trick also used at various times by the British, Italians, French, Germans, Americans, and others—they generally loathed Islam, and once their power was secure, they did their best to lure their Muslim charges toward "scientific atheism." They established Atheism Museums in the Asian republics, taught atheism in schools, promoted books like *The Little Dictionary of Scientific Atheism*. They, and modernist Asians, railed against the "black *mullahs*" and "forces of religious reaction and fanaticism." In the early days, they killed religious leaders wherever they could be found, destroyed religious materials, closed mosques and *madrassas*, and extirpated the perfidious *tarikatlar* as ruthlessly as possible. *Shariat* courts closed; *waqf* property was taken. The Soviets instituted a dramatically reduced system of official mosques and *madrassas* under four Spiritual Directorates.

In the 1980s, Gorbachev raised the spectre of "Islamic fundamentalism," and the possibility of Islamic revival clearly preyed on the Moscow mind. It must have been strange and alarming to consider that a modern, secular, Western, progressive ideology such as Communism could lose to backward, feudal, reactionary, obscurantist Islam. Such simplistic fears have also preyed on minds outside Moscow.

They prey on Uzbek minds, on those many Uzbeks who enjoy certain aspects of non-Muslim life (a completely secular legal system, alcohol, not wearing a *paranca*, a thorough separation of church and state), and on those who have power and don't want to share it with anyone. The latter group, essentially neo-Communists, constantly threaten that if they are unseated the "black *mullahs*," aided by Iran, Saudi Arabia, Pakistan, Libya, and who knows what other power, will propel Uzbekistan into some unspecified but very distant past.

Yet organized Islam is reviving in Uzbekistan, and is perhaps the one possibly constructive thing that most Uzbek citizens have in common. In fact, the government itself encourages some kinds of Islam—Islamic tourism (a hard-currency earner), and a more expansive version of Soviet official Islam. The government tries to be pro-Islam and anti-Islam at the same time, seeking to distinguish carefully between an Islam that supports its authoritarian power and an Islam that doesn't.

You go to visit a young *imam* at a new mosque in the old quarter of Tashkent. Fakhriddin takes you. The *imam* is around thirty, bearded, slender and strong. His little office off the mosque courtyard has a tape player and loads of cassettes, books, an unusually up-to-date telephone, and a suitcase. He lives here even as the mosque complex is being constructed. The mosque was the home of a rich man but now belongs to the neighborhood. Since the Soviet collapse hundreds of mosques have been built as this one is being built, with the money of local people who sought to worship and to do something together.

The *imam*, who was himself able to study in Libya, is concerned about education. "A law has been published giving freedom of conscience, and it is written that you may teach Islam privately. But they don't allow it in state schools. It is impossible to reach by private means everyone who wants to learn privately. Only the state schools can satisfy this desire. The government allows teaching in mosques, but this is impossible, because mosques are only for praying. You need materials, books, classrooms. All the money raised from the people is going to repair mosques. It's too difficult to teach the young people because all the money is going into mosques, and even then, sometimes people who come for Friday prayers still have to pray out in the streets.

"If it were allowed, we could teach kids in the state schools. We're suggesting that Islam be taught as one subject in the curriculum. It should be compulsory, since otherwise students wouldn't always attend. This is how it would work: first, parents would have to agree, since some parents might not want their children to study Islam. There would need to be a written agreement. Then the children whose parents agreed would attend Islam classes.

"One problem is that teachers now don't allow children to pray in school, even though it only takes ten minutes. There have been scandals about this. We would like the schedules to be rearranged so that prayer time would be free time, and children could pray if they wanted.

"They should open wide the way to teach Islam in this country.

222

Because there is one thing I can one hundred percent guarantee: A society with no morality will end in disaster. There's no future in that society. And no one can provide morality except religion, neither the government nor other people. Only Islam will give morality."

The young *imam* enjoys a high reputation in Tashkent, and so he has had his problems with the new government. "I was prohibited for a time. I could not appear on radio or television. Now I can." Doing the right thing before God hasn't been easy for him, and he believes strongly that it shouldn't be easy for others, either. He fears that hypocrisy has become ingrained in Uzbek life. "People are used to living an easy life. They don't want a difficult life. They lived in the Soviet regime and they also said, 'I am for Lenin, I am for Stalin.' They were inside that society. They didn't want a hard time. Now they talk about Islam but they don't really believe this. They speak only in their words. They don't like the hard life [of actual belief and practice]. They don't like to do those things that Islam actually requires of individuals. It is too hard. They have the appearance of Muslims—but inside they are sneaky."

Opportunities for sneakiness abound, as the government and captive press emphasize the danger of "fundamentalism" and of "Wahhabism." Muhammad ibn Abd al-Wahhab (1703–1787) of Arabia believed all Muslims other than himself and those who followed him closely to be infidels. "Wahhabism" is the word used by non-Wahhabis to describe the austere religious methods followed by, for example, today's Saudi Arabian government. The existence of actual "Wahhabis" in Central Asia is unlikely, but the term is applied by some people to others. The Sufi *tarikatlar* have also come in for suspicion, mainly from outside Uzbekistan, of involvement in "fundamentalist" activities. "Many people," the *imam* says in his moderate, authoritative voice, "say that the *tarikatlar* have gone through many stages, and that the earlier stages were good but the more recent stages are not good. I am not especially interested in the *tarikatlar*. It's impossible that Sufism will exist among the religious. Islam should stay as a whole religion, one religion.

"It was God's will that Islam kept its place in the hearts of our people. Even if you harm them, you cannot take away that belief.

"Wahhabism is an instrument which the Devil gave to the enemies of Islam. There is no danger of Wahhabis of Islam. People who

223

speak about them are really just afraid of Islam. People who don't know anything about Islam are trying now to put the old, Soviet-era generation against the young. The old generation didn't know Islam very well, owing to the Soviet influence. Using words like Wahhabi, they have tried to put the older generation against the young.

"People talk about Soviet Islam, Red Islam. Now they talk about Wahhabis. They may talk about Naqshbandis, *tarikatlar*, Sufis. Why do they talk of all these things? There is only one Islam. Islam has many people, of all colors and nationalities. If there were only Englishmen all over the world, you wouldn't have come here. People all over the world eat many different kinds of food.

"The world was created this way in order to make it interesting."

You walk through the narrow serpentine streets of the old city with Fakhriddin. He's a little testy about the questions concerning Wahhabis and *tarikatlar*—Fakhriddin, this extremely likable, kind, intense, heavy-smoking young man. He finds the neo-Communist offensive against some religious leaders to be insane, and frightening. "The point is that, if something happened, like a war, everyone would prefer to follow the religious leaders. *Of course* they would. How could anyone really want to follow the leaders we now have, if anything *really serious* happened? But the religious leaders don't want to mix in politics. And of course the politicians don't want them to, and neither does the intelligentsia. But the religious leaders do want *freedom*. And the government is afraid of them. Because the government knows the people respect and like their religious leaders, and don't respect or like the government."

Fakhriddin has wondered if maybe the Sufis have something to offer. He wants to look into it someday when he has more time. But he emphasizes, "Islam is one, as the *imam* said."

For Muhammad, Islam certainly was one. He received the Koran from God, and there's only one God. That has not, however, stopped some Muslims since Muhammad from fighting other Muslims and indeed claiming that other Muslims were not really Muslims. Sufi *tarikatlar* have been accused for centuries of seeking to divide Islam, which is a sin. Muhammad laid enormous emphasis on the oneness of Islam.

And yet...Muhammad also honored the right of Christians, Jews, and others to worship in their own way, as long as they recognized that there could be but one God. And there's that passage from the Koran: "Men, we have created you from a male and a female, and made you into nations and tribes, that you might get to know one another." What was God thinking? Was he joking, or being mischievous? Was this a divine challenge? What a divine challenge it has turned out to be.

You travel by train to Namangan, considered the center of renascent Muslim piety, or "fundamentalism." Namangan has the look of other Ferghana valley towns, if with a bit more Russianness. Enough cars drive by, enough shops have plate-glass windows, to show that someone has made money here. The Ferghana valley was the Soviet Union's chief cotton-growing area, so local governments could, on occasion, get extra rubles out of Tashkent or Moscow, by means straight or crooked.

You visit an impressive local mosque, which faces across its courtyard a resplendent new *madrassa*. The *imam* leads worshippers in the noon prayer then gives a talk urging them to reject Western clothing and Western habits in general. Then he greets you, and you sit down in a small room to sip tea and talk.

"When the Soviets first came to Central Asia they attacked Islam in the centers, in Bukhara and Samarkand, and they thought that Islam was weaker in other, more rural places such as the Ferghana valley. That's why people here were able to keep their traditions alive. Naturally here, as everywhere, many Muslim leaders were repressed. Many were sent overnight into exile.

"During the Soviet regime parents couldn't even teach Islam to their children. But in spite of state prohibitions, many parents did risk their lives to teach their children Islam. And for the sake of their parents many of the middle generation [the generation that hadn't known pre-Soviet life] studied Islam.

"I learned the basics from my parents, while the deeper knowledge I learned from my grandfather. I never studied in a religious institute or a *madrassa*. My grandfather was a scholar and a *kori* [one who can recite the Koran from memory]. Of course, my grandfather was afraid even of his neighbors, who could have informed the police and he would have been punished. When I was in the sixth form, teachers came to my study to see if there were any Islamic slogans or not. Of course, my grandfather knew the work of al-Bukhari and other great

225

[Central Asian] figures, and that is partly why he struggled to impart this knowledge to others."

As the *imam* says, given these conditions, "after the end of the Soviet regime there appeared many opportunities to teach the younger generation."

Once the Soviet grip loosened sufficiently, his own mosque became the focus of Islamic activism. "The mosque began to be built in 1902 and was finished in 1921. Since 1936 it was used as a vodka and wine factory. In 1989 we made a great demonstration, demanding that this mosque be returned to the people. Since 1989 many people have been coming here to pray to God. This building was constructed only with the money of the people and with their manpower. A lot of people knew me and that I had a good knowledge of Islam, and they chose me to be the *imam* here. The government didn't pay anything toward the construction. We built all of these buildings ourselves. If one does something for the sake of God and in God's way, everything will be good."

The *imam* is keenly aware of charges of fundamentalism and Wahhabism. "Enemies of religion created such words as 'Wahhabis,' because they wanted to pit Muslims against each other. Enemies of religion can be many different people. They may just be journalists or politicians or KGB. Naturally, the enemies of a nation will attempt to divide that nation, and the enemies of religion naturally attempted to divide the faithful. They didn't want Muslims to live in peace and a good life. Only they themselves know why they don't like Islam.

"But people soon understood that all was one and that Muslims were not setting themselves against each other. People just ceased to listen to the gossip.

"People should understand and study Islam, not listen to people who judge Islam but don't know it and who create names like Wahhabis, extremist, fundamentalist. There is no fundamentalism or Wahhabism in Islam. There is one Islam, and people should study it before they draw any conclusions."

The *imam* invites you to stay as a guest at the mosque, but you must go. A tall, jolly, tubby man you met earlier accompanies you down the blazing hot street, past a butcher's stall with its deep red meat hanging on hooks, past boys playing in the gutter, past the ice cream stand under the trees. "How can you understand Islam?" he asks, smiling and laughing. "Islam...Islam is like an orange. What can you know about an orange if you look at it from across the street? What can you know about an orange if you hold it in your hand, even if you smell it? But if you peel an orange, bite into it and taste its fruit—then you know what an orange is. *It is very sweet.*" He laughs again.

The next time you hear of the Namangan mosque it has been closed as a hotbed of fundamentalism, along with other mosques in the Ferghana valley and elsewhere in Uzbekistan. The *imam* has gone underground. Once again, people teach their children about Islam at home, showing their children the holy book, explaining about the five prayers and how there is no God but God.

28

THE GREAT FIGURES of Central Asian Sufism are known as the *Khwajagan*, sometimes translated as "Masters of Wisdom." "The spiritual dynasty of the Masters of Wisdom lasted for five centuries," notes the Turkish writer Hasan Lütfi Shushud. "Its political contemporaries were the Khwarazm Shahs, Jenghis Khan, Tamerlane, and his successors. In the guise of the Naqshbandi Order it has continued in existence to the present day. The title of Khwaja or Master was first given in Central Asia, where it was conferred upon great scholars and sages....

"What did the Masters of Wisdom discover and what did they impart? They found that which is discovered by all who escape from illusion into Reality. They never withheld their discoveries from seekers who showed signs of promise.... Even today, they are ready to bring their truth to the aid of all who are capable of receiving it. Divine abundance neither increases nor diminishes with time....

"What doctrine or method is responsible for the mature development of the saints and sages we call the Masters of Wisdom? It is the path of realization followed by those who cannot accept the Creation as a *fait accompli* and who reject the space-time world system.... The goal of those who take this path is the shedding of all that is merely relative, escape from the cosmic illusion, attainment of absolute liberation, detachment from individualization. The starting point is Annihilation in God (*fana fi-llah*) and the destination is the Most Sacred Mystery of Non-Being (*ghaib*)....It is bestowed upon the Masters of Oneness, who have been divinely guided to 'weariness with being.' "

The first *khwajagan* was Yusuf al-Hamadani, who died in 1140 at the age of ninety-two. From Hamadani extend the great *tarikat* lines, the Yesevi and Naqshbandi, and indirectly the Bektashi. Hamadani's fourth deputy was Khwaja Abdulhaliq al-Ghujdawani (d. 1220). In a famous letter of advice, Ghujdawani wrote: "Make a profound study of the Islamic classics. Learn jurisprudence and the Prophetic traditions. Steer clear of ignorant zealots....Do not frequent the company of kings and princes....Speak little, eat little, and sleep little....Treat everyone kindly and look down on no one. Do not embellish your outward appearance, for ornament is a mark of inner poverty....Place no trust in this world and do not rely on worldly people....Wear old clothes and choose a poor man as your companion...."

Ghujdawani transmitted his wisdom to young Bahauddin al-Naqshband in a vision. (Naqshband was born in 1318 near Bukhara, ninety-two years after Ghujdawani's death.) "I was shown three lamps," Naqshband later wrote. "Then I saw a high throne, in front of which a green curtain was stretched....I then heard a voice from the throng crying out to me, 'Listen carefully! The venerable Khwaja [Ghujdawani] will tell you things of great importance to you in the way of Truth.'...The curtain before me was raised and I saw a luminous saint. He accepted my salutation then gave me instruction...."

Young Naqshband attempted to follow Ghujdawani's instruction. He faced one major difficulty. For unknown reasons, he found he did not want to recite the Sufi prayers, the *dhikr*, out loud. He wanted to keep his *dhikr* silent. Other Sufis found this off-putting and thought Naqshband odd and unsocial. But Naqshband had found his own way. "A special awareness arose in me when I began to practice silent *dhikr*. That was the secret I sought." From that time until today, the Naqshbandi *tarikat*, unlike other *tarikatlar*, practices silent *dhikr*.

Yet Naqshband was hardly antisocial, and Bukhara at that time was filled with Sufis seeking both knowledge and companionship. He wrote, "Our method is to work through friendly intercourse. Seclusion fosters repute, with all its attendant dangers. Welfare lies in association....If I noticed the faults in my friends, I would not have a friend in the world. For a faultless friend is nowhere to be found. Everyone loves good people. What takes skill is winning the game of friendship with bad people." Naqshband seemed to waver between the blessing of community and friendship and the beauty of God. He emphasized work and poverty. He scorned worldly things yet loved to learn from worldy people. "It was from a gambler that I learned steadfast devotion in the quest for Truth. This man lost everything in the gambling den and his companion advised him to give it up, but he said: 'Ah my friend, I couldn't stop playing this game if I knew it would cost my head.' When I heard this, my heart was filled with an enthusiasm that still fills my endeavor."

When Naqshband grew old, his beard was more white than grey, topped by ruddy cheeks and dark chestnut eyes. He had many followers in these later years, people with whom he could practice his silent prayer and also with whom he could talk as much as he liked. "One day the venerable Khwaja [Naqshband] was riding along on horseback, while many of his dervishes and friends accompanied him on foot. He wept so much that his followers were also moved to tears, though without knowing why. At length he explained: 'I am inwardly such a worthless failure that I do not deserve to have anyone accept my salutation. However, the Exalted Lord has put me to shame by making people take notice of me. None of them knew what I was like inside.' "

29

MURAT BRINGS OVER a rickety bench and you sit down, drink tea, and watch three young brothers cutting a small field of wheat with hand scythes. "You see?" Murat says, gesturing toward the men. "Technology!" And the brothers laugh. From left to right they are, respectively, an economist, a musician, and a technician. Murat is a teacher and writer, a talkative, somewhat domineering man in his thirties, who lives in a Tashkent high rise but grew up in this village outside Bukhara. You drink hot tea in the afternoon sun. The brothers chop away, covered with sweat and dust. One of them plans to build his house here. His little plot is surrounded by other plots, stretching over the vast Bukhara plain, separated by rows of trees and by canals.

The plain has fed Bukhara for centuries. A boy on a donkey appears in the distance, riding slowly toward you alongside a drainage ditch.

Murat wants to show you everything, country and city. He takes you to a *kolkhoz* to meet an eighty-year-old man who has three wives and fifteen children. Past an outdoor display offering the usual hammer and sickle, Lenin, and rain-soaked photos of Uzbeks who fought in World War II, past a large decorative pond, the old man takes you to his secret: a small dank room, its dirt floor well below ground level, with a pole in the middle surrounded by a huge doughnut-shaped stone. Here he mills cottonseed oil — the mill is worked by a horse — thus making the illegal (until recently) income necessary to support three wives and fifteen children. He takes you to his vast orchard. "This is initiative!" Murat says. The old man says almost nothing, just points out each variety of tree and the grafts. "He has produced thirty-seven different kinds of apricot and twenty-seven varieties of apple. He never went to school. This is his university!" The man listens to Murat and smiles proudly. "All this land belongs to the *kolkhoz*. But one day it may be private."

"Yes, I hope it will be private. Then it will all be mine," the man says beneath one of his apple trees.

"You can see," Murat says confidentially, "how hard he works." We stop in the orchard, Murat says a prayer, we move on. How and why this exceedingly fertile octogenarian has managed to run a not-quite-private orchard and cottonseed-oil mill on collectivized Soviet land is never fully explained.

Indeed, figuring out how *anything* worked in Soviet Uzbekistan, or in independent Uzbekistan, strains one's imaginative capacity. For while state planning certainly existed and determined the broad outline — cotton monoculture, huge irrigation projects, environmental disaster — the local details seem to have been rather distant from government intentions. To a great extent, people governed themselves, and still do. Family and friendship ties determined much of who got what and how they used it. While agricultural land has not been privatized — most *kolkhoz* managers prefer keeping control themselves — it was never, in a sense, fully taken over by the state either, at least not once the initial elimination of landownership (and landowners, and the owning/managing class in general) had been completed under Stalin. The Uzbek Soviet government, much less the Moscow planners, could not entirely control its local subordinates. The system was more like communist feudalism, not an especially profitable economic form—trade, for example, was and remains negligible, even between cities—but one which did provide a certain autonomy to the Party princelings, their families and friends.

This odd, covert way of organizing society characterized not only the provinces and poorer class, but the Uzbek Soviet government itself. For example, Moscow would normally send Slavic babysitters out to watch the higher functionaries. Moscow found that it had to rotate these minders, because if one of them stayed too long in one place he would tend to become ensnared in the web of helpful relationships that distinguished Uzbek life; he would, in Moscow's terms, become corrupt. But rotating the Slavic minders, of course, only made the Uzbeks' task easier. The pale emissaries of Moscow Central would be shuffled about from post to post, never understanding anything, not even understanding Uzbek—they would be moved about like clueless stooges, empty symbols of state authority. When Gorbachev finally sent investigators from Moscow to root out Uzbek corruption, they found, to no one's surprise, that just about every Uzbek Communist with a shred of power, including the highest Party officials, was as crooked as the day is long. The figures for cotton production, the single most important economic statistic from the all-Soviet point of view, were ridiculous fantasies, dreamed up by Uzbek Party leaders as a simple way of getting large payments from Moscow for nonexistent cotton. Such was the nature of Communist feudalism at the upper levels.

And such was the nature of Uzbek loyalty to this unusual system that, when investigators announced that Uzbekistan's leaders were by and large crooks and caused thousands to lose their posts, the Uzbeks responded by doubling their hatred for Moscow, protesting Gorbachev's infringement on Uzbekistan's right to self-government, and lionizing their recently deceased, undeniably corrupt First Secretary Sharaf Rashidov, the leading figure of postwar Uzbek Communism. (He ran Uzbekistan from 1959 until his death in 1983.) Today Rashidov is regarded almost as a martyr.

So the eighty-year-old oil-maker, horticulturalist, and father of fifteen, though exceptional in many ways, was also recognizably a part of the system, a system in which everyone cooperated to bilk the state and mislead the Russians. This system lasted for decades and continues today, except that the Russians aren't around to bilk anymore. "The orders used to come from Moscow," an old, over-fed Communist in Bukhara tells you, "now they come from Tashkent. There's not much difference." The difference is that where people once resented imperial Moscow they now resent their own government, and each province does its best to keep Tashkent Central from having its way.

At his parents' house, Murat sits you down on the floor to his father's left. His father sits at the head of a rectangular eating-cloth, sons arrayed down either side, women at the end. Children mingle or stay out of sight. The cloth is covered with bowls of nuts, crackers, and preserves, plates of tomato-and-onion salad, fish, a bowl of potatoes, and hunks of bread, all tended by a fearless horde of flies. Like nearly everyone else in this and any other Uzbek village, Murat's parents live in a one-storey compound, a garden in the middle, animals and an outhouse on one side. (Wealthier families may have a second storey and outbuildings.) Some of their married children and all the unmarried ones live here, too. When a couple acquires the necessary capital and land, they will move and build a home of their own.

Murat says the prayer, and we eat. We brush away the flies, chew, and talk. "Russians don't live in the villages," Murat says. "They all live in the cities. They don't have land. They never learned Uzbek. They never learned how to cook Uzbek food. Their food is awful. They can barely cook. Like this fish—put flour on it, cook it in oil. Russians wouldn't even know how to do that."

We're all having a pretty good time. Murat's parents seem happy to have him visiting; and, thankfully, his wife likes his parents and siblings. Having everyone live this close together and not get along would be disastrous.

"There were no sincere Communists in this village," Murat says. "In their soul they were not Communists. Look at my father here. He was a Communist. He was director of the *kolkhoz* for four years. In his soul he was not a Communist."

Murat's father gives an unhappy look. Then he makes a gesture, looking at you. He passes his hand once in front of his face, palm open, from top to bottom, as if he's pulling a veil over himself. When his hand stops, his face has lost all expression. He stares at you. "It means that something has stopped," Murat says with a slight nervous laugh.

30

MURAT WANTS TO SHOW YOU everything, and over several days he takes you to farms and offices, to friends' houses, to monuments. One day you borrow a motorcycle with sidecar and tool around with Murat and his wife; on another day you borrow a car, then take a bus. You're never allowed to pay for anything, not even an ice cream or a beer. (Cold beer is available from vendors at the side of the road.) You meet the somewhat distrustful and taciturn former Communist leaders of the area, who are now the distrustful and taciturn People's Democratic Party leaders, still ensconced in the old CP building. Each one of the many wall-clocks in their building shows a different time. The Communist decorations remain, and on each official's desk is an abacus for making official calculations. These strange men—they're all men—seem at once impatient and listless. You attempt to extract some notion of their plans for the future, but they appear not to have any, or at least not any they're willing to share.

You meet farmers, who alternate between loving descriptions of their fruit trees and pained visions of impending doom owing to mistaken irrigation policies and wild overuse of pesticides.

You meet merchants, who alternate between lively scenarios of entrepreneurial plenty and morbid admissions that as yet there's very little to sell.

You meet a doctor, who cheerfully explains that his hospital has virtually no supplies. Relaxation on outdoor benches appears to be the main treatment available to his robed, bandaged patients.

You meet plenty of Tajiks, especially given that Murat's wife is Tajik and you stay one night in her parents' home. Persian-speakers but Sunni Muslims (unlike Iranians), Tajiks have lived in this region since well before the Uzbek invasion. Uzbek officials have begun encouraging ethnic rivalry by acting against the Tajik minority, while some Tajik nationalists have claimed that much of the pre-Soviet Bukhara emirate should be part of Tajikistan. The civil war in Tajikistan, which has caused many Uzbeks to flee that country for Uzbekistan, doesn't make these problems easier. But in the villages you visit out-side Bukhara, Murat's wife assures you, "We all live together without trouble. We've all been here for centuries and know each other. And of course we do sometimes intermarry!" Looking at a Tajik and an Uz-bek, it's nearly impossible to tell them apart.

One day you go to the city of Bukhara with Murat. You see the summer palace of the emir, which would be spectacular if it were bet-ter maintained. You climb up a wide staircase to the top of a tower that overlooks a vast rectangular bathing-pool. "The emir," Murat says, "would come up here and observe his women swimming in the pool. He would throw an apple down to the most beautiful girl that day, and take her away."

You sit at an outdoor cafe eating rich ice cream. Boys play in a large bathing-pool, one fed by canals that flow among and beneath various buildings either reconstructed or built from scratch to simu-late the environment of Old Bukhara. Pop songs play over loud-speakers.

"Eastern buildings, Western music!" Murat says.

"But this isn't a Western language."

"The style is Western." Murat listens carefully. "It's in Russian." He sits up. "Isn't Russia in the West?"

"It's a difficult question."

"To us, Russia is in the West. To England or France, Russia is in the East. Anyway, here this is Western music with Eastern buildings. It's a *synthesis!*"

Murat has become fond of the word *synthesis*. At his parents' house, he pointed to the glass in his parents' windows and said, "Syn-thesis!" Their living room had a European landscape on the wall, a Russian calendar with a rendering of feudal European peasants out-side a castle, a small bust of Lenin, a wood stove, and a television on which you once watched Walt Disney cartoons dubbed into Russian. Synthesis!

You wander away from the central square, through narrow back streets, across empty lots, to marvel at some of the massive structures that distinguish parts of Bukhara: the *madrassas*, mosques, and bazaars, all built from stone. There's little in this neighborhood except these implacable buildings baking under the sun, and they produce an odd effect of authority and emptiness. Most of the mosques and *madrassa*s have not served religious purposes for generations, and by now they seem almost foreign. Here and there a stork's nest sits atop some high tower, but all the nests are empty, and most of the monumental buildings are empty, too.

In front of one, several men and women lounge in the shade. You give greetings, a young man comes forward, a thin, jumpy young man. You enter at his invitation. The courtyard inside is crammed with *kravatlar* at crazy angles, more or less facing a stage. "This was a *madrassa*," the young man says, "but in the Communist period it was used as a theater. A *theater*, with concerts and plays." There was even a souvenir shop near the entrance. You climb up narrow stairs in one corner and clamber into a tiny room. "This was a *çilahana*, where a student would spend forty days in isolation. It was very hard."

Murat looks around him. "No, it wasn't a *çilahana*. It's a student's room. You can see where he would cook. He'd put his things over here."

"No, I think it was a *çilahana*. Students would perform various practices during their forty days of isolation and reflection."

Murat looks at him. "I think it was a student's room, or maybe for more than one student."

You clamber back out of the room. "No one," the young man whispers to you, "knows anything about Islam now."

Out on the hot street, you attempt to change the subject by asking after the storks. The young man explains: "There had always been storks here before. They came every year. In 1978, they didn't come to Bukhara. Not one. But in 1979 they did come. They flew over one day, then left. After that, there was an earthquake. Buildings fell. Bukhara's goodness had disappeared. The storks don't come anymore. Our belief is that earthquakes happen in bad places. Now, I would say that there are a lot of storks in Namangan in the Ferghana valley. They could be the Bukhara storks. Because in Namangan Islam is now very strong. People are praying, and Islam is powerful there. It could be that the storks left Bukhara for Namangan for that reason."

Yet Bukhara has been a sacred city for centuries, in large part because Bahauddin al-Naqshband was born, taught, and died here. His Naqshbandi *tarikat* spread through the world. The emir used to walk from his palace to Naqshband's tomb and back, an extraordinarily humble act for an emir. Allegedly, Tamerlane himself followed the

235

Naqshbandi Sufi path. For centuries, Muslims would make pilgrimages to Bukhara, and it was said that three Bukhara pilgrimages equaled one pilgrimage to Mecca.

"In the old times," an elderly man explains one perfect afternoon at the Naqshbandi shrine near Bukhara, "the Naqshbandi *tarikat* was very strong because the government supported it. The rulers were interested in it." Under Communism the *tarikat* fell apart. But now, "new *tarikatlar* are coming into being. They won't be like before. They will be different. We have to work on behavior, on etiquette and methods. To do this you need property and money. But to be a real *tarikat*, there should be a *şeyh*. There are no *şeyhler* now. And the religious establishment is against Sufism. Islam itself is against *tasawwuf* [Sufism, mysticism], because if *tasawwuf* is developed it will work against religion. Thus, religious people are against *tasawwuf*."

Hundreds of people have come today to the Naqshbandi shrine, which stretches over several acres, to pray at Naqshband's tomb or at one of the mosques, to sacrifice an animal and prepare pilaf for other visitors. Everyone comes hoping to give away food, so there's too much food.

You sit down with Murat and the head *imam* of the shrine on a *kravat* shaded by trees. Birds sing, a breeze keeps you cool. Tea is served. The *imam*, a trim man past middle age, calm and confident, recites a prayer, then begins his story:

"Until the [1917] revolution, the Naqshbandi *tarikat* grew. Via the Naqshbandi *tarikat*, respect for Islam grew until the revolution. After the revolution, the government fought against *tarikatlar*. All the books, everything was destroyed. All functions, the way of life was destroyed. During seventy years of Communist rule, they didn't allow any rituals to be observed. They didn't allow anyone to visit the shrine. Anyone who dared to come, they would take his license plate number then report him to his workplace. Then he would be discharged from his job and thrown into despair.

"This place [the Naqshband shrine] became dilapidated. The door was locked. Everything fell apart.

"This situation was created because it was known that whoever came with his children and prayed with a pure heart and asked for help—they would not be left empty-handed. Their wish would be fulfilled. It was well-known that whoever came with a pious heart always reached his goal. That's why a lot of people came—at night. They would jump over the fence.

"If people wanted to make an offering by slaughtering a sheep, they would do so at someone's house. But they were always afraid of the militia. If they were caught, they were punished.

"With God's mercy, Gorbachev came to power. The first thing he did was give freedom of religion. Then people started coming to the shrine. In Gorbachev's time, we were allowed to hold celebrations. After independence, all these old customs revived."

Like every other Sufi-minded person since Islamic mysticism began—perhaps since the Prophet himself—the *imam* has to consider certain classic problems: What is Sufism? What is the relationship between the Sufi path or the *tarikatlar* and the wide path, the *sharia* of mainstream, sometimes bureaucratic, Islam? What happens to *tarikat* practice when there's no proper *şeyh* to learn from? And finally—a more recent question, but one with ancient echoes—what is the relationship between Islamic mysticism and "modern life"?

"When you talk about *tarikatlar*, you have to talk about *tasawwuf*. A revival of the *tarikatlar* depends on reviving *tasawwuf*. *Tasawwuf* is based on two foundations: *zohut* and *mohabati*. *Zohut* means you shouldn't dedicate yourself completely to the world, and you should not forget about Judgment Day. *Mohabati* means love of God, to strengthen your love of God.

"The *tasawwuf* of Hizrat Bahauddin [Naqshband] is congruent with the Koran and *hadith* [reported sayings of Muhammad]. Let me give you an example. Bahauddin's motto was"—the *imam* recites it twice in Persian, '*Dil bayar, dast bakar*,' then translates to Uzbek. "The heart should be with your beloved, and the head at work. Your heart should be tied to God, but your hands and feet should be at work. The origin of this is in the Koran."

The *imam* continues, quoting in Arabic from the Koran, then translating: "Mankind, do not eat the food or wear the clothes if you don't work. Whatever you eat, drink, wear, don't use them if you don't work. The Prophet said, in a *hadith*, 'Honest work is required for all Muslims.'

"Hizrat Bahauddin observed these rules, and whenever he questioned students for acceptance in his *tarikat*, he asked them the following: 'Do you have a skill or not?' If the answer was yes, then he accepted them. If the answer was no, he would say, 'Go and learn a skill, then come back.'

"The people would ask Bahauddin, 'Why do you do this? Students come to you to get knowledge, to learn God's words and the Prophet's sayings. What does that have to do with having a trade or skill?'

"Bahauddin would answer them: 'You don't understand; you don't know. If the student has a skill, then through that skill he will earn his livelihood, and what knowledge [*ilm*] he gets through me he will use only for the sake of true knowledge. He will earn a livelihood through his skill and use knowledge from me for the pursuit of truth. If he doesn't have a skill, then he will take the knowledge he gets from me and try to use it to gain a livelihood, and he will use lies, and he will bring disgrace to *ilm*.'

"Therefore, it cannot be said that *tasawwuf* is separate from the Muslim religion. The *sharia* teaches fasting, alms-giving, prayer. *Tasawwuf* strengthens these things.

"*Tasawwuf* comes from *suf*. The meaning is: after the Prophet, in the period of the *sahabîlar* [usually translated as Companions; Muhammad's close circle of friends and followers], a group formed among the Companions who knew the pure meaning of Islam. They separated themselves in order to strengthen the pure meaning of Islam. Sufis work toward purity.

"The way of Bahauddin Naqshband is just. It is not strict; it is not burdensome. Nor is it easy. Therefore the world accepted it rapidly."

The Communists, of course, did not accept it. "Nevertheless, even in this situation there were good people who kept their religion alive. They were in hiding. At night, people like me would go, after midnight, to visit them and to learn.

"We cannot say that all the Communists were bad. There were good people among Communists, people who protected the religious. I know, personally, one good Communist in Tashkent, another in Andizhan. I had contact with them. They looked like Communists, but secretly, in their hearts, they were Muslim. I know people who would invite me into their homes, at one or two in the night, to teach them Koran. Although they carried the Communist Party card, they were really Muslim. It says in the Koran, 'When a person says something with his tongue, it doesn't mean it is in his heart.' These people were not unfaithful. In Islam, the *heart* is what is considered."

According to the *imam*, even some Sufi *şeyhler*, or at least disciples, managed to survive the early massacres and steady repression of the Communist period. "In Bukhara, the followers of the *tarikat* have disappeared. Only in Tashkent did some survive in hiding. And in Dushanbe, Turkestan, Daghestan, part of Turkmenistan, and in the Caucasus. In Dushanbe, a Naqshbandi teacher has appeared. A man from Bukhara, Teşa Baba [*teşa* means "axe"] went to Dushanbe, stayed, and learned from the teacher there. After years, the teacher gave his blessing to Teşa Baba to go forth and teach. He now works in this district, on the New Life *kolkhoz*. Teşa Baba is propagating the Naqshbandi *tarikat* there."

Meanwhile, the *imam*, educated in secret during those dark years, has a shrine to look after. Whether new *şeyhler* will appear or not is an important question, since generally the transmission of mystical knowledge and practice, the central *tarikat* activity, has been from generation to generation. However, one should keep in mind that *tarikat* time has its own properties. Naqshband himself cited Abdulhaliq al-Ghujdawani as his greatest teacher—a man he never met, who died well before Naqshband's birth, but who appeared to him in dreams. As for Naqshband's shrine, it appears to be in safe hands, although the shrine management committee's plans have a curiously non-Sufi sound. The *imam* says, "On May 5, 1989, during Ramadan, the shrine reopened. So many people came, there was not enough room for them to stand. Everybody was very happy. Everybody brought a sacrifice—the sacrificing of the animals so impressed people that they had tears in their eyes. The place had been empty. But on the day, everyone brought carpets and furnishings. They brought crockery, plates, spoons, urns. The whole place was furnished. Everybody asked what they should bring. They brought bricks for building. From that day forward, people never ceased to come. Bahauddin was born in 1318. The government wants to celebrate the 675th anniversary of his birth. We leaders of the shrine said we couldn't do it with our own budget, and that the state should take over; moreover, that the celebration shouldn't just take place in one city but should be worldwide. The government has a team working now. East of the city, they are building huge gates for the procession

239

to pass through during the celebration. We are opening a Naqshbandi managing association and business center."

They plan to build a school and establish a theological faculty. An enormous guesthouse, lined with mirrors and bright floral paintings, is almost complete. They are building: a trade center, a kitchen to serve one hundred fifty people (twenty hearths), a pipeline for drinking water, a sewer system. They will restore the several mosques and reopen the *madrassa*. Eventually, the *imam* hopes to regain the shrine's *waqf* properties. The state had taken all *waqf* properties by 1930. The *imam* says that, in order to get back *waqf*, Muslim leaders will have to train "cadres," to use his Russian word, who understand enough about philosophy and law to promote Muslim institutional interests.

The *imam* has met with Turkey's president. "We talked for forty minutes. He asked me questions about the *tarikat*. Halfway through, he said, 'I am Naqshbandi. My parents are Naqshbandi. In Turkey, there are eight million Naqshbandi followers.' There are also Naqshbandi in Pakistan. Ahmed Zulfukkar Naqshbandi, the most influential of them, visited here and said he would send help. A banker named Halil came here from Pakistan and said he would build a marble platform above the shrine for viewing.

"The management committee has a list of twenty-three items. These are all plans to revitalize the Naqshbandi *tarikat* in the future. We also want to start a Naqshbandi weekly newspaper. We asked the government for fifteen hectares for a Naqshbandi garden, and they approved it. This is a very big task for us, so we asked them for help.

"Also, we want to build a Naqshbandi city. We will build houses of this city in the old style, so that whoever comes will drop by the Naqshbandi city and see how people can live."

You get up to go. The *imam* pulls you to one side and mentions the shrine's Swiss bank account (Swiss Bank Corp., Zurich, #148,011.0, U.S. dollars only). "I'd really appreciate it if you would help publicize this. We would welcome any help."

What sort of synthesis would a mystical Muslim Disneyland be? One recalls Prince Charles's plans, guided by the cutting-edge architect Leon Kriel, to build a new town called Poundbury that would hide all machine conveniences and replicate the 18th century for residents and visitors. In the West, this can go under the name "post-modernism," but near Bukhara it is Islamic revivalism.

Murat wants to show you everything at the shrine. You walk beneath the sacred log three times, touching your back to it as you pass under. You take a chip of bark; this brings luck. You visit Naqshband's tomb, Murat says a prayer. You look at the mosques, the people relaxing under the trees with their picnics spread on cloths. You go to the cemetery out back. One field has graves; another is an undulating gray surface, the roofing of vaults. Murat takes you into one, explaining how the vaults are organized. The entrances are so small you must go through on your knees or even your belly, with strange dank smells all around in the pitch black.

Abdulhaliq Ghujdawani, he who taught Naqshband via dreams, also has a tomb near Bukhara. It is presided over by an extremely dignified twenty-nine-year-old *imam* who welcomes you to sit with him on a *kravat* beneath a tree and says a prayer. On your right stands an impressive *madrassa*. "This *madrassa* was built by Ulugh Bek"— Tamerlane's grandson—"and restored by the local mayor, Salim Rahimov. After he restored it he was sent to prison and spent seven years there. Now it is a *maktap*, with three hundred students." A *maktap* is a primary school where boys learn the Muslim basics. The *imam* himself studied in secret, with fourteen other students under the *imam* at the Naqshband shrine. "We used to bake bread when I was a student. *Dil bayar, dast bakar.* The heart should be with God, the hands at work. That's Naqshband's motto. But we didn't study the Naqshbandi *tarikat*. It wasn't possible. The *imam* didn't know anything about the *tarikat*, only *sharia*."

Facing the *madrassa* are two tombs, of Abdulhaliq Ghujdawani and, it is said, his mother. A paved, planted space surrounds them. The whole setup seems incongruously tidy. The young *imam* walks you over to the tombs. "This was all a cemetery following the time of Ulugh Bek," the *imam* says. "The learned were buried here. It was a cemetery until 1960 or 1965, when it was destroyed and covered over." Some benches, fences, struggling young trees.

Well: What lasts? The older *imam* had quoted the Koran, "All of you originate from Adam, and Adam originated from dust." Was he thinking of the third sura, "Jesus is like Adam in the sight of God. He created him of dust and then said to him: 'Be,' and he was"? Or perhaps the fifteenth, wherein God deals with Satan: "We ordain life and death. We are the Heir of all things. . . . We created man from dry clay, from black moulded loam, and before him Satan from smokeless fire. Your Lord said to the angels: 'I am creating man from dry clay, from black moulded loam. When I have fashioned him and breathed of My spirit into him, kneel down and prostrate yourselves before him.' The angels, one and all, prostrated themselves, except Satan. He refused to prostrate himself with the others. 'Satan,' said God, 'why do you not prostrate yourself?' He replied: 'I will not bow to a mortal whom You created of dry clay, of black moulded loam.' "

This is the same sura in which God said, "Never have We destroyed a nation whose term of life was not ordained beforehand. Men cannot forestall their doom, nor can they retard it."

Murat and his wife take you to the second most important Naqshbandi shrine, that of Naqshband's mother and her two sisters. "One of the women," Murat's wife says, "is a solver of problems. For the second woman, you come on Tuesdays. She is called Lady Tuesday. On Tuesday evening you prepare food to remember her. You prepare it for her spirit, for the enjoyment of her soul. You give the food to poor people and neighbors. It helps solve problems. If you do this, no more problems. It works for anyone. The third woman is also a problem solver. This is all among women. These are women saints. If you have problems with birthing a child, you do a ceremony and the birth will be easy."

"Your problems," Murat says, "will be easy."

"To do these ceremonies," his wife says, "you have to know what are the right days. For that, there are rumors."

Women young and old approach the main tomb. Next to it is a mosque. Across a path lies a humble shrine marking Naqshband's birthplace, which women circumambulate—a groove has become worn. As they pray, they may stop to tie a fragment of cloth to a bush or the fence.

But the main attraction remains the three-tomb complex. Visiting women, young and old, touch a stone tablet on the tomb's wall, kiss it, touch their foreheads to it, kiss and touch, bow, hold their palms before them opened upward to God, pray, wipe their palms downward over their faces, kiss, touch.

Three poles protrude upward from the tomb, one for each

woman. Atop each pole is a large, crude hand. "Maybe this is a Muslim symbol, maybe it isn't," Murat says. "Perhaps it is a custom from before Islam. Alisher Nawaii wrote two novels about Alexander" — Alexander the Great, who once spent time near here — "one short and one long. In the short one, Alexander says: 'When I die, put one of my hands outside the tomb.' He says this to his close friends, gathered around him. 'In this world I have built a great empire and I have owned everything. But when I am dead, my hand is empty, and I have nothing in the other world.' "

31

IT'S NIGHT. You sit on the steps before your house on your leafy street in the Tashkent *mahalla*. Suddenly you don't feel safe anymore. That special *mahalla* sensation of security and protectedness has departed, for gradually you have become involved in the world outside the *mahalla*, where your neighbors and friends and the people you drink with at *gaplar* can't protect you. You have strayed outside the *mahalla*, and now you fear that the dangerous world there may reach across its boundaries. A man helped you, and now he's lost his job. The precautions didn't work, not all of them. The government's repression of dissidence, which began even before independence, is heating up. You hope to leave soon, using the same back door you came in through. But the others, what will happen to them? You sit here on the steps at night, adjusting to this new kernel of fear. "They can come and take you at any time," Nasruddin once said. "They can do it whenever they like. They have enough experience." For you, this is just a taste of fear, a little kernel. You can't imagine what it's like to live with that fear every day for decades and never be sure that it will end.

32

WHAT LASTS? Time and space change shape around us. Without having moved, we can change position. We can go overnight from the vanguard of history to its far backwaters — or vice versa. We can have all the time in the world, then run out of time. Once unchangeable borders can suddenly disappear; and new ones can be erected, whether stone by stone or in a day. We may suddenly believe in something we had never thought much of before; we may suddenly become gripped by fear. We may conclude that what we thought of as lasting does not last. We may become prisoners or exiles, without moving, hold life cheap, then precious, wake up and find that we are at home in a place that had never before felt like home, and may never feel like home again.

In all this, great forces may be at work, economic, ideological, religious; oceans lapping at our feet.

If you were a megalomaniac, or at least highly overconfident, you might look at those oceans and think they're yours to command. We tend to remember those lunatics who succeed for a time: Alexander the Great, Napoleon, Mao, Stalin, Augustus. We should also remember the failures. For one thing, even those who succeed eventually fail. The Soviet empire died. Even Alexander told his friends to leave one of his hands outside the coffin to show that one can own the world yet end, inevitably, empty-handed.

Given that even the spectacular successes fail, perhaps the spectacular failures tell us more about human history than do the successes.

One such spectacular failure was Enver Paşa, the would-be Basmachi leader, the *deli* Pan-Turkist martyr. Born on November 22, 1881, in Istanbul, Enver grew up in Macedonia—his family had originated there—then completed with distinction a military education in Istanbul. He returned to Macedonia and fought the Macedonian guerrillas who were seeking independence from the Ottomans. There he joined a conspiratorial group called the Ottoman Society for Union and Progress, a key branch in the Young Turk movement. When the sultan sent a general to investigate the conspirators' activities, they killed him and fled to the mountains. When the sultan sent troops, the troops defected to their Union and Progress targets. Somehow, this touched a popular chord. There were uprisings elsewhere in the empire, so that the sultan had to restore the Parliament he had suspended and, to make a long story short, give in. This quirky series of events became known as the Young Turk Revolution.

Enver's stock was high. In 1909, he went as military attaché to

Berlin, where he deepened an already strong admiration for German military organization and efficiency. In 1911, he fought a guerrilla war alongside the Sanusis against the Italians; he encouraged the Sufi Sanusis to call it a *jihad*. By 1913, Enver had returned to Istanbul to carry out his most theatrical coup, leading Unionist officers in a confrontation with the aging grand vizier and forcing him at gunpoint to resign. Enver, a short, small man given to careful grooming and imposing mustaches, had a sharp sense of drama.

The Unionists became de facto rulers, and by 1914, at age thirty-two, Enver was minister of war for the empire. Enver feared, justifiably, that the Allied powers would happily carve up what remained of the Ottoman empire, and decided to enter World War I on Germany's side. He had little support for this, in or out of the government. So he conspired with the Germans to find a provocation. Eventually the Germans, with his connivance, steamed into the Black Sea and blasted away at the Russians, leading Russia and then her Allied partners to declare war on the Ottomans, who responded by allying with Germany.

Enver stood second to no one in making conspiracies. In 1914, he formed the Special Organization, a guerrilla/secret service outfit that mounted raids in Macedonia, Libya, the Caucasus, and Iran. Enver would use whatever ideology suited the situation. The 1915 action against the Suez Canal was called Islamic; the efforts in the Caucasus were done in the name of Turkish ethnic unity—though here, too, the Special Organization launched an Army of Islam. The organization also backed nationalistic groups. For a man like Enver, the entire diet of ideologies composed a single meal.

Enver's talents did not necessarily extend to large military operations. When Enver led the Ottoman Third Army against the Russians in the winter of 1914, he accomplished nothing with his ninety thousand troops except to incur eighty thousand casualties. Despite some later successes, the Ottoman army lost badly during the First World War, and in 1918 Enver slipped out of Istanbul on a German boat, never to see the city again.

Basing himself in Berlin, Enver took to conspiracy full-time. He flirted with Communism, or at least Communists. Enver wished to return to Anatolia and replace Atatürk, who was then leading the war against the Greek invaders. He tried to intrigue with the British, with

Moscow, with the Saudi emir Faisal—with almost anybody. He wrote to a friend in 1920 that he desired to cause "the salvation of the Turkish and Muslim world." He set up a Union of Islamic Revolutionary Societies, with representatives from Rome to Libya and Afghanistan, that promised to promote *jihad* and international Communism at the same time. He also organized a People's Councils Party intended to stir opposition against Atatürk. By 1921, Enver had a Muslim Bolshevik army—God knows precisely what the soldiers had been told—poised to strike Anatolia and topple Atatürk. In September, however, Atatürk crushed the Greek forces and, his hand strengthened, made overtures to the Soviets. The Soviets responded by staging an elaborate revolt around Enver that so disoriented him he left for Moscow, where the Soviets reassured him that bad things happen to everyone and he shouldn't be ashamed.

The Soviets then asked Enver if he might consider going to Central Asia to conciliate the Basmachi rebels. Enver arrived in Bukhara in November 1921. Several conflicting versions exist of Enver's initial movements. One says he already knew in Moscow that the Soviets had betrayed his cause in the Caucasus, and he came to Central Asia ready to wreak revenge. Another claims that the Soviets changed their mind about Enver and tried to recall him, thus forcing Enver's decision to lead a Pan-Turkic, Pan-Islamic army against the Bolsheviks rather than face Moscow discipline.

The most beautiful version has Enver sitting cross-legged in his tightly buttoned uniform, addressing his friends in Bukhara: "It is absolutely essential to fight for the independence of Turkestan. He who puts up longer with this unworthy existence, he who is content to look on longer, and he who fears death, which in any case will one day overtake us all, deserves to be damned by the coming generation. But we, with death before our eyes, wish to take up arms for freedom, in order to ensure for our descendants a life which knows no servitude and no oppression."

On the pretext of a hunting trip, Enver left the city of Bukhara and headed east to find the Basmachi leader Ibrahim Bek. A portion of the Red Bukharan leadership, including President Osman Kocaoğlu, joined him. Unfortunately, the fierce Ibrahim Bek took Enver prisoner and detained him for weeks until the emir of Bukhara communicated to his loyal servant that Enver should be obeyed.

(Meanwhile, Ibrahim Bek allowed some of his troops to fight along-side the Russians against Osman Kocaoğlu, hardly the first time Basmachi fought Basmachi.) Enver issued an appeal: "I, who am the irreconcilable enemy of the infidels, salute you, the Ghazis, who are fighting for the preservation of religion and fatherland. I also wish to inform you that, henceforth, with the permission of the Almighty, I have declared *jihad* against the Russians, and have undertaken the command of all Muslim forces in order to clear the invading Russians out of Sacred Bukhara, Khiva, and of all Turkestan. I order all Muslim Mujahideen to strive for the victory of the Sacred Banner of the Prophet Muhammad against the Russians." He signed himself Deputy of the Emir of Bukhara, Son-in-Law of the Caliph.

Enver succeeded in taking Dushanbe, now the capital of Tajikistan. Basmachis rallied to him, and he tried to organize all of the Basmachis under his leadership, an idea they at least entertained during a conference on April 15. Moscow sent negotiators. Enver dispatched them with a demand for total Soviet withdrawal, saying, "The freedom fighters, whose commander I am, have sworn to fight for independence and freedom till their last breath." In May he sent an ultimatum to the Soviet government: "I have been commissioned to announce to you the unshakeable will of the people of Bukhara, Turkestan and Khiva for a free and independent life. This independence must be recognized by the Soviet Union. The Council advises the Government of the Soviet Republic of Russia to recall to Russia within fourteen days the Red Army..."

The Soviets' only response was to call Enver "an agent of British Imperialism" and continue their offensive against him. Two columns marched, pushing Enver into the mountains. He first attempted to brake their advance at Denau. After three days he retreated, leaving 165 dead. Enver dropped back into higher, more desolate country, the Russians pursuing him until August 4, 1922, when he was killed in a tiny village, probably while charging the Russians' advance cavalry. In a letter to his wife nine days earlier, Enver had written: "I am closing this letter with these last sentences: in addition to the wild flowers of this place, which I have been sending you, I am also enclosing a small twig from the tree under which I have been sleeping for so many nights...I entrust you and my children to the Almighty...I have engraved your name on the tree with my knife...Your Enver."

You travel south with Fakhriddin, far south, through Samarkand down to the Afghanistan border—the land is farmed right up to the barbed wire—turning at Termez northward to Denau. There you and Fakhriddin walk through town, past the Great Patriotic War (World War II) monument, past a machine repair shop, through stone walls into a round clearing. The place is sometimes used as an animal corral, sometimes as a meeting place for lovers. It was once a fortress, and the Basmachis had fought from it. Today the place is empty except for, near one wall, a few sticks, a fluttering scrap of white cloth—a little shrine to someone. You climb to the top of the wall, look down at the river, imagine the Red Army's columns approaching.

You go with Fakhriddin to spend the night in a village. You're in a valley—beautiful mountains rise above you—a valley tucked against the border with Tajikistan. Across this border there is war, a chaotic conflict among provincial strongmen, Islamic activists, and ex-Communists, further divided between Uzbeks and Tajiks.

A local man tells you that the Basmachis here, under their tribal leaders, never trusted Enver because he was a Turk, and "we've been fighting with the Turks ever since Tamerlane took Bayezid prisoner. It's not that the Turks are enemies. We just don't trust them."

You go with Fakhriddin to see an old man, his wispy beard entirely white, his belongings stacked next to him in an outbuilding of a farm, his family sitting on piled-up carpets. Yesterday he fled Tajikistan. What does he say? That he was told that Muslims must fight. That one by one the men in his village fled, and the women too, until it was just his family in the village. That men came by and fired their machine guns into the ground around him and threatened him. That he cannot understand why this has happened to him.

You go with Fakhriddin to a friend's house to stay the night. This village, the men say over dinner and drinks on the *kravat*, is ninety percent Tajik, and so they, as Uzbeks, feel safe. But in the next village on, they say, a village ninety percent Uzbek, people are afraid. Will the war spill over?

It's night. You lie awake on the *kravat*, outside. Fakhriddin lies next to you. You can't sleep. The sky is full of stars as you lie awake in a deep valley on the *kravat*.

"Look how beautiful the stars are," Fakhriddin says.

"Think," you say, "it's so peaceful here, but there, one hundred kilometers away, there's war."

"Look at the stars," Fakhriddin says.

"But the sky, the stars," you say, "they're just as beautiful there."

"No, they're not. Those are different stars."

Index

INDEX